Eagles and Evergreens

A Rural Maine Childhood

By Robert B. Charles

Eagles and Evergreens

ISBN 978-1-943424-33-7

Library of Congress Control Number: 2018943168

"American Heritage"
Cover art by nationally-known patriotic and wildlife artist, Rick Kelley.
www.Kelleyfineart.com

North Country Press
Unity, Maine

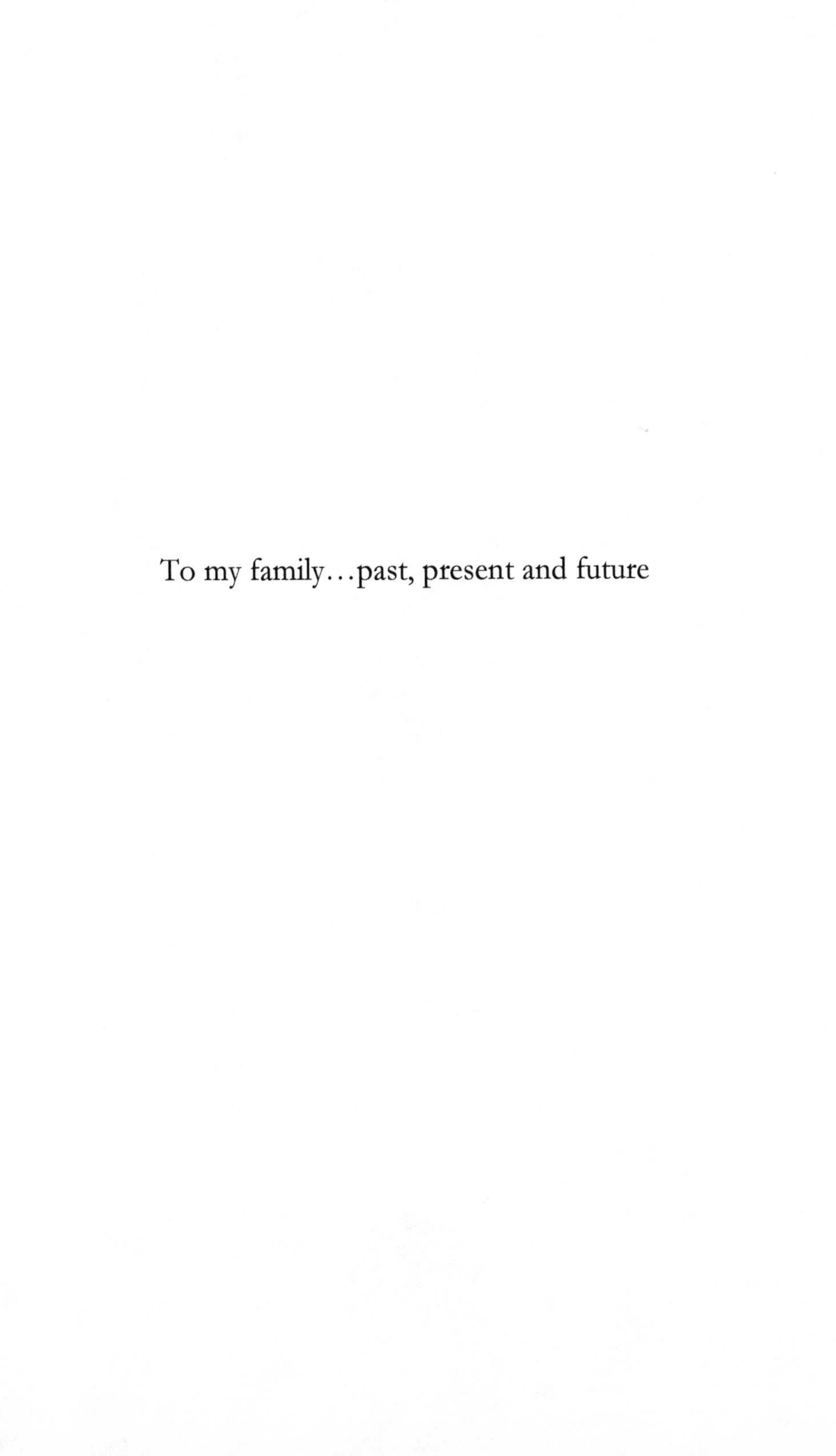

To my family…past, present and future

Table of Contents

Introduction

These vignettes are a nod to simpler times, and to small towns. Generation follows generation, and life whizzes by – mostly unrecorded. Memories fade. Stories of mirth and meaning disappear. In lieu of stopping time, this collection of essays is a snapshot. One town, 500 people. My youth, informed by the World War II generation. Eagles, among evergreens. Some tales dart and pop, others dig and dive. My hope is none drag. All are entirely true. In their truth, they describe rural Maine, but also wonderful America.

If you like reading about the North woods; if you don't mind an occasional line of poetry; if you revel in new snow and the muffle; if you like adventures "just because," love Maine for more reasons than you can count, this volume may be for you. It goes back half a century, as do I.

In that day, childhood was unfenced, if not totally free. We took the four seasons as they came, never skipped one. We went smelting at midnight, dared the ocean in daylight, flashed down steep mountains on skis and runners, sometimes fell into a frozen stream, literally hunted emeralds and tended pigs. We chased moose and gazed into the campfire, under uncluttered night skies. We could find and describe constellations and the Milky Way, spiral arm and all. With freedom, we tripped, fell and learned – all sorts of things. Mostly, we came to understand that life revolves around people and risk taking.

If Paul Bunyan wanted a town to call his birthplace, ours might have worked. Deep snow covered everything in winter, including the general store, two lakes and a slow-moving river. Abundant logging fed paper mills in adjacent towns. A hand-pulled church bell rang from the steeple of our white church. We had a shoebox post office, two bald eagles, several dozen World War II veterans, and a gaggle of irrepressible outdoor kids. We had more "pointed firs" than Sarah Orne Jewett could conjure up, plus plentiful deer, raccoons, porcupine, even ermine. No oxen, alas. All this was nothing special really, not uncommon for Maine.

Traditions counted double with us, of course. People enjoyed trout fishing, bass and perch, hunting in season, and snowshoeing for the fun of it. They listened more than talked, and walked place to place, visiting. They liked to smile. We shared holidays, all with everyone. We kicked mud off our boots each spring, worked hard all summer, ran distance each fall, rollicked and shoveled in winter. In every season, we climbed granite outcroppings, poked about the glacial caves, and watched those eagles.

Once snow melted, we ambled under cathedral pines, down paths matted by wide-eyed, white-tailed deer. We knew the saw, ax, maul and sledge – all good friends. We felled, split, stacked and lugged wood to stoves, which heated the house. We told stories, played cards, enjoyed homemade meals, laughed easily, took our lunch to school in paper bags, reused until they became dust.

We learned to value a dollar, and even a penny. One penny bought a hot ball or foot of red licorice at the general store. One dollar bought some fraction of a snowmobile or college education. We cut down our Christmas tree most years. We figured out hutching and husbanding rabbits, rather by accident, when four became sixty-four in six months. We learned to understand people and compass, in deep woods and on the sea. We knew the rat-tat-tat of falling rain on cottage roof, tent wall, and in open air. We shoveled snow where it fell, including the roof.

Each year, we had countless deer in the dooryard, raccoons up trees, partridges by the pump house, and a skunk who lived under the kitchen. I once encountered an ermine on our piano; this was unusual. But rural Mainers learn to accommodate what comes along. No one had to remind us to pick peaches, or to grow vegetables. We made much of our own bread, along with fruit pies, baked beans with salt pork. Actually, I am being loose with words. Mom made those things, you know, the royal "we."

So, if you rather like Maine – and surprise endings – come along. This collection will not make the *New York Times* list, but these tales are true, and some timeless. They pick up where Edmund Ware Smith and Maurice Day left off – but humbler fare. Nothing jarring here, except the peaches. Nothing excessive here, except maybe an old-time Christmas. In this age of ambivalence to paths less travelled, you are now on one. Here's to hoping you find some history, mystery and memories – to trigger some of your own.

The gist is this. Four kids moved to Maine at ages of two, four, six and eight – back in 1969. Roland (known as Charlie), Cynthia, Anita and me, all newbies. "Our town," to borrow unabashedly from Thornton Wilder, was Wayne, Maine. The town was a buzzing metropolis of 577 people in 1970. Founded in 1798, the name came from General Anthony Wayne, one of George Washington's trusted few. General Wayne toured the northern outposts in 1796. History gives no hint of his visiting our town, and no local sign says he slept here. So if he did swing by, he kept on going. Seems he left an impression though.

Emerson and Thoreau spoke of simplicity, and its virtues. These stories celebrate those virtues. Some are contemplative, others historical, most joyous. All are personal. No one is to blame for inaccuracies, except me. No politics here, just musings, some campfires, calamities and comedies, one lost emerald, several blizzards and moose, chickadees and scattered Scouts. Here is rural America – or "life as it should be" – in a few pages. Enjoy the trip. Taking it once again, I did. I even think Paul Bunyan would, if he could fit into our town.

Spring Comes

"Those who contemplate the beauty of the earth find reserves of strength that will endure as long as life lasts. There is symbolic, as well as actual, beauty in the migration of the birds, the ebb and flow of the tides, the folded bud ready for the spring. There is something infinitely healing about the repeated refrains of nature – the assurance that dawn comes after night, and spring after winter."

–Rachel Carson

1. *Under the Snow*

Life crept forward invisibly, imperceptibly at first. March, maybe April. Somewhere under the snow, a different world prepared entrance. First came mud, then blooms. Poets say the world sleeps in winter, wakes in spring. I suppose they are mostly right, but the first awakening is much earlier, humbler and hidden. As the blanket thins, air warms and refreezes – life stirs. That is the *real* beginning of spring.

We seldom kicked snow in search of grass. But when a boot laid bare a patch late winter, we saw spring coming. Rolling giant snowballs for the last fort, we got to grass. New life lay there – cracked acorns, slits of lime green, purple crocus buds, white snowdrop tips, maple helicopters bloated, preparing to burst. All awaited the cue. Spring was assembling, like a great orchestra seating itself for the performance. All the world was stretching, testing bow strings, mouthing the reed, finding chops, warming up.

This was a part of spring, often unseen. Here was the beginning of the beginning, appreciated by those who imagined the coming concert, felt mounting energy. Pre-season set snow-weary minds tingling. Those attuned to back-theater prep and what was to come liked it. Late winter, much was happening below the snow, prelude to spring. Not exactly Aaron Copeland's "Appalachian Spring," this was Maine's pre-spring.

Most people did not talk about it. Pre-spring was a non-season. It was pre-mud, pre-bud, pre-melt, pre-ice out, just a feeling of winter's closing and something opening. But if you dug, you found signs, seedlings getting ready – an entire, beautiful world getting ready.

Animal feathers and fur began changing. Warm intervals replaced constant cold. Legions of hibernating mice, bats and woodchucks, restless black bears, skunks and raccoons twitched and nuzzled, shivered and mulled the change.

Frogs deep in mud ponds felt their hearts suddenly quicken, body temperatures start to rise, torpor fade. Ice above them began to melt. Soon they would swap skin breathing for lungs, but not yet. This was the last phase of winter slumber, no noise above thinning ice.

Long gone were the mid-winter booms of ice "being made" by the lake, sub-zero freezes all night. Gone the extended stretches of frost, and gone day freezes. Smells, faint and wet, caught southern gusts and made sunny days "spring like," although no one dared say the word.

Smells told a story, left untold in words. Smells were the first paragraph, first page of spring. The world prepared to celebrate – to leap and play. Tree branches became aromatic and supple, no more stiff and breakable. They were pliable by midday. Frost might paint dark glass, but by sun-up it was gone. Outer sills no longer cradled crescents of snow in their corners.

This seasonal transition was fleeting. The world stretched, preparing to wake. A shift in temperature and temperament could be felt by all. The line was fine, but discernible. Even then, one had to be careful – of wishful thinking. As soon as we felt the shift, we began imagining flowers, unfrozen creeks, buds bursting, fishing holes open, everything cascading into spring. That might not be just how it happened. Sometimes months of winter remained, weeks anyway.

All the while, we knew that unseen world was tuning up for the big concert. On reflection, there was more to pre-spring than we understood. In a sense, every future spring lay right there, under the snow – not just one spring, but all of them. Each seed, thousands upon thousands; every cluster of wild bulbs; craning crocus and tight fiddleheads, nesting birds and denned animals, evergreens and hardwood shoots, scents and sounds of the living forest – depended on spring. Each and every spring was essential; seeds of all lay in the one. Without the one, there would be no more. With it, the chain of rebirth remained unbroken.

All future unfurling and blossoming, flirting and mating, generation and regeneration depended on the irreplaceable, pre-spring season. There was no skipping it, not really. No way to restart the chain, if we missed this season. Beneath us lay the entire future, coiled and ready, quiet and uncelebrated. Life itself lay dense and condensed, just waiting.

No one commented on this, not usually. Life below the snow hardly seemed worth conversation. Maybe the pre-season was too fleeting, too quick to warrant comment. Still, it was a discrete moment, spring's own gestation, before the arrival of color and sound, before strong scents and sneezing, before renewed wonder and warmth, before the Conductor raised His baton.

I liked the pre-season season, tried not to miss it, even if we did not speak about it. Everyone knew the feeling. Pre-spring was an open secret. Maybe that was why I liked it. We knew and held our breath. We waited. A magnificent world stirred, just beneath the snow.

2. *The Snowplow*

Winters did eventually leave, but not always fast. After pre-spring, life did pop. But spring could take its blessed time arriving. In a given year, the town snowplow might be parked for good – only to be suddenly recalled to service.

For spring to arrive, winter had to quit, cash out, hang it up, and stop snowing. We could have warm breezes, get all excited, and suffer another snow dump. We might hear songbirds, then whoosh – more snow. Frogs might coax crocuses up, only to meet more snow.

Winter and spring were like poker players. They played against each other – at our expense. They met, bet and raised wildly for a time. Over weeks, both laid claim to our affections, winter promising more ski runs, spring dangling the finish of lake ice. At a certain point, spring won, of course. Spring converted us from skiers and ice fishers to planters and boaters. But winter seldom gave ground easily.

More often than not, snow started melting, and then another nor'easter hit. The prevailing weather pattern changed and changed again, chasing away promised warmth, making us go back to shoveling. Late winter storms, early second quarter, could be frustrating and ferocious, even if big flakes. We had to be ready. That is why we did not change our snow tires until May.

Of course, we loved the winter. We just longed for spring after the 229th storm. Some years, winter got greedy. It refused to go. It started homesteading on months to which it had no right. We knew winter was capricious, so took nothing for granted. Snow was to be expected, right to the end, whenever the end was. If another blustery storm blew in, we addressed it. We never fretted, not really. We counted on the snowplow, always reliable since driven by … Chris.

There is Chris now – I can see him! He is riding high in the seat of the mighty plow, as it sweeps on by! School is out and there he goes! The rumble of his double blades, unstoppably pressing snow to the sides, rattling over frozen pebbles, dislodging diagonal drifts, clearing the path for those who follow – if we dare. That was Chris, true as the day was long, then some.

Like Kris Kringle in the old Christmas special, Chris's wavy hair and congenial smile lit our forest for a moment, flashing *en route* somewhere that mattered, bringing tandem gifts – the clean road and example of civic duty done. Chris was up before dawn, tunneling through blinding blizzards, riding out each treacherous storm, indomitable and indefatigable, indifferent to darkness. He was on the job while we slept. Chris was an institution, embodiment of the town's civic connectivity, determination and interdependence.

He was here and gone, seen again whenever snow settled for a second plowing, then a third. In the wake of his rumbling plow, powder flew everywhere like pixie dust, swirling and dancing into the woods, a long whisper. Without him, we could not get anywhere. With him, we did.

Out for winter runs in my teens, I was alert for trucks and cars. I could see and hear them before they picked me out. But all trucks were not equal. One carried a bouncing smile and quick wave – Chris's plow. His truck never bothered me. He made me proud to be out, and lifted my pace.

When those in whom we vest trust keep it, and with unfailing good cheer, we are lucky. We had this sort of luck. Chris's wave and smile across the frosty dash personified it. His truck and double blade were here and gone, conscientious and energizing. He was on the job. The whiteout could kick and fuss all it wanted. He rumbled on.

Funny how time speeds by when you think it has hardly budged, how people grow and change, then reappear later in life. Old smiles, new crinkles, mix of purpose and joviality, twinkling eyes the same, lights in a storm. You see them again, and everything is gratitude. There is joy in reconnection, peace in what is timeless – reflected in just meeting.

There is Chris, again! He is on his festive "party boat," out on Androscoggin Lake. That is where the family spent many happy years. How can so many years pass so fast, without more than hellos and exchanges of news, words in the general store or along a roadside, across a yard or at a yacht club dinner? But there it is – time has passed, took us by surprise, accelerated when we were not looking. Not like Chris, who waved and waited.

Here he is again, bounding across the lake – plowing waves where once he plowed snow. He is happy to find me and family on the lake, puttering and enjoying the sun, just as he is. He sports a well-earned tan and hallmark smile. Around him, relatives and friends, each following where he leads, happy for his leadership – and summer breezes.

We talk of kids and old times. We laugh at how I once flubbed my lines, as John Hancock, in the high school play, *1776*. He doubts it, but I recount that his brother John (playing John Adams) rescued me, and his father (playing Ben Franklin) helped … We laugh. Then we laugh some more. We talk of the lake, times gone and to come. It is all as if no time has passed, yet we know – it has.

For me, Chris was the soul of cheer and heart, a living example of commitment to big things, bold and unapologetic – family, friends, and what mattered most in life. From his driver's perch, through so many storms, he never failed.

He kept connections alive, banked good will, exemplified what small towns are, and what we should be – in that smile, wave and lift. If he did that for me, for how many others? Just one individual, Chris lit the forest for fleeting moments, flashing and dashing, *en route* somewhere that mattered. How do you say "thank you" to such friends? Only by remembering, vividly. I think that is the best way.

Central to our village, Chris filled days solving problems for others, leveraging what he knew to assure safety and peace. In that, he found peace. Bored with the idea of college, he became Maine's youngest Road Commissioner, at twenty-one. He never looked back. Years on, paying everything forward, he and his brothers built a construction company. The company rested on simple things, determination, hard work, inspired service. To this day, it thrives.

According to one of his brothers, Chris dubbed himself "Number Four" – ordinal rank among six brothers. To us, he was Number One, the beacon in every storm literally. We got our storms too – early and late. But he was always on them, even if winter refused to go without a fight. He was ready. Chris and his plow broke the night. Storms had no sting. They could not hold us. Once his plow was in gear, winter was on the run. Spring would soon be here. Double blades and smile – they vanquished night and drift, in their place peace and lift.

Chris, example of entrepreneurial spirit, civic commitment and determination, son of a D-Day veteran

3. Among Eagles

Richie Lincoln (left) and Paul Manter (right), just kids observing Wayne's Flood of 1936. Behind them, Masonic Hall (left) and Crutch Factory (right). Eight years later, Richie was a First Scout in the Italian Campaign, winning a Bronze Star for heroism. Paul was on a B-24 flight crew, winning a Purple Heart on September 11, 1944. On November 26, 1944, Paul was killed in action, when his plane was shot down. Paul's name, with Priscilla's brother Joseph "Ford" Berry, and George E. Dodge, are etched in granite – a stone's throw from where this photo was taken.

Edgar Rice Burroughs, the onetime war correspondent, wrote: "We are, all of us, creatures of habit …" We prefer our routines, patterns and above all, a bit of predictability. Who can blame us? We like our excitement bite-sized. We grow accustomed to our family and friends, surroundings and rituals. No shame in that, either. We look forward to morning coffee, regular meals, pages at bedtime, our birthdays and holidays. We strive for balance between burdens and joys, take risks as and when we choose. We have the cozy corner, to preserve sanity. Challenges are recognized, and responsibilities. But most have habits – what we call "home."

Sometimes "home" is yanked, or we get yanked from it. Routines are abruptly interrupted, replaced with uncertainty. Unlike in books, no foreshadowing. The future just comes and keeps on coming. We are like a Katahdin hiker in fog, straining cairn to cairn, left hoping for the best.

Probably, the worst place to be yanked into – is war. That happened to a whole generation during the middle of the last century, actually more than once. World Wars I and II, then Korea and Vietnam. By all accounts, "home" stayed important to those yanked. Routines changed, what with training and deployment. Every day was uncertain. But knowing "home" existed helped.

Once released from war, those yanked searched old routines – had to integrate new experiences into them. If "home" was routine and security, people did change. If sameness could be found, things did evolve. Still, peace resided in small towns. The return to habits offered a degree of affirmation, even comfort. Like other towns, ours was important to those who returned.

In every generation, war seems to make a grim appearance, sometimes farther away, sometimes closer, always with fury, cost and loss. Last century, we got quite a lot of that. Small towns, including ours, knew war's meaning. On return from World War II, most veterans stayed close to family, many to faith. They worked hard, lived fully, attended to little things with noticeable discipline. They were often untroubled by what troubled others, and troubled by what others were not. Having seen what others did not, they eschewed pettiness; at the same time, they might have preoccupations, frustrations and short-temperedness. Every big experience leaves a mark, and war does that especially.

In our town, World War II era veterans were can-do, optimistic and almost universally un-self-impressed. They were far more quiet than noisy. To kids, they seemed unbreakable, like oak. There was much we did not know, of course. There was a great deal we never asked – and they never thought to tell. Only later did the burdens borne become clearer. In a sense, that generation rose to protect us twice, once going away, and again back home. We walked among them, unaware of what they had seen. Only later did things crystalize. By then, we were grown.

Those who lived in the shadow of their wings, learned from their calm and optimism. We were often protected by their decency, inspired by their hard work, lifted in ways that elude a pen. While these veterans differed from one another, most were cut from one cloth, intent on being individuals, thoughtful and unsung, less interested in attention than helping the town thrive. They were consistent, too. If they had pride, it was not boastful. If they made errors, they were human. As a group, they were contributors and leaders, content with a return to bite-sized excitement. What the young did not realize until later, was that this group greatly defined the town, even as the town preserved the peace for which they fought.

Richie served in World War II. He is one of many townsmen who did. His life and service are emblematic. Thirty-five years before I was a kid, he was. Vigorous in his 90s, he sports a quick smile and dishes corny jokes. He likes telling them. He must have been a cheerful kid; he is a cheerful old-timer. Richie had three brothers. All went to war, barely able to shave. All four came home, too. On Memorial Days, the town's World War II vets – including Richie – are honored. Honored first are those who did not return, but vets all sit beside the Mill Pond, where many played as kids.

Some boys signed up to be Marines, like Jack and Richard. Jack marveled, late in life, that an eagle frequented his tallest tree. Richard was another local rock, quiet and smiling, father of four, American patriot to the end. He personified the Marine Corps motto, *Semper fi.*

Others signed up for the Army – including Walter, Harry, Charles, James and Bob. Some ended up in the Navy, including George, Ed, Fred, Stan, Leonard, Tom, Dick, John and Lincoln (Linc). At least one WWII veteran joined the Army Air Corps, Homer. Two kids stood Coast Guard duty, Fred and Bonnie. Unbeknownst to most, the Coast Guard produced 50 Office of Strategic Services (OSS) members, no telling if Fred or Bonnie were among them.

Collectively, this generation taught us our life lessons. I worked directly for Tom, and later George. In high school, I learned to write from Linc, who became our English teacher. Charles, Bob and Bill were brothers – and distant cousins. Charles was a veteran of three wars, World War II, Korea and Vietnam. Bob received the Silver Star, discovered by many only after he died. Bill was a veteran with musical talent. Some we knew less well, but in small towns, even the quietest veteran is known.

Ecclesiastes reads: "To everything there is a season, and a time to every purpose under heaven." The World War II veterans seemed to know that, uniquely. Immortal in their youth, vigorous in middle age, they were quiet in old age. Maybe we all are, will be. Richie, however, keeps his wit and humor – drawing on it regularly to entertain passersby in need of a boost.

Three boys did not come home from World War II. One was Joseph, known as Ford. He was the only brother Priscilla had. Priscilla is Chris's mother. Putting that in perspective, neither Chris nor his five brothers ever knew their maternal uncle. Ford died on a battlefield in Europe, before any of Priscilla's children were born. Such is the cost of war. One of her sons got his name.

Meantime … in February 1944, age eighteen, Richie arrived on the coast of Italy. He was part of the 88th Infantry Division – which drew heavily from New England. That division was so fierce in combat the Germans described them as fighting "like devils," leading to their nickname the "Blue Devils," a reference to their blue shoulder patches.

With other Americans, Richie faced rough terrain and German gun emplacements, artillery and machine gun nests, strafing and snipers, all the way to Rome. It took a while. The 88th Infantry Division arrived on June 4th, 1944, the first combat unit into Rome. That day, Richie celebrated his 19th birthday. His story, if similar to thousands of others, is still worth telling. It opens a window on those who grow up in small towns, maybe sheds a little light on our town.

Many American, British and Canadian boys arrived on the coast of Italy in early 1944, from Naples to Anzio. They knew nothing of war. Their intent centered on duty, then coming home. Winston Churchill, Britain's Prime Minister, hatched the Anzio idea. Richie did not know Churchill, of course. Or Franklin Delano Roosevelt, for that matter. Nevertheless, FDR thought Richie would be more useful in Italy than fishing in Wayne, so Richie went.

FDR was probably right. Richie turned out to be valuable "over there." In close combat, pushing Nazis from Naples through Rome to the Brenner Pass, Richie earned the Bronze Star and other medals. He never spoke about them. In dozens of battles, ranging from Minturno and Formia to Monte Cassino, Anzio to Rome, Volterra to Florence, Allied boys paid a terrible price for freedom. Richie was there. Stories are legion, gripping and everywhere of a similar nature.

If battles were unique, Anzio was emblematic of the fierce fighting, long odds, unremitting Allied pressure, high losses, irrepressible character of the individual soldier, and Hand of Providence. Within two days of the American landing, Germans had the beachhead surrounded by eight divisions. By day six, the beachhead was badly outnumbered. On that day, the Germans were supposed to launch an attack. The American boys did not know it, but if that attack came – they stood little chance. Then, something odd happened. With Nazi troop strength double the Allied landing, the winds of war shifted. Like the Magnus effect that takes a spinning missile off course, Nazi plans slid sideways. God had a different plan. For no good reason, German High Command delayed the attack.

They decided instead, to reinforce their position. The attack date slipped. By the time the Nazis were ready, Allied forces had drawn nearly even.

That Italian battle, and ones like it, became legendary. The Italian Campaign, objectively, saw the worst fighting in Europe. By late May, elements of the Fifth Army, including the Blue Devils, had swept northward. Allied successes, of which Richie was a constant part, came at enormous human cost – from Monte Cassino and Anzio to Rome and all points north. Overall, between 60,000 and 70,000 Allied troops died in the Campaign to liberate Italy, total casualties topping 320,000. German casualties were on the same order.

At Anzio, breakout attempts were costly. Examples are sobering. Of 767 men in the 1st and 3rd Army Ranger battalions attacking German lines in one breakout attempt, only six men returned. Put differently, 761 Americans were killed or captured from two battalions in one attempt. Still, the Allied assault there, and in locations south of Anzio, continued until successful. In the end, Allied casualties at Anzio numbered 29,200, Monte Cassino 55,000, and so it went.

Richie was what the Army called a "Scout." Scouts drew a luckless assignment. That did not appear to bother Richie. His job was to sneak to the German frontlines, under cover of darkness, and shoot a flare into the sky illuminating German positions for US artillery – then run like heck. For obvious reasons, the Nazis hated Army Scouts, like Richie. They rained machinegun fire and mortars on retreating Scouts. Richie came to count on it, kept him alert he said. To his advantage, he had fleet feet, small stature, and a resilient disposition. He never quit, and was never hit. His helmet was once grazed. By day, Scouts moved ahead of the advancing troops, guns always up, eyes keenly peeled.

Mid-way to Rome, Richie's unit got trapped in a farmhouse. Terrain was mountainous. The farmhouse backed onto a ravine. Pressed by the Germans, his commanding officer ordered them to hunker down, believing that offered the best escape strategy. Richie thought a soldier might slip back through German lines for reinforcements. This was only possible by descending the ravine. No one wanted the assignment, so he volunteered. Permission granted, he jumped, tumbled, brushed off, and went after help. By the time he returned, his unit had been captured.

Richie stayed a Scout, returning to the frontlines and marking German positions at night by flare. At one point, he took refuge in an elbow-shaped culvert. A passing German unit stopped to look into the culvert. They examined it from one end. He hid around the corner. When they crossed the road to peer from the other end, he slipped around the elbow. They missed him.

His record is one of honest daring and simple resilience, the sort of can-do that became critical late in the war. Turning nineteen in Rome, Richie was a small part of the eventual Allied victory. Still, his spirit is illustrative. Like other kids who were from small towns, he was intrepid, could be single-minded. He was not deterred or outwitted. If nothing prepared him for war, and nothing did, he managed to survive. When President Roosevelt asked, Richie defended our freedom. Today, we remain the beneficiaries.

By late 1945, Richie was home again, as were his three brothers. They all had stories. In time, one brother became our town postmaster. Norman Rockwell captured the seminal nature of returning home in "The Homecoming." "Home" was big. Today, Richie still ambles in and out of the General Store, making new friends, telling old jokes. He does not talk about the war. Only on a quiet day did he share these stories, and only when asked.

In my youth, eagles lived on the lake below our home. They spread their wings, caught thermals, rose and returned. They were methodical, and magnificent. They did what they had to do, in any weather. Sometimes, they went far. They never forgot "home" – or duty to their young. Come nightfall, they were always back. Sometimes, I think we were lucky – growing up among eagles, living in the shadow of their wings. Only later – much later – did I learn that there was *more* to Richie's story …

Richard Lincoln, WWII-era photo, age 17. First Scout, 88th Infantry Division, awarded Bronze Star, later recognized for his heroism by Secretary of Defense James Mattis

Richard Lincoln, enjoying Maine life at age 87 (photo credit Dean Gyorgy)

4. *Smelting!*

It began quietly, almost unnoticed. No crickets yet. Lake ice would break up, blow ashore, and melt back to water. From atop the Heights, we could see ice "going out." Sometimes it went all at once, in one day. Other times, black swatches lingered, but never for long. It was their time. Winter was closing up, finally. Everything was going to mud. Frost heaves retreated, until next year. Roadsides needed picking up. Boy Scouts stepped forward. Unpaved stretches got ruts. In these first days of spring, an annual rite awaited. *Smelting!*

Each year, on some random day, this activity commenced. Knowing when smelts would "run" was a mystery – at least for me. It was like predicting when the ice would go out, hard to do for mere mortals, especially teenage mortals. Not like predicting a new moon or meteor shower. Smelts came when they wanted. The season ended two weeks later. That said, it seldom began early as March, or late as May. Those who wanted to eat smelts watched and listened. We did.

Suddenly, without any ceremony, something clicked over. A pick-up truck came up the hill, usually around suppertime. Lights flickered through roadside trees. It came by at a good clip, too. That was the first sign. One truck bouncing, wiggling down into the woods past our house. Behind the truck was a give-away – a noisy trailer. On the trailer, listeners could hear an aluminum boat. It banged on potholes. Zoom, rattle, and gone. We knew what those sounds meant. It was time. People did not haul boats for any *other* purpose this time of year. *It was smelting time! Season had begun!*

Smelters were an enthusiastic lot. When they passed, most were smelting – in their minds. That's how we were in season. Another truck and boat would pass. A third, then a car filled with fishermen. Another truck and boat, another loaded car. In the backs of trucks, if you bothered to look, you would see nets, some with broom handles, tall buckets. In the buckets, loose tarps, flashlights and lanterns, occasionally brown-toed, knee-high boots, folded waders.

These cars and trucks, passing in ones and twos, were headed to water. They crested the mountain, eyes peeled for the side road. Most knew it by sight. An unmarked dirt road doubled as human tributary, sweeping fishermen down in season. Cars and trucks migrated in schools to the lake. The human migration lasted for hours, synchronized to schools of fish swimming, with equal vigor, toward the same brook head.

No fishing poles, ice augers or traps accompanied these spring fishermen. They came to net fish, just as children net butterflies. This was a different kind of fishing, done by flashlight beam, dipping for darts and fins. For reasons that elude my understanding, the moon was almost always full. Maybe it had something to do with when smelts ran. Maybe it was the first full moon after the vernal equinox, or Ecclesiastical full moon. Anyway, the lake was always high, water ice cold. Excitement radiated from truck cabs. This was serious business, time was precious.

The draw was a silvery fish no bigger than a pencil, and thin as a MacDonald's french fry. Lake smelts were smaller than ocean smelts. When "running," they were twitchy, fast and exciting. Dozens could be netted in a swipe. Adding to the excitement, smelts moved like a covey of birds; they flew in all directions when surprised. Schooling fish, freshwater smelts populated many Maine lakes. Androscoggin was just one. Each year, they ran up inlets and feeder streams to spawn. The frenzy – of men and fish – lasted a fortnight. Then, fast as it started, it was over.

Only a fraction of running smelts got caught, but the sport had resonance and true believers. Participating was a time-honored ritual. Those who smelted looked forward and backward on the season, talking about it longer than it lasted. Darkness and unpredictability, hunting the clever quarry with good friends, getting out on the lake – all made this sport popular, even sacred.

Cool nights cast part of the spell. Smelters were daylight fishermen who reveled in being night owls. That was part of the fun. Night changed everything. With hoots and bright eyes, these owls arrived in noisy vehicles, turned them off, and turned quiet. Engines were not good for fishing. Smelters liked to fish by moonlight and lantern, some with oars, others in waders. Absent moon or lantern, they settled for flashlights, some ambient light and peripheral vision.

Smelts came in bunches, stirred the water, made it boil, turning the surface to frenzied ripples. Responding to an inner clock, they spread out by the thousands, flooding inlets in frantic quest of sandy-bottomed spawning grounds. One or two perfect spots lay along Androscoggin's southeastern shore. Every smelt seemed to know where these spots were. In a mysterious leap across species, fishermen did too. Without exaggeration, both parties arrived in comparable high spirits. For those with no inner clock, well … we just waited for the passing truck, trailer and boat. That was our cue. Once we heard them, we headed for water, laden with lanterns and nets.

Down by the water, people just settled in, the way they did for fireworks. They took up positions and waited, like observers scanning the night sky for shooting stars. Stillness ruled. Golden waves undulated, reflecting wicks behind rounded glass, disturbing flat water. Some fishermen held lanterns high, creating big circles of illumination that got fuzzy at the edges. Others held them low, hopeful. Most fishermen scanned from a rocking boat seat. Some chose to be knee-deep in darkness and wet, closer to shore.

No one really knew where the smelts would start a night's run – or when. Voices conjectured and murmured. Guesses came in whispers. Grunts and giggles could be heard, not too many. Smelting was fun – but serious, too. If noise level got above some undeclared ceiling, a booming voice would bring our communal volume down. Huddles of humanity bobbed close to one another, half visible. Taken together, boats, lanterns, nets and clusters were more in the darkness than in the light, which made the whole experience enchanting, especially for kids.

In the course of an evening, the moon was often obscured by passing clouds. Light wind rocked boats. Nodding branches broke up the moonlight. Smelting had a cadence to it. It was unhurried, until it was frenzied. That cadence was part of the culture, and part of our spring. No one wrote about it, but the culture of smelting was widely understood, almost tangible. Like going to the ballet, expectations attended this event. We were quiet, and then activity consumed everyone, until it was again quiet. Anticipation came and went, then came again. Before the curtain opened, before the first fish flashed, anticipation ruled.

Like searchlights on a dark sky, flashlights swept cold, dark water. Beams were held by hopeful hands, some big and rough, some small and just curious. Everyone was ready. In stark contrast to the icy water, warm beams were comforting. We were on a quest, together. We were separate of course, each in our own boat and pool of light, but also one.

The ambience was that of a campfire or candle-lit dinner – with one important difference. Behind the sweeping beams and flickering ripples, enormous energy was being held back, ready to burst. We knew explosive action lay just ahead. The fish were coming. Everyone knew it. This was the time. This was the night. Like Spain's "running of the bulls," we had a "running of the smelts." Pamplona's festival was renowned and in July; ours was renowned and in April. Light and shade blended, everything became electric. Somewhere under the water, headed our way, was a herd of finned bulls.

Shapes played with the mind. Every ripple became a possibility. The world shifted as boaters wiggled and jiggled. Lights shimmered. Shadows danced among rocks, leapt into trees, disappearing into the woods, long and short, gone. Lights jumped about and licked the sides of boats, vanished. Dark forms prowled shoreline crags. Lapping water could be heard nibbling at waders. Nets were ready, still. Everyone was poised, children restrained, all eyes straining.

Occasionally, nervous laughter broke the waiting spell, but briefly. A laugh line somewhere offered an outlet for everyone. Banter followed, but not for long. We ached for trumpets, the curtain pull, the arrival of smelts. About this time of night, one heard pleas of "quiet" and "keep it down," usually from the same boat as a noise maker.

The view prevailed that fish did not like noise. Supposedly, it scared them. More likely, it just spoiled the atmosphere and broke the spell. There was a touch of superstition to fishing, and smelting was no different. Boats drifted on a mix of moonbeams and lantern light. Here and there, a boater chopped the moonlight with movement. Floating constellations filled the liquid sky, stars and shadows merging, all waiting for the flash of comets and tails. To some, like me, it was surreal. To others, it was just what you did at this time of year.

Minutes would pass with little or nothing said. A new boat or wader might arrive. All were welcome. Another bobbing beam, another old joke, more friendly banter. Catching smelts was both purposeful and an excuse – for companionship, bundling up and having an adventure. Just *being here* was three-quarters of the fun. The last quarter came home in buckets, if we ever filled them. But the comets were coming – we knew they were coming.

Most nights involved a build-up. Smelts were not running when people arrived. Civility mixed with a frontier feel. Some parents had kids in boats; others came alone. Fishermen rehashed past trips and catches, hoping for new stories. Spontaneous jokes popped, some funny, others only funny to the tipsy teller. We steadied our boat and soaked up the "enchantment." In the night, opinions sounded on odd topics. Mostly, they centered on when and where, from what direction and how deep – the smelts would run tonight.

Then, without warning, *they struck!* Hoots and hollers followed, warnings and alerts, plunging nets and near tips. Excitement burst out everywhere, unbounded. Wildly swinging arms produced splashing sounds around all boats. There were calls for more buckets, arms diving into the blackness! *Game on!* From somewhere, smelts by the thousands threw themselves at our cove, a blast of warm air in cold. They darted and dashed in schools of hundreds, spreading like birdshot from a gun barrel. First sparse, then dense, they came like lightning, vanguards of the storm. Soon, the water was boiling …

In seconds, we were surrounded, caught in the swirl of underwater fireflies. We swiveled to meet them, trying not to fall overboard. They charged among us, incomprehensibly synchronized. Silver sides gleamed bright in lantern light, twisting against jabs of flashlight. To us, if not them, it was dizzying, as if we were flushing flocks of birds, confronting a swarm of underwater bees. Smelts flew everywhere, escaping and plunging forward, reversing course and surging *en masse* again. For minutes, they came on, undaunted.

Catching them took presence of mind. "There they are!" went up the shout, then "Over here!" and "Look, on that side!" Boats swayed and oarlocks clanked. Oars clattered, some falling in, some out. Plastic buckets were dragged and rolled across aluminum bottoms. People shifted their weight, leaning over gunwales, hanging onto seats and each other. With resolve, fishermen pulled their nets through the water, some with broom handles, others shorter. "Sweep deep!" came shouted advice.

With the smelts' arrival came inevitable crashes, along with darting and dripping. Everyone had instructions for everyone else. "Watch the bow!" "Pass the bucket!" "Hold the light!" "Don't lean!" "Got some, put 'em here!" Buckets and sawed-off milk jugs were held aloft, dropped between boat ribs. Nets got filled, lifted up, clamped tight, turned over a bucket or jug, released and re-dipped into the cold black. "They're runnin' thick tonight …" "Here, too!" "Try toward the back, don't lean too far!"

In time, all this planning, anticipation and excitement produced a catch. "I'm full up … got another jug?" "How many you got?" "I got some on the last go." "Try the other side of the boat … they seem to be coming that way." "Yes sir, they're out tonight!" There was growing confidence in the night's harvest. The town was out, hearts pounding, all part of the adventure. Excitement grew dip on dip, until boats approached their limits, somewhere between two and four quarts. *The smelts had arrived!*

For days – sometimes years – we remembered a good night of smelting. The thrill of sudden sub-surface flickering, eyes pouncing on a ripple, the commotion … All this signaled change of season. Smelting relit some inner lantern, burned low by a long winter. Freezing was done, buds, flowers and planting not far off. Warm days would be along.

Strapping fishermen with young families loved these evenings, right along with achy old anglers. Some came to stock the freezer, others just to restock memories. Either way, we hunted together, laughed and dipped, celebrating a rite of spring. Every heart caught what it came for, then gingerly bounced back up over the Hill, aluminum boat in tow. By the time the last truck rattled past our house, well after midnight, we were asleep – dreaming of smelting, lanterns and dancing shadows, ready for spring!

5. *Entering Emerald Woods*

From the air, our house lay on the upper west flank of what maps call "Morrison Heights." From our modest peak, emerald woods spread in all directions, interrupted only by logging roads, farm fields and glacial boulders, here and there an impassable bog and fertile frog pond. A bushwhacker could expect to confront towers of granite. Everywhere, the woods were tied together by thin ribbons, aimless streams, meandering stone walls, ambling deer paths. Now and again, there were nascent wetlands, unexpected caves and crevices.

From one end of town to the other, rocky glacial deposits produced sprawling creeks, rounded ridges, massive horsebacks, small cliffs and granite outcroppings. Glacial deposits pocked the biggest lakes, Androscoggin and Pocasset, sometimes above water, sometimes below. They could be boating hazards. Amid boulders and fluttering pines, bristling spruce and quaking aspen, kids explored a geologic wonderland, vertical cliffs to sandy deserts, forested glades to fresh springs. And sprinkled throughout the mix were caves, some big, some small.

Calling our pockets of adventure "caves" is a bit of an overstatement. Their size was generally modest. Most were glorified collections of tumbled, randomly reconfigured rocks. Still, we called them caves. These caves – found anywhere – tended to be smelly. They were often occupied by porcupines. This fact made exploring them twice as exciting. We got to practice "spelunking" – and rapid retreats.

Vast, undeveloped woodland touched the outer limits of town in all directions, providing us with an inexhaustible area for exploring. That is how we happened, on many weekends, to be footloose and fancy free in the Emerald Woods.

In neighboring North Wayne, Fayette, Leeds, Monmouth, Winthrop, and Livermore Falls, the story was similar – lots of space. Kids ambled about mixed forest, picked their way among boulders on the way to fishing, hunting, camping or just exploring. They climbed crinkling veins of granite, here and there entwined with grabby roots of pine trees. On wet days, slippery expanses of ledge made us cautious, some ending in drop-offs, others tapering to pine needles.

By late spring, after smelts had run and before black flies appeared, we would press our luck in the Emerald Woods. The rich, heavy smell of damp leaves mixed with fresh ferns. Sweet, irrepressible milkweed and tree buds now flavored spring air. Breezes were welcome, no longer despised, as in winter. The woods constituted our playground, filled with mysteries large and small. Several friends made it a point, along with me, to spend time there.

One entrance into the woods, aside from logging roads and established deer trails, lay near a towering maple not far from my home. I climbed a short path through the woods, and came out on granite flats with a vista of surrounding lands and bodies of water. From this high ground, young explorers saw it all. Healthy eyes picked out Androscoggin, Pocasset, Wilson, Dexter, and Berry Ponds. Far to the west, they saw New Hampshire's White Mountains. On a clear day, Mount Washington was visible. To the east, thin bodies of water blended with greenery, fading to layer on layer of teal.

From the air – since our stepfather flew light planes – we picked out landmarks, favorite islands, crescent beaches, homes of local friends. Two local friends often explored with me, brothers Mark and Karl. We also skied Sugarloaf together, but that is another story! Friends do not come any better than Mark and Karl. Their house lay close enough to visit, far enough that visits needed planning. Their parents were always accommodating, even if I showed up in muddy shoes. Their father was an Army veteran and avid outdoorsman, their mother a cheerful veteran of raising rambunctious boys. They brought the green indoors, with a ping-pong and pool table. On rainy days, we spent hours over those. They hunted birds with German short-hairs, later took up horseback riding – again throughout the big woods.

We three boys were at ease in the vast forest. We liked climbing in spring, becoming part pioneer, part Indian, part frontiersmen. Our imaginations came alive in the forest. Here was no modernity. If shadows and caves could spook, they also inspired. We entertained ourselves traversing vertical and horizontal granite, going up trees, inventing games as we crossed tens of acres of uneven ground, hiding among gray shapes, in cave-lets, under overhangs.

Unpopulated woodlands were common fare. We never met anyone. Free of humanity, we remade the woods into whatever period of history we wished, earliest America to futuristic foreign planets. Thankfully and somewhat insensibly, our parents were content to let us explore. That too was common. Kids were expected to spend weekends outside, first working hard, then playing hard. We could go anywhere, as long as we came home alive – by suppertime.

So, we got to know these Emerald Woods around town. We tramped square miles of knobby, climbable nooks, ducked into dark crannies, pushed our noses with care and caution around uncertain corners. Pine trees, with their perfectly spaced branches, invited climbing. Cliff walls got hand-over-hand, foot-in-notch attention. Then, we reversed course.

Brambles were swatted and crushed with ease. This was a northern, not southern, forest. Bear, deer and mammal sign, but no poisonous snakes, spiders or crocodiles. Nevertheless, in these woods, mysteries required solving. Imaginary combatants lay in wait, and required besting. Hideouts and forts had to be built. Slingshots, knives, rope and compasses were brought, seldom needed, just enjoyed. Caves had to be sniffed out and poked through. Lichen-covered rocks and veins of milky quartz, carpets of packed pine and moss lay everywhere. Our world, seemingly unbounded, was an open book – for miles and miles. We dived in, wrote our own stories.

Then, *one day* our focus changed. By chance, we learned a curious legend. The legend was part of the town's unwritten history, simple and enchanting. The story – and what it portended – immediately caught our attention, and held it for years. Central to the story was all that undulating terrain, the glacial deposits, hideouts, forgotten cutaways, caves and crevices, which numbered in the hundreds.

Talking with an old-timer, he chuckled and relayed the old story – never proven – of another old-timer, a local explorer. We knew his name. Intrepid, the old explorer had nosed among town outcroppings for decades, convoluted rock piles, caves and crags that lay under dense bramble and wood cover. In one crevice-rich tract, thick with trees and chunky granite, he had reported finding a cave. In the cave, he said he had seen a "football-sized emerald."

The idea was unimaginable, utterly laughable. Locally, the report produced just guffaws. Nevertheless, for the rest of his life, he swore by the account. He had seen the gem "lodged in a cave wall." The story was doubted, diminished, over time dismissed and discarded. The old-timer – who I knew from a distance – faded. Nevertheless, in some minds, the story lived. After hearing it, it lived in ours.

Even as kids, we found the tale hard to believe. Nevertheless, it exercised remarkable power over our young imaginations. What if it were true? Could there be an emerald lodged somewhere in our forested town? As teenagers, we were sensitive to "being had." Still we wondered, talked with one another, Mark, Karl and I. Curiosity warred with pride and doubt. Eventually, curiosity won. You knew it would.

We knew all this terrain, knew the caves, knew we could insinuate ourselves into the tightest spots with a flashlight. We had explored many already, although never one with "green" walls, except for moss. On the other hand, we had never really looked, not for an "emerald." We took on the mission.

Not surprisingly, the description of where he had roamed fit many places. If the story was fiction, it was well researched. From local reputation, we knew this resident had been industrious. Each year, he had propelled himself and Christmas lights to the top of an enormous pine in his dooryard. He loved that holiday. We surmised no project would have been too daunting, although we had no way to judge credibility. As far as we knew, he might have been speaking truth – or just a good storyteller. But what if …

The story did not stop with his initial discovery. As retold 40 years later, the local resident had mounted a full-on return to the cave, complete with equipment. Technology however was limited. There was no GPS. His discovery had occurred by chance, no map, diagram of crevices, topography or relationship among geological features. He had mounted the return from memory, hoping to re-find the cave, somewhere in hundreds of pockmarked acres.

Gathering luggable equipment, he had enlisted help, searched and searched but to no avail. He could never relocate the "football-sized emerald." The area was just sprawling, a virtual township. He was on foot, with equipment. This was during the first half of last century. The area was strewn with angular and uneven boulders, miniature caves, everywhere overgrown. Disappointment followed repeated efforts to re-find the gem. The local explorer's elation dissolved, turned to dispirited frustration, eventually silence. Even on retelling, the story produced chuckles. The local explorer never located his "emerald the size of a football."

Naturally, the story lit a fire. For a time, we held out hope, thought we would unearth the secret. If preposterous to adults, their disinterest only reinforced our resolve. We looked high and low, literally, for the green gem. We suspended ourselves upside down, dangled between rocks with battery-powered flashlights, crawled into smelly burrows to examine walls, pressed ourselves into tight spots – all in pursuit of the elusive green glimmer. While it seems silly to recount, we squirmed on our bellies through wet leaves to see where nooks led. We made informal notations of where we had been, launched another weekend's effort when time allowed.

Of course, these were not lost days – hardly. In the nature of being boys, we filled these wonderful outings with cliff climbing, crack jumping, rock sliding and scrambling, enough daring and near misses to make each day a success, without the big discovery. While never systematic, we knew where we had been – and widened our search. We worked candidate areas – with no success.

Coming up short, our exploring missions got less regular. Eventually, they fell off entirely. Enthusiasm dwindled, but we never forgot the Arthurian quest – or story behind it. Now and then, we mulled the specter of that "football-sized emerald." The whole concept of a treasure in our midst, somewhere in our town – a local "wrinkle in time" – was fanciful, fantastic and hard to shake. The idea got into one's thinking like a rhyme or tune. It reappeared, even doused by rationality. Inspirational and impossible, the gem was real and absurd, as we chose. It was whimsy to be outgrown, or never to be outgrown.

We kept one eye out – for years. We never poked fun at each other for mentioning the gem, or for looking into a cave. When we tired of chases, hunts, shooting and slingshots, tracking and hide-and-seek, we would sometimes spend another day "exploring." For all our efforts, we never found it. The older we got, the more foolish it seemed. Doubtful, it seemed kid fun.

Years passed. We learned to temper youthful enthusiasms, leave them for their season, and laugh at ourselves. We grew up, became circumspect, sensible and less naïve, although not entirely. Who believed an emerald *of any size* would appear in Maine? What ridiculous odds would put it in *our town?* The old-timer had been funning, just reeled us in like a big fish. The story had names, dates and places, but most memorable tales do. Details make the improbable possible, even if no there, there. As young adults, we ribbed each other, laughed – then suddenly stopped. And wondered.

At Mark's wedding, I painted a football emerald green – and presented it to him, declaring I had *found it!* We all got a laugh out of that! Kids' stuff, hoodwinked, good joke. How many hours, days, and weeks had we spent in rocky gaps, under granite overhangs, holding our breath in porcupine cutouts, gullible and unschooled kids? What kids won't believe! What old-timers won't cobble together! No more apocryphal nonsense, no more being snookered into snipe hunts. Never again.

Then came … the "wrinkle." It happened slowly. Reading old papers, I discovered a strange coincidence. While we had been exploring local woods for that silly gem, a discovery was being made in another part of Maine. In the early 1970s, an abandoned Maine mine turned world famous overnight. The mine was Newry. The Old Dunton Mine was up Newry Hill, near Plumbago Mountain. Someone had found a rich vein – of *green tourmaline.*

That vein was "deep grass green," according to public records. Curious. To call the find rare would be an understatement. Nothing of similar magnitude had surfaced anywhere in Maine, not even in that mine. Suddenly, from the Old Dunton Mine, Maine produced nearly a metric ton of the finest quality tourmaline ever extracted by mankind. Geologists call it "watermelon tourmaline," pink crystals encased in striking green "rind." In geological circles, Newry became famous. Even beyond those circles.

Historically, Maine had produced other semi-precious stones. Gems linked to the state included beryl (and variations morganite and aquamarine), smoky quartz, amethyst, and – in one or two other locations – small caches of tourmaline (found within many Maine pegmatites). The largest tourmaline previously unearthed in the state was on Mount Mica, in Roxbury. The more I read, the more interesting Maine's geologic history became. Mount Mica was apparently the first mine in America to produce crystal tourmaline. Still, nothing like the quality and quantity of Newry's "deep grass green" tourmaline had ever surfaced – *anywhere in the United States!*

In the 1970s, Maine's profile with the US Geological Survey was high. The Newry find refocused attention on the state's gemology. Among subsequent discoveries was a flawless, 10-inch tourmaline crystal. That emerald-like crystal, officially blue-green tourmaline, was so large that it was unofficially dubbed "the jolly green giant." So rare was that one crystal that it ended up in the National Museum of Natural History, in Washington, D.C. It is still there. But there is more.

The US Geological Survey records that the largest tourmaline crystal ever cut from Mount Mica – a separate location – was also a "giant." For convenience, and a nod to Fenway Park, it was named "the green monster." Cut from a non-descript cave wall, this Mount Mica crystal turned out to be a 256-carat stone. It measured 17.8 centimeters in width, 39.4 centimeters in length – and was *all green.* That "green monster" weighed about 14.3 kilograms. If you were counting, that is two green giants from two simple Maine caves.

Now come facts that give real pause. All the tourmaline ever found in Maine was extracted along a swath running southeast from Oxford County, down through the Auburn area, sweeping off to the north toward Roxbury's Mount Mica and into Rumford. Rumford and Roxbury lie northwest of our town; our town lies southeast of Rumford and Roxbury. That means our town lies *within that magic swath,* along the line that runs southeast from the Newry mine to Mount Mica – the exact part of Maine studded with discoveries of green tourmaline. Unbeknownst to us, the forests and caves we trekked as kids – lay smack in the middle of Maine's tourmaline zone.

Finally, consider this: The "green monster" – that enormous green tourmaline pried from a cave wall at Mount Mica, Roxbury, is exactly 17.8 centimeters wide and 39.4 centimeters long. How big is an American football? An American football is seven inches wide and 11.25 inches long –exactly 17.8 centimeters wide and 28.58 centimeters long – four inches *smaller* than the enormous green gem found in Roxbury.

And this: Discovery of tourmaline at Mount Mica was not the product of detailed mineralogist surveys, seismic testing, expensive over-flights, core samples or sophisticated excavation techniques. The initial discovery of tourmaline in our state, like so many gem discoveries, was an utter accident. Quoting from a leading authority on the mine: "Mount Mica, America's first gem mine, was discovered in 1820 by two students, Elijah Hamlin and Ezekiel Holmes; while taking a shortcut through the hills of Paris, Maine, the boys noticed a glimmer of green in the soil-covered roots of an upturned tree." Boys!

These many years later, here is what we know: "Deep grass green" tourmaline is not an emerald, but emeralds and tourmalines are deep green crystals. Maine has a disproportionate abundance of green tourmaline – including the largest two pieces ever found in the United States. Our little town is neither Roxbury nor Newry, and not close to either. It has no mines and no history of gem finds. On the other hand, it lies on that rough line between Roxbury and Newry, the only swath of Maine known for generating tourmaline. We know that a football-sized gem would, by coincidence, be four inches *smaller* than Mount Mica's famous "green monster." And we know this: Old-timers love to tell tales.

So, who knows? Maybe a giant tourmaline (or perhaps beryl) lies undiscovered – or un-rediscovered – somewhere within our portion of the state, in a damp cave or forgotten crevice, part of an unassuming boulder pile or granite drop, on a quiet desert perimeter or adjacent to some lakeside path in the forest. Maybe three scrambling boys were not so far off, after all. But until someone finds the elusive football-sized emerald, or proves it cannot be found, we can only dream and wonder. Confidentially, I still do.

6. Finding Solutions

Beyond dreaming of football-sized emeralds, we had our chores. Real problems needed solving. Most bore some relationship to the calendar, putting things up, out and on, taking them down, in and off. We liked to think ourselves resourceful, able to find solutions to problems others thought insoluble.

Mainers also tended to be deliberate, intentionally unhurried. Most were, by nature, circumspect and self-contained. There were exceptions, but most did not acknowledge ever being in crisis. People admitted only to being in a fix, jam or muddle. Rumor had it, the word "crisis" had long ago been scrubbed from the lexicon upstate. Problems had solutions; you just had to find them.

Behind this confidence was another truth: Mainers had to be capable, as they often faced problems alone. Rural Americans had to be clever, learn self-reliance. With long winters, muddy roads, leaves to rake, they had to make their own luck, manage their muddles.

Patience was part of it. Like a kingfisher, they were content to wait until shadows fell this side of the fish, then dive. There was always time. In the farmer's gait, woodsman's swing, artisan's brush, we recognized a certain wisdom. Old sayings were true, "haste makes waste," "a stitch in time saves nine," and that "watched pot never boils."

Sometimes circumstances did test a Mainer's reserves of resourcefulness. In a blinding whiteout, axle-deep in mud, lost in the woods, or worse at sea, Mainers tended to keep their wits. But some days, trouble doubled and time got short. Those were real tests. One year we got one of those, right at the end of winter, beginning of spring. It was a doozy. Emerson said, "Trust thyself … every heart vibrates to that iron string." Whether they do or not, we had to. The fix we faced took confidence, pluck and a nod from Providence.

Suddenly, it was decision time – late spring, ice shack still on the lake. Without warning, temperatures shot through the roof, ice became slush, snowmobiles useless, and bad news just kept coming. No one wanted to lose an ice house. That is why most pulled them early. This year, the elements conspired against us. We missed the window. No excuses, our ice house was half under and headed down. If it stayed that way, it was gone. Getting it off the lake was now a top priority – almost overnight. And the ice was thin.

If this process sounds ho-hum, it was anything but. We had to think hard and fast. What lay before us was a gamble. We needed tall boots, crampons, more than a pocket full of luck. Retrieving an icehouse from slush late season is, by definition, dicey. Hearts quicken. Ours did. After a soaking rain, things only got worse. High temperatures and vanishing snow, deep slush, lake holes and thinning ice meant a dilemma: Let the precious house go, or take a big chance, and try to get it ashore. We decided to go for rescue – but it was complicated.

The night before was telling. Heavy rain pelted our mountainside home, no letup. My brother and I shared a bedroom, one window. It rattled all night. Once the world grew light, snow was gone. We knew the ice house was in trouble. Rescue was today or never. I got on watertight clothes, prepared to work with my stepfather. This would be different, no room for error.

Ice would soon be out. No action taken, meant we lost it. We depended on this ice house, a nice one. Our race was now hours, not days. Down the hill we went, through mud and fog, over exposed pebbles, holdout crescents of snow. Fog is not a good sign, headed onto a frozen lake. At the lake's edge, our eyes scanned the endless mush, dark spots and puddles. Winter had lost, spring won. We just asked for one more chance. My stepfather was intent. We had fished, thought there would be time. Now, smelts would soon be along. That was how late it was, frightening.

Out there was the icehouse. We could see it, a dot. It was a gem, built with care, filled with years of pulling up fish, hunkering against wind, snow and sleet. No bigger than a small car, it held a wood stove, table, foldout chairs, two windows, four corner holes for droplines. It stood half a mile away, on a questionable lake. There was no time for doubt, and no sense in cursing our misjudgment. We should have brought it up earlier – and here we were, now or never.

Out there was a thousand pounds of wood, solace and sentiment. From the beginning, our conundrum was clear: How to get the ice house up and out of the slush. Only then was there any chance of getting it back to shore, and up the hill. Any other year, we would have ridden snowmobiles onto thick ice, hooked up the ski-footed house, and zipped up the hill. The whole thing might have taken two hours. Not this year. This year, it was not that simple.

A plan had been hatched. Our rescue would occur in stages, discrete steps. We had to get onto the lake, assuming that was still possible. This could only be done by foot. The lake was impassible by snowmobile. Knee-high slush and holes marked the variegated, unstable ice. Snowmobiles were useless, no traction. Even if they got us out, they could not get the icehouse back. Here and there, the ice was wide open; that happens after a big rain. This too was not encouraging. While we could see the holes, knowing they were there sent shivers.

Today's goal was specific: Lift the icehouse out of the slush, stabilize it above the slush. The whole thing was a crazy gamble, but without that act, nothing else was possible. *If* another freeze came before ice went out, we *might* return and haul her up the hill. If we could not get leverage out of the slush, it was over anyway. End of icehouse.

From the get-go, this was like fourth quarter, seconds to play. Our plan involved a string of "what if's," all calculated risks. We had crampons, teeth strapped to boots for gripping ice. We had tall boots, tall enough. My stepfather had waders. He spoke little. He always spoke little, but less today. I hoped the slush would not jump boot tops, drench my feet. That would scuttle the mission. We brought a chisel and hand-held hydraulic jack. The jack was for placing under icehouse corners. We had a stack of sawed-off two-by-sixes, some rope. With toboggan behind us, we started out …

I knew, as lake conditions deteriorated, the rescue was tenuous. Weather had shifted wholesale. It did that sometimes. Breezes blew from the south, drizzly and wet. Warm air predominated, blowing spring north. Long term, that was good. Short term, it was bad. We needed to get the house out of slush – today. That was step one. Absent that, all else was academic. We might get a last freeze; you never knew. For sure, you could not hack out an icehouse half frozen under, so it had to be lifted. As it was, another freeze was unlikely. We were under no illusions.

One step at a time. For the rest to be possible, we had to lift a one-ton house, put boards under all corners, and defy the slush. We had to lug things out and not fall, avoiding open water. We had to lift by jack, keep it stationary. We had to insert boards by ones and twos, until the whole edifice rested above slush. Finally, we had to work our way back off ice – and then pray fervently for a freeze. Theory is clean, practice messy.

In practice, we were waterlogged before we got out there. The slippery structure weighed as much as that small car. It was in feet-deep slush. The slush resisted our efforts. Fingers got painfully cold after a time, started not bending when told. Wood bits stack poorly on land, worse on ice – and in slush. Wood floats. Think about that. Our wood bits had a mind of their own; they did not even agree with each other. They went in different directions, unannounced. If we could not lift the icehouse; not get a stack under each corner; not stabilize it above slush, we were wasting our time. But … if we did not try, we were lost anyway. So, we tried. If we got through step one, we could think about step two.

We strapped crampons to boots, began the trek. It was half a mile of ball-bearings in Sunday shoes, only worse. Slush kept trying to slop over boot-rims, while the under-ice tried to topple me. If I fell, it was over. Each step forward – dragging those blocks, chisel and jack – amounted to an advance of inches. If either of us tried longer steps, we slipped, almost going down.

The icehouse continued to look miles away. Slowly, it crept forward. The dot grew corners, then windows and a roof. Crampons were like shark's teeth strapped to the feet; planted just right, they could bite. Leather straps encircled both heels, crossed over and buckled. Tightened down, these made walking possible. Without them, no way. Still each step tested us. Gradually, we got closer. If either of us fell, the mission had to be aborted. Ice and slush would win. Every step was a chore. We proceeded. Gradually, we gained on the ice house. After an hour of shivering and shuffling, we arrived at our semi-sunken house. Just arriving seemed a victory.

We dumped wood at parallel corners, began lifting. The aim was to get this soggy structure up – simple, but hard. The process was new to both of us. We had to innovate, correct and rethink, as time and numbing hands allowed. We chiseled out the skids, each a rounded two-by-six, frozen down – under the slush. We got the jack to stay still, but not without frustration. It was like catching beads of mercury, enervating. Turns out the jack, like the wood, had a mind of its own.

Once stabilized, we started with a corner. As we did, the icehouse threw in with the jack and wood. It ran away from us. Free from the ice, the house slid off the jack. I shuffled to the opposite corner, held the icehouse firm. Slowly, the jack and house rose. We got one corner above ice, tried to slip a stack of wood under it. Another mistake. The icehouse creaked, floorboards twisted, wood blocks were uncooperative, and whole thing slid away. Seconds later, wood began surfacing on slush. Slippery blocks did not like stacking; they resisted the weight.

We began again. The process must have looked like a Laurel and Hardy clip, or Marx Brothers. Nobody was watching of course. The shoreline was empty. I remember thinking how odd to see the lake devoid of human activity, except us. After an extended battle, with wood blocks slipping and sliding, hands numb from ice water, we steadied one stack under one corner.

We then removed the jack, no words spoken. The next corner was hoisted. We tried to get the blocks to stack, lost them again. But the first stack held. The second corner was tougher. We got it up, but blocks again slipped. Something about physics. Time and again this happened. With persistence, we eventually got the second corner up. In the same way, we wrestled up corners three and four, finally stepping back, exhausted. The icehouse was above slush line.

That had been our day's goal. By the time four corners were above slush line and on blocks, we were soaked. Not a little, either. We were drenched from inside out, cold and tired. But the job was done. Step one was finished. We gathered chisel, jack, and rope. Crampons held the ice. We looked things over a last time. The icehouse was steady. We headed for shore – very slowly. This was what we had aimed to do. This was all that could be done. An hour later, we dropped toboggan behind snow machine, bolted them together, and headed up the hill. I recall the sun being low. Step one had taken all day.

Many times that day, we had reason to quit. There was no guarantee the icehouse could be pried loose and put on blocks, above slush line. No guarantee that we could even get out and back. No guarantee the icehouse, once up, would stay. Even if we got all this done, there was no guarantee weather would turn, that we would get a last freeze. The freeze had to be hard enough to allow snowmobiles back on the lake, letting us drag the icehouse home on its makeshift skis.

The truth? It was a giant gamble. A solution was imagined, believed possible, and somehow it all worked. Mother Nature then threw us a bone, the hard freeze. A day later, weather shifted north. Temperatures dropped. The icehouse stayed up on wobbly wood piles. Lake refrozen, we returned and hauled the lucky house up the hill, by snowmobile. Mission accomplished.

That spring, as in previous springs, the ice house rested at peace in the backyard. To solve a novel problem, you sometimes need a novel solution. The possible must be envisioned, believed and tried. The whole crazy idea might have failed. With a nod from Providence and Yankee luck, it did not. Sometimes trying was rewarded; the improbable proved possible. Old-timers said you made your own luck. Mainers swore there was no such thing as a crisis. Mostly, it was an attitude. Problems had solutions, you just had to find them.

7. *Deep Water*

Sometimes, all the resourcefulness in the world, like all the king's horses and men, will *not* put things right. Sometimes, we got in too deep, too far over our head. Solutions thinned to nothing, became hard to imagine. In those situations, we had to breathe deep, keep our head, and stay the course. There was no other choice. Providence got an extra call. We hoped for a solution. Sometimes, the mind thought – or tried not to think – this might be your time.

That happened at sea once. I will never forget it. I was stupid as rocks, but the Big Man had mercy on me. To this day, I do not know why – or even how. We did not belong there, a high school friend and I. We were ignorant, overconfident, and almost fatally naïve. The ocean was beautiful – and dangerous. Lobstermen and seasoned sailors knew the sea's power to disorient and destroy. On a sunny day, wavelets at our feet, we did not appreciate that power. The ocean did not seem dangerous, but it had no concern. On the wrong day, at the wrong time, in the wrong place, with inadequate training, minimal equipment, we learned that the ocean is indeed a harsh mistress.

In retrospect, the signs were everywhere. We should have seen them. We did see them, just did not appreciate what we were seeing. High humidity, not oppressive. Billowing clouds, bulking like whipped cream on strawberries, very pleasant. Sunshine everywhere, less each hour. An unsettled breeze, but enough for sailing. We saw nothing to upset or forestall our trip – not yet.

Sea swells should have been the give-away. Small waves crowded big we-mean-business breakers. Maine is not Southern California. No one comes to Maine to surf. When a shore stirs with unusual froth and the sea throws up seaweed, something is up. When bubbling white curls unfurl, one on another like rolls of parchment and the sun is flanked by pillars – there is something happening over the horizon. We were seventeen. We thought we knew everything. These signs meant nothing to us.

Soon, everything changed. Within hours, we were helpless, caught on a raucous, rising sea, cloaked in impenetrable fog, imprisoned and disoriented, slowly getting chewed by the teeth of an impending storm. We faced getting swept into the north Atlantic, or worse.

We might be flipped and left wondering what had happened, until we wondered no more. The ocean, as I say, can be a serious place. We learned the hard way. They say there are no atheists in foxholes; there are also none in the flash and boom of a violent sea.

Our boat was small, one sail, one rudder, few provisions, no backup plan. The ambit of our judgment was smaller. Neither of us had ever been storm tossed, or tested in such circumstances. We were on our own, no global positioning algorithms, no hand-held devices, no cell phones. We had a compass, map and flashlight. We had the conviction that we would survive. To be clear, this was not about wisdom, but lack of it – paired with remarkable luck.

Here was what unfolded … On a breezy day in Rockport, Maine, the world was our oyster. The sea looked fresh and ready for adventure. The hour was late, later than it should have been, even on a good day. The weather was strangely southern, but the warmth welcome. With a high school friend who boasted knowledge of his tubby ten-foot sailboat, the two of us set out. Our objective was Warren Island.

Warren Island lies several miles off Maine's coast, and has a "campground" for sailors, as we styled ourselves. That was the draw. On a map, the island was less than an inch from Rockport. In reality, it was somewhat more.

By early afternoon, we were on the open sea, heading north-by-northeast, according to our compass. All was good. Two high schoolers – rulers of the Queen's Navy. In retrospect, my mother must have worried sick. We had not detailed our plans. The idea was so simple: Follow the compass. Watch the horizon until the map, compass, island and sailboat converge on one spot. Could not be simpler. We would camp the night, return to Rockport the next day. We were confident, cocky. We were incompetent kids on the ocean. What could go wrong?

Two hours into this careless adventure, the horizon, weather and surroundings shifted. The last weather forecast was for manageable seas, no posted warnings. Nevertheless, in a breathtakingly short span, we were rising and falling on massive sea swells, battling five-foot waves, completely socked in. Fog everywhere, we were in a gray-out. Worse, it was darkening.

Wind rising, it was no longer aimless, but strong and unyielding. I knew what this meant, a definite change in weather. We were in the jaws of the storm. A sudden sense of isolation and foreboding set in. I could not swallow. Being lost is not fun, less on rough seas in a little boat. The gray got muddy, lost all depth. Waves built, swells grew. We were suddenly in a different, unnerving place. Evening now rushed on.

Where were we? Another idea flooded our minds, a dark and disturbing idea. We tried not to think about it. What if we *missed* Warren Island? What if by some random accident, rolling storm chop, slight miscalculation, coming night, impenetrable fog, we kept going *due east.* There would be no obvious stopping point, no landmark or land – *before we would arrive in the open Atlantic, swept into the fringes of the Gulf Stream. From there, who knew where?* This unsettling thought was kept at bay by force of will. Neither of us mentioned it, although we later realized both pondered it. Instead, immortal boys that we were, we kept up reassuring banter, a steady stream of gallows humor, secure in our baseless optimism.

When you are sitting in a small sailboat on the big ocean, suddenly thrust up, suddenly dropped down, immersed in cold, dark fog from bow to stern, your heart accelerates. Cannot help it, mine did. My buddy seemed convinced that the little boat was security itself. I was content for the moment, but less sure about that. We had the compass, map and light – but no foghorn, no way to communicate with anyone. We told ourselves we were in control, quietly knowing we were at Nature's mercy. The situation was hair-raising, if undeniably exciting.

Under such circumstances, the mind begins to play games. Imagination gets the upper hand. Rationality gets lead-footed. You must keep moving forward. Fear enters the picture, and must be sidelined. Dispassionate review of the situation is hard, becomes harder, or did for us. Neither of us wanted to reveal that we were worried – which probably kept the other's confidence up. Still, conditions deteriorated fast. We kept rechecking compass and map, adjusting sail and rudder, watching swells rise and fall, hoping against hope on those ghastly, ghostly clumps of fog. But they just kept rolling by, not an island among them.

Every dozen swells or so, we got an opening in the fog, a few more feet of visibility, then it closed. We could see nothing. The gray was constantly darker now, near in and farther out. There was no horizon, only endless water, curling foam, impenetrable nothingness. Within a few short hours, darkness would consume us. From there, who knew what? Finding Warren Island, for starters, would be impossible – unless we banged into it, an eventuality as unpleasant as it was unlikely. We tried to stay focused on other topics, to keep the compass on bearing, to imagine we were making progress toward Warren. Our imagination wanted to go other places, and we dragged it back. No land, no humanity, nothing – just splashing, splashing, gurgles and murmurs and fog.

Officially, Warren Island lay three miles off the coast from Lincolnville, farther from Rockport, which is southwest of Warren. We tried to imagine we were moving northeast, that is, up the longest side of a triangle defined by Rockport, Warren Island and Lincolnville. In reality, we had no idea where we were. We might be on a bearing toward any point on the compass rose; there were thirty-two to choose from. We might be on target for Warren, or headed for Nova Scotia or Iceland, maybe Great Britain or France!

On our map, Warren lay to the south of another island, called Islesboro. This was a larger, populated island. By contrast, Warren was just 70 acres, a state park plunked down by a glacier in the sea. It had no people, no houses, no cars or lights of any kind. It was a big rock covered with trees, bushes, ferns and moss, perfect for camping – if you could only find it. We were now far from the mainland, so there was only one way to go – forward in search of Warren.

Knowing how to use a map and compass was one thing. Trusting the compass – as doubts built – was another. Watery valleys swallowed us, again and again. Just as fast, we were thrown up on top of another swell, crested a moment, and dropped back. We would look around, wonder aloud, then everything beneath us fell away – and we with it. Down we went, as through a trap door, until we rested again in the dark valley. And so it went. Dark valleys followed by teetering crests, over and over again. Fog lay everywhere. Darkness nibbled at the fog. We had to keep faith with the compass. That was harder to do than say. We kept second-guessing it, based on – nothing, because we had no bearings.

"Sure that's northeast?"

"Compass says so."

"Thought northeast was over *there* … I'm sure it was."

"Don't think so… more that direction. The compass says we have to keep going that way …"

"Are you sure? It's moving all over the place, maybe it's not working. Maybe it's off, wet."

"No, we have to trust it, it's all we've got."

This sort of thinking did us no good – lots and lots of no good. We eventually quieted ourselves and stayed committed to one course. The compass was our guide, increasingly our only lifeline. It had to be trusted. Boy Scout training kicked in; we did what we were trained to do, put faith in the needle and magnetic north. All other alternatives – frankly, there were none – would get us into more trouble than we were already in. We concluded that it *had to be right.*

Resolved that there was nothing more we could do, we felt better. We turned to munching junk food. This was food we had intended for Warren Island. We had two sleeping bags and a pup tent. The food was accessible, so we ate it. As long as there was wind – however little – we were better to proceed under sail. As hunks of silence passed, dark fog stayed with us. It was here to stay. The island, wherever it was, remained hidden. Was it ahead of us? Could we have passed it?

Suddenly, I recall shouting – "Look, an island!" An island seemed to lie directly ahead of us, appearing through the shroud. It had the right breadth and length, a couple of bent-over trees … was that a cabin? Forgetting what Warren was supposed to look like, we were sure this must be our island – *just in time!* The fog was now dusky. It rolled by in brooding, opaque clumps. Something rumbled far away. The sea was dirty teal.

We tried to close in on this island, but it seemed to recede, getting away from us. We just kept getting farther from it. Determined, we stayed in hot – or cold – pursuit. Suddenly, our minds adjusted to what our eyes were seeing, not what they wanted to see, but what they were actually seeing. Thoughts of Warren Island vanished, popped like a whitecap bubble. Disappointment overcame us, with new worry. A dry feeling caught in the throat, unsettled the stomach.

The island was moving! Our trees, it turned out, were mechanical cranes, crooked on giant hinges. The cabin was a cabin – a wheelhouse. Almost on top of us, then gone, this had been an *oil tanker* … A blip of humanity and then gone, it was enormous, like sailing under a skyscraper. Emotions ran the gamut, from wanting to shout at the vessel, to cowering under it, and sadly watching it disappear, then realizing that we might have been crushed or tossed over had we been any closer. Then, we were again surrounded by fog, alone.

That experience was enough to make us shiver. We just sat and watched, then sat and watched nothing. It had been close enough to swamp us, yet missed us. On reflection, it was well out of earshot. Our little sailboat now heaved on the crossing wake, as well as the continuing swells. Loneliness set in, and another pang. We must be in some shipping lane. We had no interest in being crushed by another oil tanker, even a slow-moving, tree-lined version. All we knew was this: The passing tanker was not Warren Island. We had to stay on bearing. Our only chance was to hit that island.

Had we gotten off northeast bearing in our excitement, thinking we had found an island that turned out not an island? Had we started drifting farther south, or were we still on course? We focused hard on the compass needle, and keeping the bow aligned with it. Seas rolled harder and higher. We ate more crackers, and watched waves disappear under the boat … What else was there to do? Destiny had left us guessing.

Hours seemed to pass. Time seemed to stop. Yet full darkness did not come; ambient light still lit the heaving sea. Oddly, neither of us was sick; we did not have the energy for that. We reminded each other the map and compass were by definition right. We reminded each other that we might run across other islands, if off course. We reminded each other that we were resourceful, dry and safe, right to be calm. In time, we would make landfall. Had to make it, right? Yet for all the mutual encouragement, nothing changed. The sea grew hypnotic, fog almost dizzying. The hypnosis was broken only by spikes of fear.

No more tankers. No bell buoys. No foghorns. Why not? We just floated in depthless space, made deeper by the whoosh of endless waves. Around us, only one thing could be counted on, the sea's cadence. We did not want to meet another towering prow, bump into another tanker, but some humanity might be nice. We did not want to face the deafening blare of a multi-story foghorn, but a neighbor would be welcome. We had no one about us, not even seabirds. Why no seabirds? Novelty and terror battled for dominance, neither one winning. We drifted. Wisps of wind puffing from the stone-gray netherworld, thoughts on the island. We knew we were at the mercy of big forces, really big, but still dry.

The dense fog amplified everything, making each splash surreal. Waves constantly hit the boat's side, clicking like a clock. The clock ticked toward something – outside our knowing. We were, by turns, silent and concerned, suddenly giddy, exhilarated and entertained by the experience, consumed again by emptiness, silent and concerned. Then, we were terrified. We were better off not knowing our odds, or what lay ahead. We trusted we would intersect with Warren Island, as improbable as that eventuality was becoming. It was what we told each other. It is what anyone would have told anyone.

"Pretty big seas now …"

"Yeah, four or five feet, still a fair wind."

"Fog seems dark, doesn't it?"

"Yeah, doesn't matter … It'll dissipate. My sense is we'll be on Warren before long, should be."

"See something in the fog over there?"

"Where?"

"Over there?"

A long silence passed.

"No."

"Me either. Thought I did."

"Funny how it tricks you, this fog – you think you see something, then it turns out to be … nothing. Funny how we saw that tanker, eh?"

"Yeah, that was a close encounter. I mean … loomed right up and all."

"Yeah, wonder how far from shore we are …"

"Hard to tell, but we're on course – island should be up soon, wasn't that far out …"

"Yeah …" Another long silence. Just silence. We knew that we both knew nothing.

Suddenly, fog took shape near the waterline. The shape might be anything, a boat, bell buoy, or leading edge of a small island. The shape grew, very, very slowly. It was something small, far smaller than Warren. It was foreign, but welcome. Any break in the fog was welcome. Darker than fog, this silhouette was something. It was faint at first, dirty coal, gradually turned blue-gray. Something was forming before our eyes.

As we closed on it, we realized that this … *was* an island – a desperately small, insignificant and easy to miss island. But it was an island all the same! It was more a big rock, edged with pebbles. If we had passed a few hundred feet either way, we would have missed it entirely. We would never have known it existed. A handful of trees could now be seen, real trees, growing above high water. In what was left of light, a fingernail beach lined one side, all pebbles. This was not Warren, but who cared. We were ecstatic. It did not matter. Somehow, by maintaining course and calm, we had managed to hit a small island. *Halleluiah!*

This island lay, we surmised, somewhere between Warren to the north and North Haven to the south. Or it might be further south, since there were no tiny islands on the map we had. In any event, it was a small, uninhabited, stationary sanctuary. It was land. That was all we needed, simple, God-given, unrolling, dry land! Noah and his dove could not have been happier than we at that moment. We had, after all, been saved.

That night – and it fell fast – we just rested. The sea got bolder and brasher, rougher and louder, not calmer. Lightning flashed around us, thunder banged, boomed and rolled. Did we care? No, not at all. We were as relieved as any two rescued, undeserving sailors, plucked from a threatening sea could be. Pulled ashore in the nick, we were thankful to have pebbles under us.

While off by degrees, the compass had performed magic; it had landed us. Having eaten our provisions from nervous energy, we dug clams by flashlight. Bubble holes told us where to dig. Driven by hunger and the adrenaline of landing, we found a pile. No one spoke in those days of "red tide," and it seems there was none. Not on this little island. Amassing a mess in no time, we collected driftwood, then started a fire. We boiled clams until edible, then ate. Clams never tasted so good – not before, not since.

If this was not Tranquility Base, it was darn close. We had made our moon landing. It all seemed unreal, too real, exhausting. We stared into the fire, as the sea rolled and pounded around us. But we were not on it. We just pondered the *miracle* – a little, uncharted island, waves tumbling over pebbles, plentiful clams, undeserved good fortune. We knew it was a miracle, one shot in a thousand.

We had been given this island – just in time. We reminded ourselves that we were – in fact – on ground. With each retelling, we realized more fully the gift, a real wonder. We laughed, got quiet, thought about our close call, what might have been, listened to the sea and storm, motion around us – made ourselves still. Before long, rain started. The tent was up, so in we went – well above high water. We had pulled the boat up, too, and tied her off. Adrenaline reserves depleted, we were asleep in minutes.

Now and again that night, I awoke. Rain slashed at everything, including tent and boat. High winds whistled about us, sounding loudly in the island trees. Wind and rain shook the tent. For a moment, I would shudder, then realizing I was on land, go back to sleep. We had made it, our prayers answered. Bright flashes lit the tent walls. Pebbles rumbled and rumbled. The tide crept up the beach, pushing pebbles over each other, and then receded. Thunderclaps would stir me, wake me, then I was being lulled again by the pebbles. Exhausted, we slept.

At sunup, all was different. The world was bright, light and calm. We put mustard on bread and called it breakfast. The tent, still pegged down, sagged badly. Soon we were up, tent unpegged, shaken, folded and stowed. Our boat, safely above us on the beach, was bailed. Around us, we got our first good look at the blessed island. On the big sea, it was no more than a football field or two, rounded. We had been thrust out of the water, on a glorified sandbar. We were standing on the proverbial needle in a haystack.

The bright sea was flat, with a few lost puffs. On it, we tried to set sail, but hardly moved. What wind existed, soon died, leaving us caught in irons. This was post-storm peace. Neither of us complained. We could see land to the north, likely Warren, and a thin strip to the West – the mainland. Our windless calm was beautiful, but sailing was out. We would have to paddle. We had paddles.

Our original plan had been to re-find Rockport, to the southeast. That was where we had left the car and trailer. On a mirror, we revised the plan. We pulled instead for Lincolnville, which was closer. We made progress one paddle stroke at a time, digging cheerfully into the glassy ocean. Slowly, the line thickened. As it did, we counted ourselves seadogs, and darn lucky ones. If we had not held course, not said prayers, not caught that pebbled isle, we might still be clutching wet gunwales, having staved off a black, hostile sea – or worse. The thought was almost too much. We kept paddling.

Anything encountered on this fine morning was pure joy. We had three miles to paddle. That was when we got our next surprise. When we first saw them, our jaws went slack. What were they? Sharp profiles, triangular fins, swimming together, toward us. Dead ahead, they stood out on flat water, pole pines on a ridge.

This sight was mildly jarring, certainly unexpected. There was no mistaking them for seaweed; there were no waves or clumps. Eight inches off the water at each tip, the fins were purposeful. They were headed at us. We had their attention, and they had ours. As they neared, we tried to count. Two, three, four? Each was triangular, 150 feet out and closing. They held course the way we had on Warren. This was … new.

Reflecting on the ocean mirror, their shapes and sizes got distorted. Ripples spread in the wake of their fins, suggesting sizes and speeds of what lay beneath. As the fins narrowed to a hundred feet, neither of us spoke – or paddled. We just waited. Being lost at sea in a storm was one thing, but this encounter was the capstone. What were these creatures, swimming hard toward us? We dared not guess.

Maine waters held sharks, but they were usually loners. Sightings were rare. The water was cold. Fishermen got lone makos, porbeagles, nurses and mud sharks. Once in a great while, they happened on a great white. Blues, makos and porbeagles ran a dozen feet, great whites up to eighteen. These did not look that big. Nurse and mud sharks were harmless. All these were sea stories; we knew nothing about sharks.

At this moment, what lay before us was one thing – real. Minds raced. How did sharks travel? We tried to remember. Groups or alone? Something told me they travelled alone. Always? Would a small sailboat on flat water stir a shark's curiosity, their appetite? The idea seemed far-fetched, but impossible? What were these approaching fins?

As they got nearer, the truth finally swept over us. Simultaneously, we let out sighs – the fins were rounded, not triangular. That made all the difference. These were white-sided dolphins, maybe harbor porpoises. Briefly they were bounding around the boat, inquisitive, then gone. As we resumed paddling, they plunged off. They were happy. So were we, for the second time in two days. They accompanied us at a distance, then went their own way, after herring or another sailboat.

When the journey was nearly over, we congratulated ourselves. We agreed it had been fun. Adventure happens, sometimes a bit too much. Lessons are learned, sometimes hard. The night before, we were not sure what was going to happen to us. We had imagined an island, and found one. Today imagined sharks, found porpoises. Joy flowed from the imagining, and the living, as we looked back on it.

A few more pulls on flat water, and we reached Lincolnville. Relieved to be on land, we pulled the bathtub across pebbles, right beside The Lobster Pound. We dropped to sit and reflect. Someone had been looking out for us. We hitched a ride back to Rockport, retrieved the car and trailer, returned to collect the boat. We swore to think twice before our next ocean outing. The oath must have stuck, because I never found myself again on the ocean in anything smaller than a lobster boat. That seemed a good size, that and up. When in doubt, stay the course. There is an island out there for you.

8. *Community Roundhouse*

People do not think of a general store as a roundhouse. Roundhouses are for trains, which puff in, puff out, circle and steam, chug, huff and scoot. General stores are for people, more sedate. But not ours. In my youth, the Wayne General Store was something to behold, unchanging and active, the town's roundhouse.

Nowhere did you find more reliable wonderment – or nicer people – than in our old-fashioned, anything-you-need general store. That was how it seemed to me. Everyone's arrival got noticed with a smile. Screen door banged behind you. Familiar, welcoming voices piped up. People lingered, leaned and listened. Between buying things, they mulled their common humanity. Everybody got and left something. From each meeting, we parted stronger.

A certain spirit suffused the place, intangible and hard to peg. Like dipping from a common well, people came for reasons practical and social. As much as any place in town, the General Store was inclusive. The cheer stayed, like wistfully recalling falling snow or little flames licking a log. Just thinking of the place made one smile.

No sooner had you pulled the handle than floorboards creaked and camaraderie surrounded. There was an earthy aroma of tomato vines. Reinforced baskets rose to the left, heaped with tomatoes, apples, zucchinis, carrots with dirty clefts, misshapen green peppers. Sometimes you saw turnips and beets, squash and radishes – all local. I don't recall pumpkins, but they may have been there in October. Strawberries abounded, with blueberries and raspberries in cardboard squares; kids picked many of these. All this created a roundhouse ambience.

In some towns, the favored gathering place is a barber shop or street corner, church or grange hall, ballpark or boat launch. Maybe the library, or a park. We had all those, except the barber shop. They all served worthy purposes. But for me, it was the General Store.

Here you could always find people mulling and conversation unfolding, while you surveyed candy. Red and black licorice on wide rolls, a penny a foot. Hot balls, Sugar Babies and banana-flavored bubble gum cigars. Chewy, white-centered caramels, Starburst and Milk Duds. Days when we ambled in barefoot from waterskiing at the yacht club, or swims in the mill stream, we hunted little wax bottles with flavored syrup, ice-cold Moxie, root and birch beer, sometimes orange and grape soda. Kitty corner to the candy stood a waist-high freezer, double flip top. Under the top lay abundant popsicles, and a delicious face full of cool condensation. For candy, our general store was better stocked than a modern movie theater.

Every roundhouse needs a station manager, and we had ours. While duties migrated to Skeet and Nancy, and then beyond, they started with Vern. He was a World War II veteran, as was his brother Preston, both having seen time in Germany. His wife was Barbara, children David and Jill; his brother Preston fought in the war, his brother Harold tended the home fires. Vern knew kids liked candy of all types – and sour pickles. A tidy wooden barrel held the pickles, wax bags nearby. Vern knew how to market; where kids went, parents followed. Besides, adults found what they wanted too – hammers and pliers, nails and screws, nuts and bolts, farm tools, tools to fix farm tools. It was all somewhere in Vern's store. His place secured us against every contingency, sawblades and sparklers to car keys and cat food.

The General Store was really about people. Crossing those floorboards, reserve fell away. People spoke their minds, plain and simple, honest and mostly cheering. What people conveyed was caring for each other, no head games or nonsense, unless identified as nonsense. No one was anonymous. That meant everyone was accountable, including kids, especially kids.

Conversations might be short, but no unmeant words, no brush offs. Maybe it was the era, but once that door banged, time slowed. Trust in humanity returned. We were reminded – by inclusion and including – we each mattered. We were just one town, but we *were* a town. People did not speak *at* each another, but *with* each other. I miss that era.

Between buying boxed spaghetti, ground beef and toilet paper, big news was swapped. Lifelines were thrown and caught. Over a box of Cheerios or Cap'n Crunch, stressful days were broken by humor. Little things were celebrated, disappointments acknowledged and consoled. We wrestled all four seasons together.

Nobody talked of lofty things like dignity or self-esteem back then, although we knew what they were. People suspended judgment, allowing others to live unguarded, every heart different, content to be around other authentic people. We liked authenticity, another word we never used.

Some folks shuffled through in overalls and work boots, others button downs and tidy shoes. Much of the year, including spring, people came and went in Bean Boots. These were sold – later re-soled – by Maine's own L.L. Bean. Back then, the boots were not fashionable, just close and lasted.

Without knowing what we were doing, everybody enriched the life of everybody else. Makes you wonder, doesn't it? Wheat doesn't know that yeast makes it rise. Took me years to understand why I liked that place so much. It wasn't just the good candy.

Another thing. Stepping into the General Store, you could "step in it." People chuckled and ribbed each other. Yankee jousting abounded. No one was politically correct, or much concerned to be. That term had not been invented. I think we were happier that way. People "gave as good as they got," and were prepared to "get as good as they gave." People felt included when featured in a joke. It made them part of the club, undistinguished as our club was.

Offense was not taken, since people knew none was intended. Looking for reasons to grouse was the height of pretense, pure tomfoolery; no one thought of it. Besides, back then, no one wanted to be thin-skinned; it was a waste of energy. Tailored joshing and giving someone "grief" sparked smiles, sometimes a retort, or admission. Ironically, this was viewed as a good thing, a nod to life. There were no sacred cows, or not very many; we were meat-eaters. An undercurrent of mutual support was ever-present, with un-uttered recognition of our mutual dependence. Much got said, with much left unsaid.

From behind the counter, half a rod from the door, comers got their first greeting. Might be sweet or salty, depending on the day and person. Vern owned the Store in my childhood. He owned wit, too. He was unrepentant and vocal, part of the job as he saw it. He might challenge or encourage. He might pass along an observation or ask one. He had lots of opinions. And he knew everyone had them. He invited them; if business allowed, he offered a quip.

Talk kept us honest. Vern's voice was known to all, a mix of gravel and sugar, like rocky road ice cream, good in the proper proportion. He liked to jest. Being razzed was okay, too. As I say, it helped assure no one got above themselves, or got left behind either. "Getting skim, are we?" "Ayah, trying to take off …." "Not a bad idea!" "Well, that's the plan …" "Why not, right? Good place to start! That'll be forty-nine cents." "Yup, I've got that …" "Take care then." "Ayah, will do."

The General Store's smooth, tanned, well-scuffed floorboards had their own scent. It was a good smell, like entering a bakery, coffee shop, or grandmother's home, only different. The smell was one of commerce, boot traffic, locomotion. The boards were actually oiled, then poured over with sand and swept clean. I guess this kept them from cracking, secure against moisture, got them ready for more feet. Over those planks, the town passed at all ages and stages, from little feet to big, tireless and untroubled to brimming with responsibility.

In a way, the Store was a loading and unloading zone, a place where people rode in on one track, rode out on another, a true roundhouse. We came, circled the place, got direction and connection, picked up what we needed and were on our way. All manner of trains entered and swung through Vern's venerable roundhouse, filled with news and banter, not much carping.

Sometimes a particular issue animated the town. All trains got some purchase, an exchange of views, a tighter grip. On such days, the floorboards were covered with puffing, steam and brakes. The place was alive. I liked being around on those days. I saw sides of people not usually shown. The Store became a place for swapping views, listening and absorbing, sharing concerns. Some people always spoke, others rarely. I listened to the ones who talked less; it helped me understand them. Even then, sharing was constructive, done in an effort to bring people around, swivel them in the roundhouse, as it were. Sometimes they did not move. No matter, consensus was unnecessary. There was always tomorrow. That was life.

Exchange was welcome, even sought. Differing opinions were what made us interesting, made us individuals. Respecting each other's views is what made us the same, made us one. Into the roundhouse we came, here and there a change of track, always worth the journey. Sometimes, Vern gave trains a good spin. Master of the roundhouse, he took it as a right. After all, it was his business. Everyone could speak or remain silent. But Vern might draw them out. He took a customer's measure, could sense if a conversation was within reach, or better left for later.

Maybe it was not a roundhouse after all, but a second town hall. It was certainly a study in democracy. It had a way of distilling common purpose and ironing out differences. What bothered people was acknowledged and understood. With Vern as *de facto* moderator, no one took themselves too seriously. That was good for business, apparently – and good for the town. While Vern turned a profit, he made the Store a place for patrons. No one was embarrassed, even for an unpaid bill.

Vern seemed to work hard, but everyone did. Weekday talk was short, weekend talk longer. "How you doing today?" He might get anything back, more on a weekend. "Not bad, but wish those loggin' trucks would slow down on the hill, they get goin' so fast I can't see how they'd stop if needed to." "Yup, they come like a bat outa grandma's attic, don't they? How's that foot?" "'bout same as it's been, can't complain." "Good to hear, what can I do for ya today?"

That was his cadence. Conversations ranged to weather, crops, kids, health, sports, and politics in season. Those were the big topics, where track got laid and jumped on occasion. Mainers do not talk too personally, just personal enough. Some conversations were more nod, coughs, and local sign language. I am not being funny. A well-placed cough told a lot, as did a partial answer, long sigh, repositioning of the ball cap. "Crops in?" "See your mail box got clipped …" "No deer yet?" Those questions might trigger base coach signs. Mainers let others be themselves, have room. That habit showed in the store, too. We assumed the best and if someone had something to say, they said it. If not in the mood, just fine too.

On the other hand, no one shied from comment if town meeting kicked up controversy, or the Government came asking. That was especially true if people saw unfairness afoot. Two or more patrons might get into it, or even a patron with Vern. Funny thing, no one ever left worse for this candor. Conversations were fenced, respectful. They had limits, just as meadows have rock walls. You could trust even leggy exchange would not lose the wall. If passions surfaced – and sometimes they did – they were corralled by the speaker. Hard to imagine, but that was true all over Maine and America. Civility was not a popular word, just a way of life. People got along, and conversations were of the sort that involved and expected getting along.

Vern somehow kept the balance between proprietor and participant. He liked "running the store," and had done it long before my time. Customers were always right, except when wrong. Maybe it was his blend of toughness and grief-giving, practiced wit and unexpected mercy, candor and humor. Ringing up a pile of staples, he could mediate or moderate the most animated patrons. "I can't see what this zoning's goin' ta do for anyone, 'cept keep us from selling good land and push up taxes." "Well, if we don't take some action while we can, before long people will come into town and take away the character of the place." "I think we've got plenty of character to go 'round, and I don't see where good land for building and farming should be designated for some other thing, kept from bein' sold and built on." "Well, there's sure to be exceptions, but if we don't think ahead, we'll look back and wish we had – and by that time it'll be too late." "Well, by the time I get an exception for my land, I'm sure it'll be too late. Who's got the right anyway to tell me what my land's gonna be used for, or what it's gonna be worth? That's my right, don't you think?" "Well, most of the time, but when the town's got to be protected from things happening everywhere, then the town's got rights too." "Protected from what?" "Protected from things like condominiums goin' up all over the place 'round lakes, those pre-planned things that seem to be spread like a plague, roads cuttin' through big patches of land, all kinds of contagion." "Well, I still don't see how the state or town can tell me what my land's goin' ta be worth!" "Alright … you want two pounds of ground beef, or one?"

And so it went. Customers and concerns, like rolling stock, entered and departed. That was the beauty of our General Store. It was a continuation of town meeting, the town … constantly meeting. Like the baked bread, issues went from mixing bowl to oven, oven to cooling rack. Within those walls, we found conviviality and commiseration, remonstrance and conversation. We did not have a wooden soap box, just the wood floors – and each other.

In some ways, the General Store was a message board, in modern parlance a walking blog. Facts and rumors were stirred together with merriment. Sometimes we got it right, sometimes wrong, but news was passed, no cell phones, email or Internet. On occasion, chocolate chips and walnuts ended up in the same cookie, by mistake – sweet, curious, nutty. "Well, I haven't seen them in a while, but she did look a bit tired at the church supper the other night." "It would be so nice, you know, since they've wanted another for some time." "Oh, are you talking about …?" "Yes, have you seen her lately, you know, I think she's expecting." "Who's expecting?" "Oh I had no idea; how wonderful, I guess I just didn't notice." "Ah, good to see you; say, do you know who's expecting?" "Really, that's wonderful, have they told anyone?" "Seems news is out, guess so." "Is she very far along?" "Don't think so, but imagine they'd like a boy." "Did you say, they were expecting a boy?" "What was that, they know it's a boy?" "Oh say, I guess you know by now … that's right, they're going to have a boy." "Really, that will be so nice; they'll have one of each."

By day's end, word had passed – a few times. Wheat was ground to flour, rose with local yeast, was sliced and served, until it looked nothing like wheat. "Well, well, and hello there! It has been a while since we've seen you, how is everything going?" "Oh, just fine, except that we both had to pull double shifts last week up at the mill, so I've been a bit tired." "Tired, eh? Well, congratulations all the same on that baby, and glad for you all it's going to be a boy, have you picked out any names yet?" "Baby? Boy?

Names? What? I think somebody is ahead of the curve here. I'm not expecting!"

Then a correction cycle would begin. "Turns out it was a false alarm." "False alarm, apparently." "Yes, they're not due yet." "Oh, not yet?" "Not sure who got it wrong, but they're taking their time." "That's wise, good to take your time, no need to hurry." "True enough, things happen when they should … Say, have you heard about the folks moving in next to the old white house on Main Street?" New word would pass, more wheat through the door.

What was lovely, if not obvious, was what got left unsaid. I did not appreciate this for years. Behind small talk and message passing was something more important. People *cared* about each other. This was not a mall or box store, no cavernous aisles filled with unfamiliar faces. The General Store was personal, a repository of goodwill. All made deposits, all took withdrawals.

Yes, there was idle gossip, but inaccurate rumors were corrected. More than not, goodwill predominated. Neighbors in need were visited. If someone needed a ride to church, doctor or meals, it happened. The store gave value beyond commerce and congeniality. Victories and tragedies were shared, common fare. The old roundhouse kept us informed.

Finally, the General Store was practical. Like Norman Rockwell's iconic "Shuffleton's Barber Shop", the store radiated warmth, with purpose. It sold things. We needed what it sold. It was our first destination and last resort. There was no Walmart, Home Depot, Lowes or outlet in striking distance. Do-it-yourself, fix-what-breaks homeowners went to the Store. Mostly, they found what they came for. Vern worried on that.

Need a snow shovel, rock salt, crow bar, saw or hammer? "Straight back, to the right." Quarter-inch screws, metric bolts, flypaper, duct tape, WD-40 or gas can? "Back right, before the shovels." Envelopes, white glue, epoxy, stain – walnut, cherry or oak – polyurethane, brushes and thinner? "Back left, front of tarps and post-hole diggers." Soup, ketchup, mustard, mayonnaise, boxed cereal, pastas, Hamburger Helper, baked beans, black beans, white beans, sardines? "Mid-wall, back aisle." Veggies and fruit? No one had to ask – front right, spillover from baskets in wooden crates. Popsicles? Flip-top freezer.

Need a key made? "Meet you down back in a minute!" Light bulbs, toilet paper, hinges, hacksaws, locks, even baseball gloves? "Look in the mid-section, left and right, front aisle." Fresh meat? "Ground beef right here, and what will it be?" A side hung behind him chilling.

For teenage boys, the Store was magic. Beyond candy, to the left, lay dreams. A trove of fishing lures and jack knives, flashlights, squirt and dart guns, comic books – and looking was all free. A spinning rack of paperbacks had romance covers, Maine's own Stephen King and James Michener. Then combs, brushes, shampoos, disposable razors (used for weeks), toothpaste, and antidotes to everything from poison ivy to sunburn. A spinning rack held Timex watches and watchbands, playing cards and bandanas. Nothing was particularly expensive, but we looked more than bought. Except for candy – we always left with some of that.

So, the General Store was a railyard with side tracks, part of life. Up the road was similar wonder. Toward the edge of town lay the Corner Store, a kindly place run by Harry and Pauline. Harry was a veteran and Pauline as devoted as human beings come, a smile for everyone. Those two stores bookended town. Both still exist, and their screen doors still bang. The Corner Store is now Cobbie's Corner Store; the General Store now doubles as a small-town bakery, lovingly run by Julie, mother of five, baker and proprietor.

In the decades after youth, I discovered the General Store's spirit in faraway places. Turns out, a tendency toward inclusion, humor and respect, candor and congeniality, decency and caring are not limited in time or space. Other roundhouses exist, all over the world. Put differently, the spirit of goodwill is more common than people imagine, shared by good people everywhere.

I encountered that spirit – unexpected trust and warmth – among Polish underground fighters, struggling to throw off the Soviet yoke. I witnessed it among Israeli and Egyptian families, buffeted by regional insecurity. I felt it among crinkled elders in remote Indian villages, eating chilies and rice under a jute roof. Even distant, troubled lands overflow with personal affection, including war-weary Colombia and Kosovo, Serbian enclaves, Iraq and Afghanistan, even impoverished Laos.

The human smile – despite international tension, inevitable spikes of evil and unending train wrecks – remains alive and well, absolutely universal. Can a desire to identify common ground, despite differences, lie far behind? Turns out our General Store – roundhouse for humanity – contains a spirit with global ubiquity. Comforting, that. Maybe the world is just one big roundhouse, and we have not figured it out yet.

In any event, my lodestar is America's general stores; in their calm and commerce, peace and prosperity, lies a wonderful, half-forgotten simplicity, a certain timeless authenticity, and a standing lesson in self-mediated understanding. You just never know what will follow when you start out with, "Now, what can I help you with?"

The Wayne General Store, place of magic, circa 1965. Vern ran the store from 1951 to mid-1970s, selling everything from toothpaste to local vegetables, keys and nails to penny candy and sour pickles from the barrel.

Vern Lovejoy (left), future proprietor of Wayne General Store, and brother Preston, in Germany, mid-WWII. Brother Harold manned Wayne's crutch factory during WWII.

Veteran Vern takes over Wayne General Store circa 1951, while his wife Barbara opens a local beauty parlor.

9. Animal Quirks

Animals are quirky. A circling eagle climbs hot air, slides a downdraft, glides effortlessly across Androscoggin Lake, talons out to hit an unsuspecting fish, then wings up, back to the nest. A waddling porcupine emerges unannounced from a granite cleft, smelling like the eagle's fish – a week old. An otter family totters across the yard, neat as infantry, obviously uncomfortable on pine needles. A beaver whacks his flat tail on Dead River, emphatically making a point observers refuse to take. A skunk shows up under our clothesline, getting more respect than the beaver will ever get. Flying squirrels dive-bomb the birdfeeder until empty, then ask for more. Growing up in the Maine woods, we saw it all, animals at their best and worst, a fair reflection of ourselves.

Elsewhere in the world, animals are dangerous – but seldom in Maine. In Australia, years later, the contrast was uncomfortably vivid, even stark. My wife, two kids and I drove 500 miles across the Outback. Beautiful, transcendent, strange. Nothing like Maine. Among tumbling scrub, we encountered every sort of odd flora and fauna, kangaroos and wallabies to echidnas and wild camels. The kicker was an encounter in Tasmania's Freycinet Park. No Maine animal, caught in a moment of surprise, compares with stumbling across a black tiger snake.

Guidebooks are curiously cryptic: "Look out for black tiger snakes," is all they say. Australians quietly nod. Unlike a Maine snake, this variety is poisonous – the world's fourth most venomous, aggressive, that is, attracted to movement. They grow to six feet, sport a swiveling head the size of a big man's fist, and kill their victim in an hour.

We just got complacent. We had a four-wheel drive, just like in Maine. The Tasmanian peninsula had two sandy beaches, just like in Maine. There was no one around, just like in Maine. The day was peaceful and sunny, just like in Maine. What could be so dangerous?

As we walked the overgrown isthmus between the two beaches, I got a strange feeling. I had my ten-year-old son put on his sneakers. He was in the lead, with me behind him, and my wife and daughter cheerfully following up. Suddenly, my son stopped – cold. "S-s-s-snake," was all he managed to get out.

It was a monster, six feet long, one scant yard in front of him. Thick as a stump, long as jump rope, it slithered slowly before him, looking around. "Freeze," was all I could say. I did not need to. Everyone froze. The notorious aggressor undulated by, gradually disappearing into the damp, leafy undergrowth. We knew what it was; his markings were clear, black tiger snake. We all nearly collapsed.

Snake gone, we humored each other – until we stumbled onto the *second* black tiger. Like the first, this one was nearly six feet, head of a wolf-fish, bold and menacing. That made *two* in ten minutes. While technically two hours off the trail head, we were back in one. Halfway there, we met another family. They seemed in shock. "We just saw …" I finished their sentence, "a black tiger snake?" "No …" they said, "a king brown." *Oh, great! That* was another Australian snake, more deadly than a black tiger, fifteen times the venom. We were at the car in five minutes.

People around the world can be inordinately friendly – wildlife not always. Put differently, Maine wildlife was nothing like what, years later, we encountered in Australia. The contrast was so marked that we took great solace in knowing Maine had *no* poisonous snakes, for all the quirks of local Maine wildlife.

Even ordinary critters offer endless entertainment. Not long ago, three young red-tail hawks wobbled on tree limbs outside our window. They were not interested in seeds; they were interested in a squirrel. They fluttered uncomfortably, constantly reseating themselves. They were new to hunting. Below them was dinner, in theory – a savvy, irreverent gray squirrel. The morsel kept eluding them. Try as they might, they could not catch him.

Their frustration grew until it was palpable. What would Mom and Dad say? Here was a stupid squirrel, who knew their secret. They were just young bumblers. He was ignoring them. The humiliation of it! Heads down, they fussed. We watched to see what came next.

They had dived and dived, to no effect. The twitchy rodent, brindle face had bested them. Realizing their youth, he took a devil-may-care attitude. They could not coordinate eyes, wings and talons, so he went back to foraging. He did not even look up; he was content in his own world. The scene was comical. The squirrel gave these handsome know-nothings not one iota of respect. The hawks knew the forest manual put them top of the food chain, him bottom, but not today. They drifted off, hangdog. Animals can be quirky, like people. And like people, can make you laugh.

Sometimes, the whole forest changed. One species exploded, another shrank, all in one lifetime. In youth, we never saw a wild turkey. Today, they are everywhere. Same for coyotes. Around the house, we saw field mice (white-footed and meadow voles), blind moles (star-nosed mostly), hustling chipmunks, thumping rabbits (snowshoe and domesticated), red and gray squirrels (most fearful of hawks and eagles). We had a snatch-and-run fox, always after our rabbits. Bobcats were rumored, but never seen. Whitetail deer were plentiful, with turtles and bull frogs. Closer to the lake, we had muskrats, beaver and *harmless* water snakes.

Grosbeaks lived for their ration of sunflower seeds, which we dutifully delivered before school to a window feeder. Grosbeaks, chickadees and speckled sparrows were sociable, getting along with nuthatches, who insisted on eating upside down. Skittish flickers were less sociable. Arresting in their white-tailed beauty, they would do a fly-by, clearing the feeder – then eat. More obnoxious were the self-possessed blue jays, no manners whatsoever.

Downy, harry and pileated woodpeckers made regular appearances, projecting purpose and intellect. The pileated was rare, and all business. A tall gent, he had flaming red hair front to back, white stripes on his dark neck. He was the consummate deconstruction engineer, throwing more wood chips in a minute than a gas-powered chipper in ten – and in every direction.

Some birds were prizes. Just seeing one made our day. Bald eagles topped that list, of course. Circling, hunting, sitting chin to wind on a pine bow, defiant beak, ready to order an unruly world. These birds held their own, and held our undivided attention. Next came chirping ospreys, who flew tight circles over our canoe, diving on fish – including the ones we caught if not careful.

Loons, a species dating to the Mesozoic era, spoke and sang to each other. From 100 million years ago, their distinctive call came to our ears, as it once had to dinosaur ears. Here was the ultimate "message in a bottle," mysterious, indecipherable, heartfelt, transfixing. Not to be forgotten were unhurried blue herons, and all manner of colorful ducks, especially the common merganser. And on Maine cliffs, in places like Acadia, we enjoyed watching an acrobatic dodger, the peregrine falcon.

Closer to home, crows were all quirk, and never quiet. They were nettlesome clowns, strutting about in their black feathered gowns, searching for something to eat, chattering streams of gobbledygook. They woke us at dawn, and carried themselves with the dignity of flapping tarpaper. They aspired, if at all, to being ravens. None made it. Then again, they could all fly – we could not.

Finally, we had the Canada geese, generally overhead. Everyone looked up as they honked in "V formation," slightly uneven. Years later, my son put the question to me. "Dad, do you know why one side of the V is longer?" His inflection suggested knowledge. I thought about it. "Because the wind blows harder on one side?" "No," he said with resolve. "Is it … that one side is younger, the other older?" "No," again. "One side male, other female?" "Nope." A smile began to creep across his young face. "Is it one side is tired, needs to draft, the other stronger?" He shook his head again, "no." Having exhausted my idea attic, I gave up. His smile got big. "One side is longer Dad because … it has more geese." *Boom-tick! I had been had! He was already practicing Downeast humor!*

Quirks abounded. Ravens were genuine individuals, imbued with a certain dignity, perhaps even integrity. They were decisive, robed like judges and Oxford dons, seemingly lost in inscrutable thought or observation. They seemed to radiate intelligence. No wonder Edgar Allen Poe wrote: "Open here I flung the shutter, when with many a flirt and flutter, in there stepped a stately Raven of the saintly days of yore …" From Poe's time to ours, their quirks commanded attention.

Raccoons were their opposite number, inveterate thieves, comic. They were agile, shameless bandits, nimble enough to climb a fence or woodpile, topple a ladder, jump a roof, open a garbage bag or pick corn. When caught, they blamed the cat. One day, when I was pintsized, I landed a bucket of sunfish. Proud, I toted them home in a bucket of water. I gave them names and declared them my pets. They swam big circles. Mom did not count them pets, so my uncapped aquarium was put outside.

Next morning, I was up early to visit. To my shock, I found the bucket empty, except for water. My sunfish were gone, nowhere to be found. I looked everywhere. They were not outside the bucket, but paw prints were, raccoons. Raccoons love *fresh fish* and *washing* their food. I had done it, given them a pre-washed, ready-to-eat fish dinner. My bucket was a drive-through "happy meal." From that moment, I remembered the prints, and never brought sunfish home again.

With time, I got fonder of raccoons – slightly. Years on, friends found abandoned babies and raised them, eventually releasing them back to the wild. They were adorable – and hyperactive. Little rascals climbed back to front, shoulder to head, as if we were young pine trees. They were insatiable. The troupe explored every jacket pocket and ear channel. They listened, watched and sniffed – at everything.

One pulled a wrapped cough drop from my pocket. They were all over it, each baby more excited than the next. They huddled around this strange-smelling food. Faintly sweet, it was not fish. Maybe raccoons plunder honey hives. I did not know. With their sensitive noses, they seemed to believe this invaluable. Every little nose, every pair of little hands, wanted in.

One baby was in charge. He began un-wrapping the aromatic honey drop. Soon they were all climbing down our heads, shoulders and backs to inspect his work. As the lead baby pried the wrapper open, they fidgeted and washed their faces. Not sunfish, but nice and smelly. Excitement built. Even my anticipation grew. Would they like the cough drop? Finally, it was unwrapped. There was a collective pause. The baby in charge knew what he wanted, so did the rest. Without ado, he threw away the cough drop. They descended, a chirping mass, on the crinkly *plastic wrap*. The delicious sound of cellophane was better than flopping fish or corn husks. They crinkled away.

Deer, deer, deer … Maine woods were filled with cloven hooves, white-tail. Tracks were easy to find in mud or snow, side-by-side peanuts, scuffed a bit when in a hurry. In damp soil, nimble feet sank an inch; in snow, a foot or two. When visible, the impression looked like a small heart, the hart's heart. Toes were each distinct, merged at the base. Today, we have more deer than we need, but back then sightings were rare. With their rocking horse leaps, they resembled gazelle. Prints told stories – speed, weight, age and sex, sometimes a hint at motivation. The passing doe or buck might be ambling, fleeing, cavorting or grazing. Like us, they were creatures of habit and season. Nibbling at dusk, they might spook, perform a *grand jetes*, and go crashing through the thicket. We enjoyed these deer quirks.

Porcupines, slower than raccoons, put on a show. These slow rodents wiggled and waggled, needles flowing like a hayfield as they walked. No friend of dogs, they never did us any harm. Then again, we never barked or sniffed at them. Skunks were another story. One took up lodging under our kitchen, briefly – then thankfully gone. They could be bad news. The species was a perilous contradiction, gorgeous black and white puffballs, nearsighted, and lethal – or chokingly pungent – when they sprayed. We gave them plenty of room. Now and then, a wandering skunk hit a car. The skunk usually rested in peace. No one else did.

Once, camping in a drizzle, we dug a trench around the tent. The goal was to capture runoff. Surprisingly, it caught local attention. Late at night, I heard a raccoon rummaging through our camp gear, deliberately left outside. I picked up a flashlight, unzipped the flap, and swung my beam around – no joy. I slipped through the flaps and scanned – no animal. I listened – no sound.

Then through the rain, I heard a muffled shuffling, scratching. It was behind the tent. Ah ha! Soaked and mildly irritated at the raccoon, I stooped over and snuck along the ditch, preparing to surprise the rascal. With a sense of satisfaction, I whipped about the corner, light on. As you may have surmised, my light fell on something other than a raccoon.

At three feet, it illuminated the backside of an unhappy, snuffling skunk. Luckily, skunks do not have eyes at both ends. I shut the light off, and withdrew. Thankfully, he *missed* my offense and waddled off. If your best skunk story is no story – you have done well. Maine animals do have their quirks, most redeeming, none poisonous.

I am put in mind of the old dramatist John Payne, who in the 1820s captured the sentiment of a local Maine boy. "An exile from home, splendor dazzles in vain … Oh give me my lowly thatched cottage again. The birds singing gaily that came at my call, and gave me the peace of mind dearer than all – home, home, sweet, sweet home. There's no place like home, there's no place like home!" Maine animals may have their quirks, but we have ours too. I will take the combination any day to poisonous critters Down Under.

10. *Moose Breath*

If you have never smelled moose breath, stand by! Close encounters of the moose kind take the prize for surreal and outsized. I will share only two, enough for me. One unfolded in the dooryard, the other up north. By way of preview, close contact with a full-sized, fast-moving bull moose leaves an indelible impression. Mainers know the feeling; few forget it.

Moose one. Snowdrops and daffodils were up, green grass poking through tan mat, delicate buds wishing for a southern breeze. Oak, maple and cherry trees hinted of blossoming. Mud was everywhere. This was the season. Mornings were still nippy, but lake ice was out and the water open. Memorial Day was not far off, a few weeks. We were still in school, counting down days. That was when it happened …

To catch the school bus, we followed a morning routine. Being late was part of the routine, a weakness. Some days, I beat it. This was one. We would grab our bagged lunches, then scramble up exposed stairs to the garage, which lay at road level. Mom made us bring home the bags, until they fell apart. At the road, we waited for – sometimes barely caught – the bus.

The bus came around seven. Our house lay below road level, four-fifths up the mountain. Above us, unbroken woods stretched a quarter mile, gradually turning to granite, then sky. Below us, broad meadows – used as runways for light planes – filled the eye, turning to woods that cascaded steeply to the lake. Our closest neighbors were a half mile to north, south and east. Thus, on most days, we awaited the bus in quiet.

This particular morning, my sisters, brother and I grabbed lunch, tucked books under our arms, slipped into coat sleeves, and climbed to meet the school bus – not yet here. Nothing unusual. By chance, I happened to be up the stairs and out the garage door first. Today, the bus was late, or maybe I was uncharacteristically early. Either way, I arrived alone. Or so I thought …

I opened the garage door to a tremendous crashing and stick-snapping. The cacophony was startling. All the chaos culminated in the appearance, directly in front of me – of what seemed an apparition. From that ground-stomping clatter, as from a magician's ball of smoke, appeared a massive bull moose.

The sheer volume of the animal sticks, even now. If a prehistoric mammoth had stepped forward, I would not have been more surprised. Without warning, I stood face-to-face with a big-eared, big-eyed, big-bearded bull. He was a truck in fur, a muscular body on a chassis of disorderly legs. He looked irked to have ended up where he was. This was obviously not where he thought the upper mountain led. His decent to the road was steep, through thick brush and undergrowth. Getting there was a chore. Now he laid his baseball eyes on me. I just froze.

This was a bad dream come real, facing a bull moose at a dozen feet. The moment was terrifying – and strangely electrifying. Not every day something like this happened. The moose must have imagined himself in a dream, too. Descending an unpopulated mountain, he meets a pie-eyed boy, exhilarated, baffled, and scared out of his wits. We shared this special moment for an uncertain period. Neither of us bothered with anything, except each other. Time more or less stopped. My heart could have, but somehow kept beating. We were locked on, both distracted.

For a long moment, the moose examined me – and our mailbox. We were both appealing shades of green. He stood stock-still, mid-road, just looking. He seemed to struggle with where he was, exactly what his bounced-around optical nerve was transmitting. Whatever it was, it hit the neural net, nested in that massive head – and confused him. Bravely, the mailbox and I returned his gaze, unblinking. The three of us were in shock. The moose towered over the mailbox and me. None of us spoke, or even grunted. I could not have grunted, since that required air.

On closer inspection, his eyes were candlepin bowling balls, dark. His beard hung nearly my body's length. His head was mostly nose. The combination held me like a tractor beam. I was not prepared for this moment; I do not think I ever imagined it. My mind was preparing to catch the bus, not a moose. I had been innocently mulling homework, to be done on the bus. To be fair, the moose was probably unprepared for me, too. Like me, he was not a quick thinker, at least under these circumstances. So there we stood, moose, mailbox and me, sharing our common shock, not sure what to do next.

The moose was out of breath. I could not find mine. From our separate universes, we had both been racing … apparently for the same mailbox. Now, we were both here to declare victory, only it was a tie – what did we do with a tie? We eyed each other a moment more, then noises came from below. Decisions had to be made. Others were ascending.

The moose obviously had no appetite for conversation. Of course, in my dumbstruck state, I offered little encouragement. On another occasion, in a parallel life, we might have met for coffee, gotten to be fast friends, exchanged cards – but not today. Not with siblings coming up the stairs, school bus rumbling somewhere, neither of us good with words, no common language.

In seconds, Mr. Moose was in motion. By the time my sisters and brother appeared, he was at full trot, headed for the bend in the road. I was petrified, energized, transfixed and giddy. I was tingling, head and heart pounding with adrenaline. This was fiction, made real.

Suddenly, with my moose lumbering away, I decided not to let go. My eyes tracked him, hoping he might slow, but he was resolved. He had seen enough of boys and mailboxes for one day. I tried to process all this – big head and ears, nose and eyes, chin and beard, shoulders and stare. Then I made a decision. I did not want the adventure to end. I began running after him.

Nuts, I know. When I tried to explain later, words failed me. They do again. Just skip this part. Nothing logical here. A big moose will do that – suspend logic. Stirred by adrenalin, I wanted to keep the moose in view. I forgot the bus and homework, siblings and time. I gave chase. Terrified, electrified, fascinated and curious, I threw down my books and pursued the moose.

From the ease of a reading chair, you may think this reckless, even stupid. You are probably right on both counts. But I was not in a reading chair, not grown up, and not you. Actually, I was not even me. I was under the spell of that magical moose. He might have wheeled suddenly, giving me more attention than I bargained for, charged or tried to stomp me. He might have done anything. But we had never seen a moose in the dooryard. I wanted to see where he would go. Ditching school was easy; the bus was irrelevant. As my siblings popped out the door, I shouted something incomprehensible and disappeared after my moose.

I kept pace for a time, but also my distance. Racing the moose proved exhausting. He was darned fast, faster than I imagined. A screen of roadside trees separated us. He lumbered in huge strides. The whole episode was surreal, encountering this forest mammoth up close. Even in Maine, kids do not often see a moose as they wait for the bus. This beat homework. I tried to stretch my stride. I had a lumber. I had a good view. We were headed somewhere, but he was gaining, outpacing me. He trotted, I sprinted. His long legs carried him where that chin pointed. I wanted to see where he would go. I could not take my eyes off him. He seemed to hear, but dismissed me. He was at a dog's run. It was a losing proposition. He gained with each step; his were three of mine.

As he loped along, I bounded behind my evergreen screen, wishing not to offend him, trying to stay unseen. He was purposeful, headed somewhere. I thought briefly about the bus and my homework. But this was science. As we ran, I breathed harder. I did not want to upset him, but my breathing was getting louder.

The moose did not slow for a quarter mile. Then, he abruptly turned left. He bolted down an old logging road. I knew the road well, but that was small advantage in mud. Picking my way through trees, I crossed asphalt and took to the mud. In spring, even the best logging roads got slippery, rutted and proved hard to navigate. Jumping ruts while chasing a mammoth was messy. My sneakers were soaked, moose disappearing fast, then gone.

For what seemed a long time, I just stood and listened. He broke branches, made his own road through the woods. His breathing echoed in my ears, perhaps mine in his. His long gait and swamp-swaggering legs outpaced me with little effort. Somewhere, he was enjoying anonymity again, deep in the forest. Soon all was still. He was gone. He had ditched me.

I drew a deep breath, turned around and headed back, heart racing. Splashing in mud ruts, the whole encounter seemed unreal. I was alone again with my thoughts and muddy feet – the incident replayed itself. Amazing how fast a big moose can appear and disappear, come from somewhere, disappear into nowhere, never to be seen again. He never was. The mailbox and I gave him a fright.

Moose two. Second "close encounter" was a bull further north, not far from Moosehead Lake in fall. The unexpected rendezvous also involved mud, the wet shoreline of Little Kokajo Lake. I was a young teen with my first camera, hunting magic moments. And I found one.

This trip brought the family to a remote cabin. Wherever I went, my camera dangled from a lanyard, swinging freely with flash attachment on top. At night, my camera slept in a faux-leather box. One morning, I awoke before full light. We were on a pond. I was up – before everyone.

Camera in hand, I slipped outside. The air was cool and tingled. I planned to be back before anyone awoke, no note. My camera itched to catch something. What, I was not sure, but something. In that exact moment, somewhere, a countdown began. Ten minutes stood between me and another magic moment – with a 500-pound bull moose. Like the other encounter, we did not become friends. But after that day, the north woods teemed with moose.

Surveying the dewy dawn, I blinked sleep from my eyes and took in the pond. Maine ponds are lovely at dawn. Often, they are covered with cotton balls, rolling condensation. Suddenly, my heart leapt. In the center of this pond, bobbing and dripping, was a bull moose, regal rack. I centered my camera. He became a dot. The viewfinder shrank him to nothing. Such a photo would win no prizes. I could do better. I had to.

Slowly, he swam or slogged toward the near shoreline, now and then pausing, unhurried in the dawn. He did not move directly toward me, probably had no awareness of me. Instead, he moved toward an unseen point, up the shoreline. His body weight was borne by the water. He was quiet. Even from a distance, he was breathtaking. To think he might come ashore nearby was electrifying. I resolved to get closer. Maybe I could take a photo no one would believe.

The shoreline was thick with trees. Soon, my moose disappeared behind them, somewhere off to the right. Shielded again by young evergreens, I slunk along the lake's rim, stopping to listen, hoping to see something, camera ready. I kept quiet, stayed stealthy. Periodically, I caught sight of him through branches, still at a distance. Now, I could hear him more clearly; he was picking up speed, swimming intensely or perhaps walking.

Through the branches, I could see him closing, moving diagonally. He might come ashore and be gone before I could see him. That was my big worry. He seemed headed for a spot several hundred feet to the right. This was fun, hide and seek. My camera dangled. I grabbed it, kept stalking. I could hear my breathing quicken, switched to air by mouth, quieter. Wasn't this how professionals did it? Must be, I thought. Suddenly, I had to pee. There was no time.

Light on my feet, I passed an abandoned cabin. More like it lay along the lake's periphery, empty and needing repair. I picked my way through a curtain of evergreens and alders, sinking in mud, straining for a better view. My feet were wet, but who cared. Tall grasses clumped under the trees. I crossed a deer path. Was it a moose path? A fleeting thought.

Luck was with me. I switched directions, shifting to a dry patch. The path steered me inland, but quickened my trip. It kept me hidden from the open water. I emerged near another ramshackle cabin, this one also empty. It seemed to have fallen into disuse, certainly no one near. It was perfect – a blind. Here, I waited.

This cabin separated me from the walking moose. He was closer. I could hear him kicking up water. He was stirring nearby, not far now. I got more excited, if that was possible. I waited, and waited. Studying the cabin's unstained outer boards, missing cedar shingles, torn patches of tarpaper, I could see why a moose made this an exit ramp from the lake. There had been no one here for a while. Shingles were curling and splitting. Still, the cabin's walls were solid. This was "rustic," Maine's great north, a perfect cabin for moose country, I thought.

But where was the moose? Had I lost him? No way to know. Logic said "no." Silence said "yes." Had he slipped the shore, while I studied this cabin? Disappeared back into the water? I hugged the backside of the cabin. Logically, I knew he must be in the lake, close to the shoreline. I listened hard. *Relief!* I heard splashes again. He *was* nearby. I stood *very* still. I knew he would come ashore near this point. He was snorting, splashing. From the sounds he was making, he would emerge near the other side of this cabin! I suddenly had to pee again. There was no place, no time. I had to get this photo. Funny what you remember, isn't it?

I crept backwards along the path, a dozen feet. Poking my head through evergreens and alders, I looked around. Nothing. I returned to my perch, and stood behind the cabin, hugging the back wall. I just listened. Every twig might have meaning. The moose was rustling, moving slowly, getting out of the water. I really had to pee. His splashes were close.

Suddenly, I forgot about everything except him. The cabin stood twenty feet from the water, but was small, not twenty feet square. I knew he must be coming ashore *directly in front* of this old structure, my "moose blind." I stood tight, waiting to see what he would do next. The answer was nothing. Nothing, nothing and nothing. He went radio silent again.

I recall, even now, that I checked my camera to be sure film was wound, flash attached, and bulb installed. All was good. That was what you had to do for a good picture. I cursed myself for not having gone to the bathroom before coming, but I was on a mission. The rest could wait. I had to get a close-up of this giant, and his massive rack. I was close. Very close.

Then, for several long minutes I just stood. I stuck to the wall, waiting. Nothing happened. I listened for signs of movement. None. I reasoned with myself. He had to be there. Where else could he have gone? I tried to imagine him moving, put time to gait, tried to calculate how many minutes should pass before he had land legs and balance, dripped a bit, looked about, and took stock of things – and decided to head for the path, beside me. But there was nothing. No sound of shaking. No sound of steps. No sound of returning to water. Nothing.

All of a sudden, I heard him. He *was* finally moving. He seemed farther away, farther than I imagined. Was he on a *different* course? Was there a path that took him *away* from me – away from my *camera?* Or was he just lingering, nibbling and lounging at the shoreline? Would he stay there indefinitely? Was he in a funk, dripping dry? Do moose drip dry? I had never thought about it. If so – for how long? My mind raced. I certainly did not hear him shaking. Maybe moose are silent shakers? Maybe they do not shake, given that big rack? The rack must be hard to wag. *Where was he?*

Logic told me he would not reenter the lake. Not after a good swim. Why would he, after coming ashore? If he headed back, I should hear him. No sign of a second dip. Maybe I had scared him. Maybe he could smell me. Logic told me, since he had not emerged from the other side, he must still be near the lake. If he had not crossed behind me, he must still be in front of me. He was being coy. He was standing stock still. I listened for clues. Hearing none, I edged to the corner of the cabin. If I did not hear something soon, I would just peek around the corner, see where he was, and pull back. You might think I had nerve, but really I had no idea how moose behaved. I was just enamored of my camera, wanted to put it to use, and had to pee.

Earlier scuffling, hard breathing, and splashing were all gone. In its place, no discernible sound. If the moose was walking, he was stealthy. Was he just standing? Maybe eating lakeside grass? Did moose do that? Was he sunning himself like a turtle – in cool air? Sun was rising. Was he focused on something? I noticed, on the other side of the lake, a cow moose and calf. Was he attached to them, concerned? If so, why was he over here, and not moving? I got impatient.

I was prepared to click a picture. More importantly, I wanted to see this majestic beast close up, watch him lumber by at a safe distance. For a moment, I thought my mother would not like this situation, my proximity to a moose. She would have hauled me inside. But she was asleep. The thought of returning to the cabin without seeing the moose up close, getting a photo, was a non-starter. You do not spot, track, and wait – to sigh and walk off. My moose mission needed completing. The moose needed to do *his* job, and get into my camera. *Where was he?*

No sound meant – no movement. A short look around the corner, seemed in order. He was probably near the lake. Even from that distance, his rack would make a good photo. I could watch him eating. Ok, time to venture a glance. The weathered corner beckoned. I would take a peek.

What was the harm? I would see where he was. I leaned forward, poked my head around the corner – and met my second bull moose.

Whoa! What the X&%##@&&!!!! There he WAS! Inches from me! Looking straight at me! Massive head, shoulders wide as a double refrigerator, rack the size of a dinner table, eyes of molten glass, and that warm, musty breath – right on me! A veritable tower of terror, he was less than a yard from my face! OUTA here – NOW!*

That was all I could think, all my feet thought. My feet took over, did the thinking. To the extent I can recreate them, these were my paralyzing thoughts. *Nose like an engine block, jet engine nostrils, oak tree out of his head, gobs of hair, surreal eyes, dripping chin. He was a monstrous ***%#@!!! MOOSE! AND he was in motion!* As if to put me on my way, he *snorted! He was not just breathing on me, he was blowing air at me!* That was it. I did not collapse, but should have. I should have become a quivering heap. In retrospect, a miracle I didn't. I would today. His totality was transcendent. I stumbled backwards, and took off.

Even so, the world was in slow motion. The countdown, to which I referred earlier, culminated right here. The rendezvous was now. I flew, flailing and slipping on dewy grass, stumbling down the moose path on my skinny legs, praying not to fall, hoping not to be followed, trying not to hit trees. *Where was the path, anyway? Our cabin? And the moose? Was he still there, or not? Was he following me, or not? Where was the blessed moose?* Those were the sentiments flooding my rattled brain. Camera bouncing, I forgot about it – and just made tracks.

Then at some point, I stopped. I looked back, caught hind quarters disappearing into the woods behind me. Out of breath, my courage returned. I had missed my picture. Hope, embarrassment and vanity mixed. I had not even raised my camera, darn it! *How could I have forgotten to take the picture?* I decided, in that instant, not to fail. I turned around, slipped back down the path. He was crashing through the marsh beyond. He had crossed where I stood, no interest in me.

I got to the point where I could see his tracks, and tried to follow. He was out of sight, no more lingering. I managed to get into the swamp, to no end. He was fleet, like his cousin. He was gone, branches wiggling still. I took a photo of the branches. I decided not to challenge the muck. In these Little Kokajo photos, you will see no moose. But he is nearby, I promise. The trees are lovely. A good story goes with them. At least I got that, and some moose breath.

11. *Mischievous Bunnies*

As a family, we kept bunnies. In a word, they were mischievous. We did not intend to keep bunnies. It just happened, like everything about bunnies. They showed up, and one thing led to another. I did magic tricks for birthday parties and needed a bunny – yes, to pull from a hat. Suddenly, we needed four – one for each sibling. Suddenly, we had dozens of bunnies.

What does a family do when suddenly in possession of dozens of bunnies? We built rabbit hutches. We built more and more rabbit hutches. These proved utterly useless, ineffective – more mischief. Bunnies dig. They like to "commune." They commune liberally. Liberally, do they commune, and bingo. Within six months, we had sixty-four bunnies, threatening to become a hundred. We had what *Star Trek* called "Trouble with Tribbles," only ours were bunnies!

My sister Cynthia loved our bunnies, and willingly assumed responsibility for their care. This was kind. It forestalled another fate. Years later, she founded a bunny rescue operation, her second. In our youth, she refused to let a single bunny be eaten. She would not have it.

Accordingly, we tried to quarantine the bunnies in new-fangled hutches, with chicken wire all over and under. This worked briefly. Rabbits, however, are determined. They learned to gnaw wood, claw wire, find holes, twist open gaps, dig tunnels and get out. In short, they would not have it.

Eventually, we compromised. We let them all go, every last one. Most stayed close. They built homes everywhere. They came to be fed, then happily wandered off and grazed. But nothing lasts forever. A few months after releasing them, bunny numbers started to dwindle. That was when we noticed him …the fox. He came evenings with great stealth, loitered and skulked about, then struck and disappeared. In time, bunny numbers stabilized. The two species seemed to arrive at a stalemate. Still the nocturnal raids continued. The bunnies were not happy.

One day, something bizarre happened – so bizarre that we talked about it for years. We replayed the day, tried to understand what had happened. We never really did. It confirmed to us that Nature is utterly inscrutable, at times inexplicable. Nature abhors a vacuum and maybe foxes. One day, she leveled the field. What follows … is factual, incontrovertible, and strange.

That afternoon was bright, indistinguishable from any other. We climbed off the school bus and looked around. Something was different, not right. Bunnies should have been everywhere, hopping around the dooryard. There were none. Normally, as the sun set, bunnies emerged to eat. They spread across our pebble drive and upper meadow. Today, no bunnies. Not one.

Could the fox have gone on a rampage? Eaten them all? Chased them away? The alternatives were unsatisfying. Yet here we stood, where dozens of bunnies should be standing – alone. We dropped our books and began to hunt the woods. Where were they? That is when one of us spotted them. They were a thousand feet away, gathered in an unnatural huddle. They looked to be in a giant circle. *What in the world was going on?*

Bunnies did not assemble in giant circles. They did not assemble, except in pairs. Bunnies roamed separately. They had friends, but nibbled as individuals. Yet there they all were, in a tightly packed group. Odder still, from where we stood, they appeared to be static. They seemed to be unmoving. *What were they doing? Why the distance? Circle? Stillness? What were they up to? Why would rabbits muster in a cluster?* We ran toward them.

The closer we got, the more we saw. They were alive, ears wiggling, feet shuffling, but still. Here and there a tail or leg jiggled. Every bunny – off-whites, grays, splotchy and browns – were there, and uneasy. Frankly, there was nothing *faintly normal* about independent animals jammed in a bunch. This was NOT rabbit behavior. The huddle had them pressed together. They were collected in a place smaller than a child's bedroom. As we approached, several fidgeted, ears went up. Otherwise, the huddle was quiet, almost somber.

What in the world was this open-air chapter room? Were they plotting some grand act, these industrious little bounders? Silly. Why assemble here – so far from the house? Why compress themselves into a ball? As we grew closer, we could see the mass shifting, going from ball to doughnut, back to ball. Suddenly, they were a gaggle of wagging ears, flicking legs, bobbing tails, focused noses. They had loosened, began a slow march around the circle, going nowhere.

As we neared, our curiosity grew. They became aware of us. *What were they up to? Why were none of them eating? Why were they facing inward, as if listening to a speaker?* Now and then, one would hop, as if straining for a better view. They were focused – on something.

Then an epiphany swept us. As kids, we realized there must *be something to see.* We burst into an all-out run, seconds away. As we ran, the air crackled. Something strange was afoot, and we knew it. Even as we approached, the bunnies barely moved. Only after we got close did they begin to care and disperse. They acted like parishioners, reflecting on a sermon. Or maybe like a band of knights, exhausted, departing the roundtable, pushing back from the war council.

Their movements were measured, unhurried and confident. They seemed of one mind, radiating a spirit of victory, drifting off a field of play. There was something cerebral too in their manner, unusually pensive and slow-moving – characteristics for which bunnies are not well known. They seemed to be coming out of something, emerging from another place, not where bunnies typically go. Nor did their pace hasten. They moved in time with an invisible metronome, tick per kick, tired and stopping to pause. Not one of them was eating. By ones, twos, they just hopped away. Very strange.

That was when we saw him – pastoral and inert. At the center of the dispersing circle lay a solitary figure. Surrounded by bunnies, he had been like a magnet drawing shards. The magnetism was now gone, the shards dispersing. Their grotesque attraction? *The fox.* Their predator, nightly bête noir, the animal that had terrorized them for months, picked them off, preyed on their young. At the center of the circle from which they drifted – he lay dead.

We stood for a long moment, confused. The bunnies continued to hop away from the dead marauder. Too odd for words. Here lay the fox, lifeless. Here were our bunnies, drained. We could make no sense of this. As a rule, bunnies do not kill foxes, even if they loathe and outnumber them – as far as we knew. No one bunny in its right mind would confront, let alone try to kill, a fox. Besides, bunnies are herbivores. Nevertheless, here he lay, predator no more. Here they were, quiet, triumphant and relieved.

We scratched our heads, repeating to each other what we were seeing – later what we had seen. Here were the jaw, teeth, skin, muscle and claws of a proven predator, practiced prowler, intact except that he was dead. No marks on him, he was decidedly deceased. No signs of disease, evidence of mishap or wounds. There was no indication of how he had died.

So what happened to the fox? What were these bunnies doing? What had they seen, if anything? Were they just inspecting their arch-enemy's demise, confirming it? How does a healthy fox meet such an abrupt end – in an open meadow? The bunnies would not say. They just hopped away. All the same, we knew this: Spirited, healthy foxes do not expire without a cause. This incident – simple and true – long remained a curiosity. At times, it nagged at me. I laughingly retold it – to new and incredulous listeners.

Then, a few years ago, I stumbled onto something. It was a wild stretch, but it was something. It might explain what happened on that strange, sunny day in rural Maine. Quixotic research landed me on an improbable, but distantly possible, answer to the great bunny mystery. The idea may strike you, the reader, as far-fetched. It did me. But if you consider the absence of any reasonable alternative, the idea takes on new color. It may sunset the mystery.

In short, science may finally offer an answer. You see, an infrequent phenomenon does occur in Nature. The phenomenon is well-documented, although uncommon. Like frozen fish falling from a sky post-tornado, hikers ambling into an albino moose, or a freak snowstorm in summer, the thing happens. It is a matter of record. The phenomenon to which I refer is called "animal mobbing." No joke, it occurs, albeit rarely.

This is Nature's "castling" move, changing the chessboard for one instant, suddenly reversing roles, shifting expectations and upending power – for a very short time. Once the moment passes, things return to normal. The rightful order resumes. Seen among birds, fish and smaller animals, including meerkats and ground squirrels, mobbing is "an anti-predator behavior which occurs when individuals of a certain species mob a predator by cooperatively attacking or harassing it, usually to protect their offspring." Sometimes, the predator is killed. Curious, improbable and remarkable, almost laughable. But what else could the crazy day have been?

As unsettling as the notion of "mobbing" may sound, as incredulous on a first read, the phenomenon does exist. So maybe that greedy fox grabbed one bunny too many, and wham! Who knows? Who will ever know? Only those enigmatic, mischievous bunnies know. Whatever happened that day, it never did again. Lightning, as they say, seldom strikes the same spot twice. Nature is bizarre, in ways we only barely imagine. If "normal" is more comforting, Robin Hood in me rather likes the idea of this anti-predator mobbing. Perhaps that rapacious fox got his own. Who knows? I know only this: Our bunnies were never again raided by a fox.

Sister Cynthia, with one of our 64 lovable, uncontainable bunnies, circa 1975

12. Rescue Mission

Living in rural Maine, we saw Nature up close. Sometimes, too close-reference the moose and predatory fox. We often saw life's stages playing out around us. We watched wild things born in spring. We saw fawns and bunnies learning to leap, often sideways, figuring out legs. We saw young birds being fed by parents, struggling to fly, perching, pecking and hunting. And we saw animals get older. In tracks, we saw deer come up lame and sick. We found animals expired, felled by cars and sometimes each other. We listened to chatter boxes in trees, watched stealthy hunters move noiselessly. We saw romance and sparring, budding families and lone rangers, the cycles of life. Sometimes, we even got injected into one.

We had empathy for wild things, informed by caution and understanding of their place in the ecosystem. We ate venison and partridge, but watched fawns at dawn and laughed when flushing a bird. We had no aversion to hunting and fishing, loved our catches. Still, we knew the patterns of life and respected them.

Not surprisingly, as kids, we made a habit of saving injured animals. If we could not, we got them to a vet. Maine vets treated wild animals free. We enjoyed the cycles, occasionally assisting. All this was a rite of passage. We picked birds up that had flown into windows, dropped from nests, or were nursing broken wings. I once found an injured osprey; a vet restored him. As kids, we tried raising baby mice, saving half-chewed chipmunks and squirrels (remember, we had cats), and helping turtles cross roads. If an animal was ailing, we knew the score: Wounded animals generally perish. If Nature put them in our way, they got a second chance.

All this is prologue – to one rescue mission. Why kids are drawn to animals is a mystery, especially turtles. We anthropomorphized them, superimposed feelings on them, and gave them names. Once a turtle got a name, he was just a person in a shell. Franz Kafka would understand this. E.B. White, Garth Williams, Dr. Seuss and Maine's own Maurice "Jake" Day, creator of Bambi, would too. Maybe we just liked helping, or got a solid return on our emotional investment. Who knows? Maybe our motivations were those of every child, and need no explanation. As kids, we liked observing and caring for animals. No wonder, these days we have two dogs, two cats, two birds, and a lizard. Animals are just companionable, even the lizard. In theory, so were turtles.

Climbing a tree and finding a clutch of songbird eggs inspired wonder. The wonder doubled stumbling over oversized duck or loon eggs. We left them where we found them – that was a rule except for frog eggs. Those eyeballs in jelly we collected into jars. We watched them grow into tadpoles, sometimes frogs. More often, we let them go as tadpoles. Turtles too were plentiful. But *turtle eggs* were an unlikely find.

A word about eggs. Wild ones were filled with promise. They were young life, unwritten stories, creatures waiting to be born, static ovals tapped by the Wand of Life. We had no problem eating chicken eggs, right along with bacon and ham, and loved them. We were not purists, certainly not sentimental about chickens. But wild eggs were different, and inedible anyway. They were compact packages of future wild life. That was enough. Wild eggs made us curious. That is how we happened, one day, to try hatching … young snapping turtles. Little did we know, Maine did not need extra snappers.

Most turtles were docile, storybook plodding – and peaceful. They carried themselves with poise and equanimity, lived peacefully in the woods, pausing now and then to sunbathe. They liked mud, no preening, and no star roles. Most were happy log-sitters, if regular swimmers. Bothered, they just tucked their heads in and waited things out. On the river, they dove from their log. They were eminently practical.

Snappers were different. They were swift in water, cranky and impatient on land. They liked to eat little ducks, and could get big in the process. Some were as big as a turkey platter, and weighed as much as the turkey. Ashore, snappers looked clunky and armored. They were trundlers. If you tried to pick them up, they craned their necks and tried to bite you. In my experience, they never succeeded, but always tried. They were not looking to fight, but did not tuck from one. More confident than your average bear – or painted turtles – land-bound snappers had attitude. In the water, they were something else – quick, darting, disinterested in contact, except a good gobble when they saw one, usually identified from little legs and a tuft of feathers. Why we cared about this species, I am not sure.

Nevertheless, one spring day, we landed in the middle of their life cycle. A snapper the size of two basketballs, destined for egg-laying, had come to an untimely end. About her on the road were scattered a dozen turtle eggs. Ironically, they seemed intact – and in need of hatching. We scooped up these orphaned eggs, imagined each a young snapper, and began strategizing. We thought ourselves white knights. Mom thought us nuts. Still, it was her spirit we were acting on. She was as enamored of Nature as we were, just painted it – instead of rescuing it.

We ignored the big questions. How did one hatch snapper eggs? Were snapper babes cuddly and containable? How did one sustain small turtles once hatched? Such things were secondary. Actually, we never thought about them at all. Our mission was to save the turtles, if we could. The rest we assumed would work itself out. Mom cautioned about expecting too much, then acquiesced. She did not bother with warnings, best to let Nature teach. And Nature did.

Once back home, the turtle eggs were closely studied. Little ping pong balls, they were rubbery, squishy, but stable. Not one was broken. No way to know which side was up, we surmised they needed to be buried in sand. We knew they were snappers, but had only passing knowledge of eggs.

We considered our options. We could leave them near a pond, bury them ourselves, and let Nature take its course. In retrospect, that might have been best. That idea, however, was boring. We could find a vet and hand them off, but that seemed a bit over the top. We could coddle and fuss, dote day and night, keep them warm, trying to cajole them from their gummy shells. *That* sounded exciting. We chose that option.

What followed was a singular lesson in how to fuss over turtle eggs – and almost burn a house down. Once we had chosen coddling, one question remained. *Where? Where could we place these traumatized packages, these shells within shells, to make them hatch?* Our conversation was circular, until we ended up where we wanted to be. "How about inside, then we can see them?" "No, they should be outside, maybe just out the front door." "No, they'll be eaten by birds and night animals." "It gets cold at night." "We might forget and step on them." "If we don't keep them close, they might get eaten … by mice." "How about inside?"

In the end, we decided – altogether unwisely – to keep them inside. We emptied a bureau drawer in the room my brother and I shared. That would work. "Look," I said, "this will be perfect … Nothing will get them, we can watch their progress, and if they hatch too quickly, we have them trapped – they won't get away!" My logic seemed impeccable, the way kid logic is – even when ungrounded and making no sense whatever.

We cheerfully lined the drawer with towels, closed the drawer to a slit – allowing ample air and deterring cats. *What could be simpler?* We would just wait for them to hatch. This should be easier than pollywogs to frogs. We considered putting sand in the drawer to simulate the outdoors, but that was messy – and difficult to explain to Mom. Better to keep things simple.

Days passed. Nothing happened. We began to think our turtle eggs needed incubation. Maybe the drawer was not warm enough. *If incubators and lights hatched chicks, something similar should hatch turtles, right?* Never mind that turtle eggs hatch in cold sand. We did not have an incubator, so we improvised. Heating the eggs might be the ticket. Lights were too hot, heating pads too hard to regulate, water bottles too short duration. Suddenly, I got it. We could borrow the aquarium heater, just set it for room temperature, put it in the drawer, and warm the eggs. The thought never crossed my mind that heat propagates differently in air and water. Water is fire resistant. I barreled ahead.

My brainstorm seemed practical, convenient, borderline brilliant. *What could be easier?* The aquarium heater warmed fish. For a few days, they could survive without it. Meantime, the drawer would become a balmy 75 degrees. For humidity, we would insert moist towels. Nothing catches fire at 75 degrees, right? All would be fine. Moist towels would shield our eggs from direct heat. The turtles would think they were sunbathing. Soon, they would pop out of their shells and populate the drawer. Aquarium heater plus time equaled turtles!

This became our plan. The aquarium heater was removed, set among moist towels near the turtle eggs. All was well. Keeping the heater at modest heat, we congratulated ourselves for thinking creatively. Soon we would have turtles. Plan executed, we headed off to school.

As the oldest, I was ringleader, sometimes a bit headstrong. This time, I assumed the role of executive decision-maker for turtle hatching. I was, you might say, in charge. There is a price to be paid for leading – especially leading badly. I was about to learn this. If things went badly, I could expect to be the first to hear. And I was.

On this occasion, things went quite badly. When I got home from school, my mother greeted me sternly, no smile. Straining to be patient, her eyes were ablaze. I had not mentioned our make-shift incubator, the aquarium heater and moist towel configuration. On the way to the bus, our ingenuity had not seemed relevant. I now realized that was a profound oversight.

As it turned out, the aquarium heater was not just efficient – it was incendiary. Put in that drawer, it became a pyrotechnic wonder. Innocent as an aquarium heater looked inside the aquarium, it dried moist towels, heated a wooden drawer, elevated everything beyond 75 degrees (obviously, since it was out of water!), and produced a smoky, billowing hazard in hours! When our mother got home from teaching, a strange odor permeated the house. She traced it to the bureau, where she found piping hot turtle eggs, singed towels and wood, all compliments of the aquarium heater. She got there just in the nick. Egg smoke was curling from the drawer. *Ouch!*

Needless to say, we narrowly averted a house fire. I was chastened, put on notice. The towels were minutes from flame. The bureau, room and house would have gone up in seconds. I was mortified. The experience was sobering, educational and frightening. The scorched heater was trashed, new one bought with my money. Towels were ditched, new ones bought with my money. I got a well-deserved lecture. And our poached turtle eggs were deposited outside.

And we never hatched snapping turtles. This miscarriage of altruism was squarely on me. The idea of turtle eggs in a bureau, no sand, wet towels, aquarium heater – all mine. Few redeeming features attached to this venture, except some new realism. Our own shells got a little harder. We never again tried to hatch turtle eggs.

Only later did I find consolation. Turns out, the snapper eggs were probably doomed from the get-go. *Any* trauma spoils a turtle egg. As does *any* premature release. Throw in one auto accident, some hard tar, lots of handling and re-handling – and the odds were long. Besides, turtle eggs will *only* hatch "right side up." So, good luck there. Turtle eggs also *need* outside temperatures to hatch. Placed outside, they would have been someone's dinner. In any event, snappers were plentiful. Funny thing, too – despite the loss of a dozen eggs several decades ago, they still are.

13. Memorial Day

Small towns across America stopped the clock on Memorial Day. Such was that day's power over the heart. Even in our youth the day stopped kids. We had a parade and speech, veterans in uniform, scouts in formation, baton twirlers, old cars and a fire engine with running boards. The day drew everyone out of their home and downtown. Once there, minds drifted backwards to people remembered, some well, some less well. We thought about the past, those who had marched, and those who might have marched.

The town collected at the Mill Pond, in what we called Memorial Park. Grass was always new mown, always smelled good too. We stood looking out over calm water. The water drifted gently by and curled over the dam – as it had for more than a century. We listened. Sometimes, we participated in the ceremony. A modest speech, then taps. Finally, a wreath was silently laid each year on the Mill Pond for those who had fallen. This was done by a veteran. Gradually, that wreath drifted away from the shoreline, toward the dam.

We knew the names. They had left town to fight for America, friends and family. We knew their families. We imagined their going, from right where we stood. As a town, we gave thanks, and made time for collective remembering. The day was a "thank you" – to those who gave us the day, who had fought and had died for our freedom. By definition, Memorial Day was bittersweet, a pairing of loss with gratitude. Every person felt it. Some felt so much emotion they did not come, but they too felt it. Eventually, that wreath disappeared over the falls.

Every year, we would follow the same practices, track the same feelings. It never grew old. We wound past the General Store, Masonic and Grange Halls, Elementary School, down the road and out of sight. Then we circled back to the Mill Pond for a short speech, taps and the wreath-laying. Young people rode in old cars, flanked by veterans from World Wars I and II, Korea and Vietnam, later the Gulf War, Kosovo, Iraq and Afghanistan. Some had served abroad, others closer to home. Many had signed up; all had cared. By my mid-teen years, World War I veterans were all gone. Soon the World War II veterans will be.

Gathering in Memorial Park, dedicated to our fallen, we consciously paused. To me, the day embodied a long bow to honor. It was about honoring those who had the unhappy distinction of not coming home. It was a terrible and heartbreaking distinction, yet terribly important. From

World War II, three did not come home. Priscilla's only brother was one. She always attended.

The day was solemn. All those who had fought, from Richie to Priscilla's brother, departed expecting to return. No one goes thinking they will not come home. There must have been promises, tears and reassurances. The three who did not return should have, but for war's caprice. The unfairness was that some returned, others did not – young lives, cut short.

Going back to those lost in World War I and Civil War, one dared not tally what might have been. Lost were future fathers and grandfathers, future carpenters and farmers, teachers and doctors, lawyers and whole lives – left unlived. Or were these lives lived to their fullest, just as God wished, true to their given destiny? There was no use wondering. It was irretrievable, like the wreath released to the falls. Still one did: Were those who did not come home already on an irreversible current, or swept into it by events? Only God knew.

Whatever happened, it was forever – whatever forever meant. We believed their going to war made a difference in our lives, made our lives possible. That is why we stopped on this day to remember. On one hand, we wanted to understand and appreciate. On the other, we could never understand, just strive to appreciate. We wanted to pay time to their honor, reminding each other that sacrifice matters. Life and death what they are, we could not say it to them. Some ached to.

Lincoln at Gettysburg noted that anything the living say is evanescent and unavailing, insufficient and unsatisfactory. On the other hand, a loss suffered and honor shown is eternal. It always will be so. Lincoln did not say it that way. He said, the gift given was "above our poor power to add or detract." And so it is. It was then, and is still. Put differently, St. John observed that unconditional love simply has no parallel. "Greater love hath no man than this… than that a man lay down his life for his friends." How better to say it? Not one of these young men left expecting death, yet each knew it a possibility. They assumed that risk, even if they did not know the extent of their commitment. For that decision and where it led their noble souls, we thanked them. We did that as a town, and we did it every year.

As seasons changed, Memorial Day also marked an inflection point. The day cleared spring chills for summer. Crumpled uniforms came to life, filled with recollected friends and commitments. The past got uncorked, briefly. We sipped of it. Some drank deeply of it. Then we all recorked it. The day was restorative. It awoke something in us. Once over, we did not dwell but kept it close. We paused, then we continued. And we all got it: Freedom is not free.

I think Memorial Day planted spiritual seeds. Some resolved to make their own lives better, more closely equal to the gift given – the one denied those who did not return. In small towns across a grateful nation, the day was special. In practical terms, eyes watered and watched, ears listened and hearts pounded. We drank from a common understanding, appreciated the idea of unconditional giving. We resolved not to forget. We were again aware of how others affected our lives. The moment – parade, bugle, speech, wreath and commemoration – reminded us that prosperity rested on the past, as much as present. To kids, war was far away, located in a different time and place, usually distant. Yet we knew it mattered. Old souls, around us and behind us, intersected with ours. Festivities aside, something hallowed occurred that day.

Each year, someone was asked to speak, someone with military experience. We would drop our bikes, turn off the antique cars and fire engine. We would stop all noise and listen. Dogs sat; kids stood. Everyone was at parade rest, attentive. Aging veterans sat in folding chairs. Some could not stand; others were persuaded to sit. The rest of us – dressed in everything from scout uniforms to cut-offs – stood behind the veterans. We spread ourselves across the park. The annual speech was short, usually upbeat, sometimes sobering, now and then historical, and always personal. Whether hot or cold, emotional or crusty, the words were carefully chosen.

We admired those who had signed up. That is why they sat in chairs. We admired living and dead veterans by name. The speech reminded kids that America was no accident; it was the product of individual and collective commitments made and kept. My first Memorial Day blends now with others. But they were all memorable. Looking back, they empowered us to look ahead.

Then, quite unexpectedly, town elders asked me to speak one year. The request was a surprise. It remains a cherished moment, something I shall never forget. I had to think hard, deeply. I wondered what I could say of value, and whether I was the right person to say it. *What had I to say, worthy of that platform?* Forty years after my first Memorial Day, it was my turn.

Just six years after the events of September 11, 2001, Memorial Day hit close to home. As a Navy intelligence officer, I lost six friends on 9/11. Although a reservist, I drilled with the active duty. I preferred working with them, so volunteered regularly at the Pentagon. I enjoyed my Navy service. The people and mission were inspiring. Our unit worked in a "wedge" of the Pentagon. We did intelligence work for the Chief of Naval Operations, the "CNO." Our unit, which did analysis in real time, was called "CNO-IP," Chief of Naval Operations-Intelligence Plot. There were not many of us. We were specialized. We tracked "red forces" – bad guys.

On September 11, 2001, I could as easily have been at my desk, there in our wedge. I was not. On that day, as terrorists flew planes into the Pentagon, World Trade Towers, and attempted to hit the White House but were brought down in Pennsylvania, I was not in our Pentagon spaces. Throughout that horrific event, I was in the air.

The plane that hit the Pentagon penetrated four rings. It slammed into our wedge, my wedge. It killed our entire active duty component, my unit. I knew them all. These professionals had trained me. With them I had served, laughed, eaten, joked, worried about family, and tried to protect the nation. I knew their families, what made them each tick, how they reacted to pressures, how professional each of them was, every day. Each was an expert in his or her area.

Their names tumble off my lips, even now. Dan was an encouraging Commanding Officer, Vince his Executive Officer, a seasoned aviator, father of young children. Darin was cheerful, fast-speaking, newly married, source of all the guidance a young watch officer needed. His brother, a Navy fighter pilot, had died in a mishap. Angie was a thoughtful intelligence specialist, happy and spiritual, cerebral and forever smiling. She trained me, took me through my evaluation. Jonas was a giant, muscular and quiet, top briefer. Jerry ran every piece of equipment we had, including video links to leadership. He loved coaching his daughter's softball team. He had just been recognized for his devotion; it moved him. His clear-eyed glasses were foggy; that was the last I saw him. All six perished when the terrorist plane careened into our spaces. They had drawn a terrible, inescapable straw. Their lives ended instantly, while their legacy is eternal. The trade-off is not what any wanted. But that was out of their control – like the fate of Priscilla's brother in World War II.

Throughout the event, I was on a commercial jet, headed for Phoenix. The sun was bright. I slept until awoken by the captain's announcement. I did not know it yet, and am not sure he did, but 9-11 was happening as we flew. Our plane left Washington forty-five minutes before the one that killed my friends. The irony was almost too much to comprehend.

Awoken mid-flight, passengers were told only that the President had declared a national emergency. All planes were ordered out of the sky – wherever they were. Strange and unprecedented, I thought. We landed in

Wichita, Kansas. Only then did I understand the dimensions of the crisis, and enormous implications. Within hours, I began to hear the worst about my friends, one by one. My thoughts went to their families, and mine. Our nation was at war. My friends were the first casualties. I immediately volunteered for active duty.

On active duty, I did what I could. With others, I trained intelligence personnel who arrived to succeed Dan, Vince, Darin, Angie, Jonas and Jerry. There was little more I could do, just live and give to the fullest. For years I would attend services for them, but the experience of serving in their place was formative, has remained so. I took it to heart. Their lives were an inspiration.

The day deepened my faith, too. It had to. You must understand why. Some mysteries are too deep for resolution in any other way. We control less than we think, and owe more than we know. Only pausing, do we start to understand, and then but dimly. The material world is often lightless; without faith, it makes little sense. It yawns wide, but remains a purposeless void. Thoughtful minds probe that darkness. They seek points of light, shafts of understanding, a way to penetrate it. Once found, such shafts illuminate the darkness. Put differently, absent faith we remain without answers. With faith, there is hope and perspective. For my friends and town, I tried to speak cogently on Memorial Day, 2007. In Navy whites, I looked out over two dozen veterans in folding chairs, and those behind them. Then I spoke.

"It is good to come home – thank you." Those words were easy, as it was always good to be home. "You know, this is a remarkable day, Memorial Day – in a remarkable town. Here, at the edge of the Mill Pond, I recall more than one Wayne veteran speaking … I was usually in shorts and a tee-shirt, sometimes my Scout uniform … but somehow, the day left its mark." As I spoke, memories of parades returned. I tried to stay on message. This was not my day; it was theirs.

"On Memorial Day, I used to think a little harder about Wayne's history, about the nobility of those who had served from Wayne in World War II and in Vietnam, and more recently in the first Gulf War – people who almost never talked about things like nobility. Usually, they were folks who walked a little slower, and seemed awfully proud of America, decisive people, unabashed about their patriotism, love of country. They always seemed to be the ones quietly watching from the sidelines, having been – in earlier days – right at the center … just content to see freedom, alive and well." As I spoke, I could see the veterans in front of me. And others, those who clung to shadows, uneasy with recognition.

"Today, on *this* day, we honor *them* – we honor those, some names we know, some we never knew, who died defending this great nation. We honor these patriots of Wayne for their conscious acceptance of risk – often grave risk – in the air, infantry, Marines and on the open sea. We honor them for their service to something greater than themselves, for defending freedom when it needed defending, for unselfish sacrifice, earnest and unflinching courage, simple determination, and for their love." Here, I slowed. The crowd stilled.

"Yes … love is part of it. We don't talk about that part. They didn't generally talk much about it either. But what does honor really mean? Honor is another name for taking action – often dangerous and difficult action, but in all cases taking action with higher purpose, for the sake … of others, for love of family, town, state, nation and ideals. That is where love and honor intersect – and it is why we treasure these patriots so much. They gave their *all* because they felt they needed to – and it has made all the difference to the world in which we are allowed to live." If Robert Frost had been right about the "road less traveled" making "all the difference," surely the road these patriots took made all the difference to us. I tried to keep my voice steady, but emotion crept on me.

"I want to pause and tell you about a few of these patriots – just a few, because there are so many. I was visiting Gettysburg several weeks ago. I decided to look into the role of Wayne in that great contest, the battle that decided the Civil War. That put me in mind of Wayne's veterans generally." I had walked the battlefield, quietly climbing the rocky knoll known as Little Round Top. I had imagined – just for a few minutes – what hell must be like, fear and then, beyond hell and fear, courage and the love that saved a nation. On this knoll had stood "those who here gave their lives that that nation might live." That moment was hard to compress into a Memorial Day speech. I tried to skim the top, share the best.

"I was reminded of those not with us today, but whom we honor, who have spoken from this place on Memorial Days past, patriots like General Charles Reed who served in World War II, Korea and Vietnam, and like Keith Bennett, who flew A-10s for the town of Wayne in the first Gulf War, and so many others." This was a tough moment. Those two represented many, but I knew them. For a moment, my voice quivered, just for a moment. I continued on my theme, echoing others around the Nation.

"I was reminded of those who are part of the Greatest Generation, who wore our nation's uniform in World War II, like George Richardson, Lincoln Ladd, Richard Lincoln, Fred Moore, Homer Towns and Tom Lane." As I spoke, some of those men sat in front of me, others in quieter places. I pushed on.

"In my own generation, I am forever proud of Wayne patriots like Perry Jackson, who flew F-4s and the F-18 for America, Carroll Lane who flew helicopters for the United States Marine Corps, and Carl Lincoln who is flying Blackhawks over Afghanistan today, who commands the American C-17 wing in the Pacific, and who flew strato-tankers in the first Gulf War." Those three came to mind because they were not far from my age, had been more than active. All three were aviators, volunteers ready to answer the call, as prior generations had.

I switched gears. "Wayne patriots fought in the Revolutionary War, the War of 1812, wars defending freedom of the last century – and prominently in the Civil War … after which Memorial Day became a national day of observance." I wanted to bring the history of our town to life for those sitting and standing. I dived in.

"During the Civil War, 99 young men from Wayne signed up and defended the Union. They fought with some of Maine's most famous units. You will recognize their names. There was Charles Lovejoy who fought with Maine's first regiment, heavy artillery, a group of 1800 men. In one battle, they lost 476, in another 580. They were present at the surrender of General Lee, and they mustered out – on September 11th …1865." In the audience to which I spoke, were a number of Lovejoys – including my two first cousins.

"There was Benjamin Berry, who fought with Maine's 7th Light Artillery, and saw action in countless engagements at the front … and there were names like Elijah Knapp and Charles Gott of the 2nd Cavalry; Albion Frost who joined the 4th Light Artillery and Edwin Foster who fought in Maine's 29th Infantry." To show how unbroken the lineage is in many small American towns, a close scouting friend was Benjamin Berry, likely relative of the Civil War veteran. And Frosts and Fosters stood in the assembled crowd. Roads in town were named Knapp and Gott.

I rolled out the profile of Wayne in the Civil War. "There were those who fought side by side, brothers in arms, with the 11th Infantry, including names like James Stetson, Sewall Pettingill, and Silas and Andrew Maxim, and their kin, Benjamin Maxim, who was in the 1st Heavy Artillery. What they might have done with Hiram Maxim's later invention, the machine gun, we will never know …" The General Store had once been owned by the Stetsons. The farmer who gave me my first job – and first dollar – was a Pettingill. The three Maxims who fought in the Civil War were likely related to future resident Hiram, who just missed patenting the light bulb. Someone named Edison … got there first.

"There was a William Stevens in the 3rd Light Artillery, who got deathly ill a year into battle and died, like Thomas Wing, of disease during the war. And long before Wayne was inspiring young men to fly, there were four other Civil War Wings, Llewellyn, Leonard, Charles and Lewis." The organist for years in town was Nell Stevens. The four Wing brothers were all buried in a special spot in Wayne.

"Lewis [Wing] was one of the three Wayne boys killed in action. He died in the battle of Bull Run, in Virginia … The Wing name is one you see a lot, since Wayne's founder, Job Fuller, himself a Revolutionary War veteran, married a Wing, Elizabeth Wing … and Moses Wing, a Revolutionary War veteran and Elizabeth's brother, was Wayne's first town clerk and postmaster. Some of these heroes are right up Pond Road, today, in the only circular cemetery of its kind – Wayne's own Wing Cemetery."

In places like this town, family names, national battles and geography are interwoven. I felt the point would not be lost on this clutch of patriots. "You know, when you look back, you discover a lot. There were islands of special interest, sounding oddly like islands we know today, Wayne's own Daniel Lothrup, who signed up at 44 to be part of the 9th Infantry, and then Grafton, Nelson and George Norris, all of whom joined the 11th Infantry … Nelson would be wounded, but fight on for five years to defend the Union, mustering out as a First Lieutenant." Norris and Lothrop Islands, specks on a map of Maine, are large on our local horizon; they are two of four major islands in Androscoggin Lake. Lothrop is home to bald eagles, even today.

"There were other names that ring bells … Davis Lane, Edward Richardson, George Hall, William Johnson, and Elhanan Smith who all fought together in Maine's 24th Infantry. They fought in New Orleans, and of the 900 men that went out in this regiment, only 570 returned. Wayne's members of the 24th all came home." Again, with families that lived for generations within a stone's throw of where their Civil War predecessors had lived, these names rang bells.

"And then there was Seth Jennings, age 38, who signed up with Maine's 30th Infantry, the same unit Robert Sturtervent joined, at age 39.

Jennings came home to see this Mill Pond again. Sturtervant died as a POW. By contrast, Wayne's William Raymond signed up at 36, was captured, held in Virginia as a POW until 1862, was released, re-found his unit, fought valiantly at Gettysburg, was wounded, and stayed on for another year, until coming home. And then there was Cleveland Swift, Wayne's only member of the Coast Guard Infantry … Like Raymond, he also came home." Love of home was a great motivator. It still is.

"In all, 20 of Wayne's 99 brave men did not return alive, one dying as a POW, 16 of disease, and three killed in action. Of the three killed in action, one was Lewis Wing, who fell at Petersburg, Virginia, one was Valentine Cumnor who also fell in Virginia, and one … was Lyman Richardson, who gave his life at the Battle of Bull Run. In a remarkable twist, since life is full of ironies, this young man died on 9-11 … 1865, and in yet another twist, he enlisted in the Union Army on May 28, 1861 … exactly 146 years ago – today." That so many residents of a Maine town that even now numbered little more than a thousand souls would take up arms, join the Union troops, and battle – some never to return – so far from home is a marvel. Yet, 99 men from this little town did so. And tens of thousands from other Maine towns did likewise.

"So, there have been many true patriots from this little town, and on days like this, we do them honor by remembering that they rose from this soil, from beside this Mill Pond, to defend their family, their town and this nation."

I needed to sew up the speech, and so threaded a last needle. "Finally, I want to note that service … to family, town or nation is not exclusively the province of the military. We honor our nation's fallen heroes today, but service comes in many noble forms: Some support the war effort, some serve by enforcing the law at home, some teach, some care for ailing family, some put food on the table. It all counts."

I wanted this faithful group to remember the day. I reached into the recent past to tell a story that struck me as apt. "In that vein, I am reminded of a thought uttered, in passing, by Colin Powell. I will leave you with a story. It was always a privilege to be in his company. He has a special appreciation, to this day, for the people of Wayne, not least because so many showed up in the midst of a terrible blizzard three years ago … to honor him and one of their own [at my swearing-in as one of his Assistant Secretaries of State]. He never forgot that day. I will certainly never forget that day …Working with him sent me to Baghdad, Kabul and other vacation spots, but on the day I want to recount for you, we were in Washington ..."

The story I told was short but emblematic. "It had been a long night. In the night, we had learned that a US ally, a leader of a small country who made tough decisions and had been pushing his country toward democracy had been assassinated. Powell did not dwell on that event. Instead, he observed with hallowed simplicity, 'He was a man equal to his time.' Somehow, that assessment, coming from Powell, resonated with me. That said it all. On this Memorial Day, no matter how we act on the inspiration we draw from the sacrifice of others, we honor them most by striving, in whatever way we can, to be 'equal to our time.'"

I closed with a hand-off. "When I told General Powell that I would be delivering this speech in Wayne, I got the impression that his connection to Wayne is still rather strong. I told him a little about Wayne's patriots ... and he gave me something for you – for the Wayne library. It is a photo taken in January 2004, when he was speaking to the assembled Wayne contingent in Washington, and he has inscribed it – 'To the Patriots of Wayne, Maine, on Memorial Day 2007, signed Colin Powell.'" And I handed the photo off, for later stewardship by the Wayne Library. "For letting me say a few words today, about a very special town – a town I will always consider home – thank you."

That was it. That was all I had to say. In places like my hometown, little remembrances and Memorial Day mean a lot. To those who have fallen and their families, the day can never replace what is gone. But to those living, it is a chance to say 'thank you.' The invitation to speak meant a lot. That is how little towns are – they remember.

That year's wreath was then walked to the edge of the Mill Pond. It was placed gently on dark water by a retired Navy Captain, crisp whites and sparkling sword a bright contrast. When he placed the wreath, all eyes were on him. There was a silent splash. We watched it disappear over the falls. Then we returned to each other. It was Memorial Day, and summer knocked.

Postscript – In 2018, my old elementary school classmate, Carl Lincoln, was the Memorial Day speaker. Although selected for Brigadier General, he chose to retire as a Colonel from the U.S. Air Force in 2012. During his long career, he flew more than 6,100 military hours and 12 different airframes – including Blackhawks and C-17s. He commanded the 59th Expeditionary Rescue Squadron in Afghanistan, during Operation

Enduring Freedom. Flying Pavehawk helicopters, his unit is credited with 41 combat saves. Like Wayne relative Richie, he won the Bronze Star. In 2018, I was honored to place the town wreath on our Mill Pond. Don Welsh, retired U.S. Marine Corps Colonel, was our parade's grand marshal.

Wayne Mill Pond, view from footbridge across dam, Memorial Day 2018.

Wayne Mill Pond, looking toward dam, Memorial Day 2018
Masonic Hall (left), as seen in 1936 photo of Richie Lincoln and Paul Manter (see page 7), currently being restored. For details, see: www.SustainWayne.org/hallproject.

Memorial Day 2018 (left to right), the author (USNR, former), Col. Don Welsh (USMC, Ret.), and Speaker Col. Carl Lincoln (USAF, Ret.)

Col. Carl Lincoln, flying Pavehawk missions over Northern Afghanistan, 2003, saving lives with as little "bent metal" as possible. Total of 41 saves credited to Col. Lincoln's unit. Wayne Elementary School classmate.

Perry Jackson, US Marine Corps A-4 pilot, later flew F-4 and F-18 fighters. Wayne Elementary School classmate.

Taught to take risks and serve others, John Wood, Master Maine Guide, takes disabled veterans fishing on Maine's rapids every summer with "Project Healing," from which other programs, such as Wounded Warriors, have sprung. Here kayaking West Branch, Pleasant River. Wayne Elementary School classmate. (photo credit, Scott Underhill, Canoe Magazine)

Robert D. Reed, one of Wayne's three Reed brothers, served in WWII, Korea and Vietnam. Bob won the Silver Star in Korea. He also earned the Legion of Merit and Purple Heart. The Korean War Silver Star citation reads, in part: "First Lt. Robert D. Reed...distinguished himself by courageous action...on 9 February 1951." Fighting was "exceedingly bitter." Reed's company had to "dig the enemy from his positions with hand grenades and bayonets." Reed went "immediately to the area under most intense enemy fire, seeking means to eliminate them without loss among his men," and "totally disregarded his own safety." He led an initial "fierce bayonet attack," reorganized his men to repel a counter-attack, then led a second "fierce bayonet charge." His charge "halted the attack of overwhelmingly superior numbers" and "through his inspired leadership, the platoon held the ground until ordered to withdraw." Notably, he was "the last of his platoon to leave the hill." Despite knowing Bob all my life, I never knew this. I learned it reading his Silver Star citation, long after his death. Photo circa Korean War.

William C. Reed was drafted in 1943, served as Staff Sergeant, later performed (sang) at USOs around the world. Bill and Bob were twins. Photo circa WWII.

General Charles Reed, Bob's and Bill's older brother, also served in WWII, Korea and Vietnam. The three Reed brothers were first cousins, twice removed, to me. In a small town, this made them "Uncles." Each took time to impart values to my generation, including love of country.

Summer Fun

"And so with the sunshine and the great bursts of leaves growing on the trees, just as things grow in fast movies, I had that familiar conviction that life was beginning over again with the summer."

–F. Scott Fitzgerald

14. Alive on Dead River

She is just a place … but what a place! Dead River is anything but dead. She is the embodiment of life. A bit fickle, this quiet river perambulates like a lady of leisure, wandering here and there about her lovely delta. She dimples around corners, happy under a canopy of lazy, leaning trees. She kicks up her feet, twirls this way then that, teases all comers with tight baroque curls, then reverses herself.

Actually, this lady has two beginnings and two endings. River water flows in both directions, first one way and then the other. As a result of this unusual habit, the river is almost unique. Most springs, water rises gently, extending out over soft riverbanks, backing into Androscoggin Lake. Then, as suddenly as it rose – in a handful of days – it recedes.

Like many rivers in southern Maine, this one takes her time – whichever way she is going. There is no danger of swift current, no rapids creating untoward interruptions in the flow. Sometimes the river retreats in one direction, sometimes it barely flows at all. Most of the time, she stays steady and polite, focused and coiled. She wanders freely among wetland grasses, following a preset course. Cartographers draw her channel on their maps, but she pays no mind. They draw tidy lines. From whimsy or independence, she jumps them as she chooses.

Without fanfare, this river rises ten feet on a good snow melt. Her water reclaims property around the adjoining lake. She swallows embankments, and gobbles up lakeshore. As a factual matter, Dead River absorbs Androscoggin River's back-up from below, as well as runoff from multiple lakes above. When she decides, she is unstoppable. She begins to move with care and purpose, becomes hard to dissuade. With fixed stare and pursed lips, she stalks rocks, trees and beaches. In summer, she excuses herself, rediscovers her limits and returns to the channel. Perhaps all this is what made her so enchanting in our youth. She drew us in, was captivating.

Given this river's strange and quiet personality, lack of volubility and tendency to imperious changes, she was intriguing. She was intolerant of development, and still is. Nothing is built on her double delta, two delicate fingers extending into Androscoggin Lake, wagging at passersby.

For a moment, allow me to offer more context. What we called Dead River was actually a strange geographic anomaly. For thousands of years, snow melt and rain pressed water into Dead River from the larger Androscoggin River below. At the same time, upstream water poured down a ladder of seven lakes into Dead River. Caught between these two forces, Dead River rose and fell with caprice. Her height was based on rain and snow. The result was a nod to her quixotic nature, a trade-off of uncommon beauty for unpredictability. Gradually, a grand delta formed as waters flowed first one way, then the other, alive with soil and silt.

As locals know, this special river does exactly as she chooses. Humanity is hard pressed to change her course. That is fine. Side to side and end to end, she shifts in response to forces beyond human control. So expansive is the river in some years that kayakers in early summer can cross her double delta by parting brush. So narrow is the river's gauge by fall, and so tall its banks by comparison to late spring, that rocks and logs jut from the bottom as hazards. The river has what geologists call bi-directional current, two-directional flow constantly building the delta.

At Wayne's center, defining one end of the Mill Pond, a dam holds back water from six lakes above, beginning with Pocasset. That dam does not permit backflow. Thus Androscoggin Lake never returns water to Pocasset, once that water flows over the dam. Water gushes in spring, dumping hundreds of tons into the lower lake, eventually into Dead River. The result is a very special ecosystem.

Dead River has long been a *de facto* refuge, teaming with wildlife and lush undergrowth, undeveloped banks and fallen trees. Not to be missed are laboriously built beaver lodges. The river slinks among mud walls, edged with wild grasses and water lilies. The imperceptible current slides around turns, prowls the delta, and hides more than she shows. All this is atypical for Maine or New England, actually the nation. Bi-directional rivers are rare, and unsung.

So here – in the name of recognizing a river's beauty – is her song. She has no mesmerizing waterfalls, no glitzy rapids, and no famous lookouts. Except for occasional flooding, she is gentle and unassuming, perfect for canoeing, kayaking, and quiet motoring. Entering this river, one is instantly – and obviously – in a hushed world. Between strokes or engine bursts, drifting visitors are cloaked, part of another world, if also spied by wild eyes. Drifters feel as if, almost by magic, they are moving on a windless canvas, no current or chop. At first, all seems inert. Then, as ears and eyes adjust, things happen.

Sun filters through overhanging tree leaves, creating lifelike reflections on the water, as if water were land. The silence rings. River banks are muddy and dark, extinguishing thoughts of disembarking. The woods beyond are rich with shadows, deep and mysterious. They are part of the river, part of being here, yet say nothing.

On the water, logs appear without warning, submerged, another mystery. They are a boating hazard, unmoving as the endless reflections, only harder. A visitor's focus is divided between land and water, a division often unclear. Time seems unchanging. Dead River is another world.

When water gets low, hazardous logs pop up more often. They brush the underside of unsuspecting boats, triggering a need to swerve. Otherwise the tributary acts like an oversized runnel. She is a squiggly rill, hardly rough and tumble. In this way, she is only more bewitching.

Leaving behind the lake's whistle and whitecaps, we found ourselves cloistered among prayerful trunks, an almost monastic setting, what with kneeling, bent and brooding branches. Now and again, we brushed against these hooded figures, pensive monks strolling a long, open abbey. Some days, these tippy trees seemed more like lazy sentries, a few standing at attention, most just leaning, lollygagging and sleeping. The overwhelming sensation was unnatural stillness. About us, no whirring, banging, ringing, or talking. That such stillness existed was refreshing.

Whether the river was flat or rippling, small turtles lounged on logs. Edging toward them, we talked in hushed tones. "Stay quiet … go slower." Visitors proceeded slowly, wanting not to hit anything, not to miss anything. Big vessels stayed clear of the river. She was notoriously hard on propellers and sheer pins. "Watch that log, go left!"

The river was engrossing, with good reason. Like it or not, she could grab visitors – and hold them. Just being here, drifting along the double delta, was an adventure. Gradually, as one watched, banks came to life. From the corner of an eye, movement. Suddenly a blue heron was snatching a fish, leaning forward, taking off, twisting to look back, wings slowly beating what seemed heavy air. Then, as if that heron had never existed, all was again quiet.

On any given day, turtles feigned indifference to visitors. But if a canoe got too close, plop and they were gone. More quiet. "Whoa, a beaver at one o-clock!" Warning calls led to a cut engine, more drifting. Surprises lurked. Suddenly the embankment disgorged a beaver the size of a fox, little muskrat in a hurry, or a kingfisher diving for dinner.

Yellow lines were etched on tree trunks, as if sedimentary rock. These were Nature's chalk lines, pollen that fell and stuck to trunks at different water levels. Drifting through the mix of reality and reflection, one felt an inner two-way current – excitement and peace, first the flow one way, then the other. The river's double delta squiggled on for a mile, meandering without movement. If a leaf fluttered down, it stayed, floating in place.

To newcomers, the vicissitudes and unpredictability could be unnerving. But to those who knew her, she was always a friend. The only irritations, which were seasonal, were mosquitos and horseflies. The river asked no admission, offered no poison critters, just an abundance of amusement. In many ways, Dead River was a buffer. It was a place to which anyone could paddle or motor, and get away. Within this echoless ecosystem, the modern world did not exist. Here one found no human dwelling, glint of glass or metal, sign of mankind, or indicator of time. A visitor's eyes relaxed among muted tones, moss and mud, amber logs and hanging leaves, still water, and a slice of sky.

But the river was deceptive, too. That was part of her excitement. She encouraged daydreams, stilled the heart. Surrounded by quiet, little things sounded bigger – a beaver's slap, wings rising, an osprey's chirp, a turtle's dive. We did not come often, not often enough. When we did, we collected what we could. We saved the moments like shiny pennies, flashes of intimacy with nature's least accessible elements. Have you ever stepped suddenly into a forest glen – and looked around? Emerged from woods near dusk? Straddled two ecosystems? Maybe something simpler. Have you ever risen at dawn, walked a dewy meadow or gazed across a foggy inlet? In such places, at such times, for just a few seconds, the world can stand still. Silhouettes appear. Something ineffable, intangible, possibly unknowable is present. To such moments, there is a certain synchronicity, as if for just that time, all makes sense. At the intersection of such times and places, peace dwells. It does predictably on Dead River.

On any given day, the river's shifting shoreline was alive. Curling tendrils and broken branches blended with crossing tree shadows. J.R.R. Tolkien or C.S. Lewis would have loved this place. One could imagine Gandalf or Shadowfax, the dragon Smog. Around the next bend, one might encounter Tumnus, or even Aslan. Such was the power of the place to awaken sleeping, stagnant, stifled imaginations, to wonder. First peace, then a wildly wandering mind.

Like no other river on which I have floated, this one transcended all cacophony, closing up behind the humble entrance. It was a bubble in the universe, a place to find what one had lost, lose what needed losing. Other rivers were special, but none cast this spell.

Later, I would float South America's Amazon, India's Godavari, Egypt's Nile and the Monkey in Belize, overlook Baghdad's Euphrates, but no river was as bewitching and mysterious as this humble offering. She topped them all for the great escape. No trumpets, no complex or quixotic, rare or exotic fare. She had her contradictions, overflowing yet reserved, imbued with energy but still, slow to move if exhilarating, straight forward and baroque by turns. Shafts of light came through the canopy, time's lines creating uncertain depths, wisdom in the shadows. Those who knew her felt her depth. Every visit brought something new.

Then we returned to the world. Through water lilies and jade grasses, we paddled or puttered. Soon we were back on the rolling lake, awash in unfiltered sunlight, bouncing on chop. Waves and wind met us, whitecaps punched at the gunwales. We set course for a far shore, faces to the wind. The air was different, redolent with humanity's scents, wood smoke or pancakes. Those things were good too, just different. We had been somewhere. That is how we always felt. We had spent time on the precious double delta. We were more alive. We tipped our hat to the lady of leisure, bid her adieu until next time. Dead River was just a place… but what a place! As the world rushes forward, just nice to know such places still exist. And they do.

Central Androscoggin Lake, Dead River delta, from Morrison Heights

Dead River delta, from air, mid-winter (credit Steve Ritzi)

15. Hard at Work

Summers were entirely different from springs, falls and winters. Beyond warmer weather, more tourists, a chance for canoeing, waterskiing, camping and fishing – we got a chance to work. Hard work for pay was welcomed. It was an opportunity. Young as we were, we took it. Looking forward to hard work may sound an oxymoron, a concept in conflict with itself, but not in our town.

We looked forward to being productive at a certain age – working, earning and saving. Putting something away and being responsible felt good. But first, we had to learn. Members of what Tom Brokaw has called the "Greatest Generation," taught us how. Three members of that generation put me through my paces, all three WWII veterans, Old Man P, Tom and George.

Initially, I dreaded work. It got me up early, made me sweat and ache, took away my lazy days. But it was also habit forming, reinforced by an unexpected sense of accomplishment and pay. Soon I developed the taste. I liked getting things done, solving bigger and bigger problems, taking on a mission and finishing it off. With small accomplishments – weeding peas, splitting wood, hauling brush, mowing lawns, pounding nails – came confidence. Exhaustion made sleep sounder, and dawn that much easier to meet.

The real secret? Hard work was motivating. It was a pony engine that started a virtuous cycle, even in reluctant kids. Commitment, risk and effort produced outcomes and rewards, in turn motivating more commitment, risks and effort, producing higher outcomes and rewards. Simple and powerful, good when taught early, and best with callouses. Jobs undertaken and finished created toughness, physical and mental. The "next task" was always easier. Self-worth tracked sweat and blisters, rose with every push to finish. I liked work, then liked myself for liking it.

Harder projects produced more accomplishment. Hard work was ruthlessly fair. No discrimination or divine intervention could alter the balance. Effort in, accomplishment out, along with confidence and muscle. Plus time and sweat produced a paycheck. From Maine to Montana, rural kids knew the value of hard work, and tended to work long summers. A story is worth a thousand lectures, so three stories follow.

–First Dollar

Terms of employment were clear: Ten cents for each thousand-foot row. Having never weeded a thousand feet of anything, those terms seemed fair to me. What did I know at twelve? I was not sure of the difference between a hundred and a thousand. I knew a dollar. So did the farmer. Ten hours later, feeling bent, spent, and red as a steamed lobster, I knew the difference. I was also happy. I had earned my first George Washington – by weeding peas.

To the farmer, my work must have been inconsequential. To me, the day was pivotal. I had apprenticed to a man whose life was the land – whose life depended on it. His entire family worked pre-dawn to past dark, daily. They knew how, when, where and what to plant, under what conditions, with what follow-on through harvest – and then some. They knew excuses were unavailing. They knew nature moved the goal posts, always forcing extra labor.

They knew how to fix a dozen things on the spot – everything that rolled, hashed, dug, dragged, cut, ground, pulled or seeded. They were efficient, and had to be. Time was crops. Crops were life. They planted, fertilized, weeded, nurtured, watered and harvested. They got harvest to market, which was a roadside farm stand – and the General Store. These were not small feats. I knew and respected what they did – more after my first day of weeding peas.

The farmer, tall in his blue-jeans and tee, stood before me in muddy boots. His face wore a half-smile, part grimace, part gratitude, but unchanging. Furrows crossed his brow, seemed filled with endurance and hope, drudge and satisfaction. Whatever lay behind that face, he was essentially content. And he was a teacher, of his own kids and me. If anyone believed in hard work, he certainly did. That day, he offered a chance to get dirty, tired, and to learn. Some may not see the bargain, but I did. It felt good to be trusted, and to earn. He also taught attitude. Life can be unfair; never let that slow you. Droughts and floods, weeds and diseases, birds and bugs, rot and regulations challenge the day; unyielding flexibility, optimism and commitment win it.

In our town – until farms started disappearing – farmers were hopeful, paragons of planning and doing, persistence and patience, faith and fortitude. To a one, they believed in the future. How else could they rise at dawn, year after year, perform backbreaking labor, entrust themselves to God's mercy? They fed their families, and then put food on our table. We had several *bona fides* farming families. If everyone had a back acre or two, those were gardens. Big turned fields were different, the province of farmers. We knew the difference.

Local farmers were all in, "24-7-365" with the land, wearing it down and worn by it, building it up and built by it. They knew miracles, but knew not to count on them. They were grateful for sun, more for rain, breathed after the last harvest. They saw seeds sprout, sprouts become flowers, flowers turn to fruit, and fruit ripen to harvest. They were all about commitment, risk, and effort. They seeded the far corners, but tried not to get cornered. No escape from an ill-timed frost or extended drought, washout or deluge of bugs; that was farming. If disaster chose them as its dance partner, that was it, no exit. Providence shined or shunned; they knew the bargain – and accepted it. That is why farmers were special in our town, and everywhere. That is why working for one was a privilege. Decades on, little has changed, just the value of a dollar.

The tall farmer's income was tied to sweet peas – as well as string beans, corn, tomatoes, zucchinis, beets, squash and pumpkins. They sprang from dirt, so my introduction was to dirt. I swore to be efficient, no idea what the oath entailed. That morning, his family was in motion before I arrived. My chief preoccupation soon became distinguishing young peas from weeds.

Unlike me, the farmer's family knew the difference. They lived the adage, "If anyone will not work, neither shall he eat." To eat, they had to know young peas from weeds. To me, the idea was new. Ready to work, I had to learn. In our town, there were four farm families, the B Family, D Family, S Family and Old Man P's family. On this day, I was working for *Old Man P*. I did not realize it at that time, but he was what you might call "the real thing." I never wanted to be a farmer – not before, definitely not after – but I respected the way of life. These farmers helped to feed us, taught and quietly inspired. They seldom complained and modeled can-do. What they harvested showed up at the General Store. What Old Man P taught, I never forgot.

Very early, I jumped on my bike, pedaled downhill, clutching a lunch bag in one hand, brake in the other. I was in cut-offs and a tee. Down the mountain I sped, past friends' homes, all a blur. I wanted to be on time. Rounding the bend at hill's bottom doing 30 mph, I pumped the last stretch of woods, closed on the field with stone walls whipping by. I was excited. This was my first job. I dropped the bike in tall grass, leaped the stone wall, and met the farmer. We had arranged all this. I was here, surrounded by young peas, at 7:00.

Man of few words, he greeted me kindly. He nodded to the first row. Terms were set. Already hunched forms hovered over rows at staggered intervals, shrinking toward the horizon, some only partially visible. The farmer's family knew how to do this thing, to weed at speed, and they were about it. They were into their workday. Exhilarated by my downhill ride, I was flush with entrepreneurial spirit. Wasting no time, I just leaned over and started weeding.

I resolved to win the farmer's respect. I did not want him to think me ignorant, so held my tongue. That was probably unwise. Truth was, I had scant experience distinguishing young peas from weeds. This was an immediate problem. I tried to work quickly, constantly fearing the mortal mistake, pulling a precious pea. Nose-to-plant, blood-to-head, distinguishing was tough. Only crumpled over can you fully appreciate the uncanny resemblance between these clover-green youngsters, juvenile peas and weeds. They are virtually interchangeable. One becomes food, the other blocks sun and produces nothing.

At first, their natural similarity slowed me. I pulled with caution, weighing each pull. Eyes compared leaf shapes, plant heights, differences in tint and root depth. This was time-consuming, but I feared pulling one of his miracles, a half-grown pea. Sorrel and dandelion were easy, as were crabgrass, ragweed, milk weed and lambs quarter. But other weeds were deceptive, clever imposters, meant to confuse me – and they did. I tried to hurry. Before long, the whole row became a fern-colored blur. What was a weed? What was a pea?

I began to think I was in over my head. Getting this wrong might be catastrophic. I slowed down. An hour into this process, I looked up and was shocked. For all intents and purposes, I had gone nowhere. But beyond my row, all the world had changed. The farmer's family had disappeared out of sight, over the horizon. They had finished countless rows, as I still plodded my first. I was trying to be pea-perfect; it was not working. At ten cents a row, I had made less than a dime in my first hour. I got better returns collecting returnable bottles on the roadside. I needed to pick up the pace, yet not disappoint the farmer. *I had to speed up!*

Over the next couple of hours, I tried all sorts of tricks. I gave up perfection. I went systematic, putting the whole row on a conveyer belt, setting the belt's speed to fast, picking weeds as they went by. I became a combine, trying not to miss weeds or pull peas. This new speed, and the focus required, was tiring. Mistakes were made, but the row sped along. Pick, pass. Pick, pick, pass – oops – pick. Pass, pick, pass, pass, pick – shoot – picked a pea! No replanting a picked pea … Before long, weeds and peas again seemed alike. The sun was higher; sweat swarmed my eyes. Each row was now a long, green runner.

The mind wandered. I was suddenly plucking lollypops and jelly beans, walking ribbons of green licorice, passing streams of lemon-lime soda. I realized, I was thirsty, had forgotten water. Back to my weeds and peas. I had to speed up, increase cadence, and get more rows done. Loiter-time shrank again. I told myself: *Step it up!*

Lunchtime came. The farmer's family returned from over the horizon. The farmer approached me. "You don't need to finish out, if you don't want to …" he offered. Quitting was the *last* thing I was going to do! Told him, I would get the knack. I had no interest in knocking off, would settle in. "I'm a little slow on the uptake, but getting the hang of it," I assured him. We ate fast, and returned to weeding. Surveying my work, one of his older daughters offered encouragement: "You pulled a few peas back there…" I thanked her, nodded, and apologized. She was an expert, a young surgeon of the soil. She was right, of course. "Sorry, they look, uh, similar," I muttered. *How did they do it, tell the difference?*

Rest of the afternoon, I strived to do better. Muddy sneakers moved faster. I snatched up weeds, downshifted to save peas. My shirt came off, and white back turned rosy. My calves itched. But people remember who quit. I was not *about* to quit. Somewhere this side of dusk, I rounded my ninth row. Tenth was done by dark. I had not covered anything like the farmer's family. They were systematic and quick. Surely, they thought me a laggard. I had accelerated, reduced my error rate, but was slow. I had learned a lot – including how hard farm families work, how not to quit, and how peas and weeds trick the untrained eye.

Trying to straighten, I also discovered something else: I was a hunchback. Darkness threw a blanket over the field. But now I was happy, even lighthearted. I had done it. I had put in a full day's work with Farmer P. His family stood quietly by as he spoke. "A good day's work, there … ten rows, was it?" he asked. "Yes sir, ten … I learned to get better." "Thanks for coming out," he said, his eyes alive. He pulled a dollar bill from his wallet, and handed it to me. It meant a lot to him; it meant a lot to me. My rows were not pretty, but they were done. Ten rows his family would not have to do. Then he gave me something better, a compliment. "Weeding is tough … you did good, put in a good day … If you want to come back, I'll put you to work," he said. High praise from Old Man P. "Thank you," I said. He had taught me the value of a dollar, at age twelve.

I did not work long for Old Man P. That particular summer, another job popped. It boosted my earning power to forty dollars a week. But I never forgot his kind words or example. When you look up "hard work," the definition is "Maine farmer." Farmer P's work ended up on our dinner table, and filled a farm stand on Route 133, along with shelves at the General Store. We ate those peas. I knew where they came from. They were worth every penny.

–Toilets, Nails and Fences

That summer, I began a job which occupied my energies for five summers. I labored at a local institution, the *Androscoggin Junior-Senior* camp for boys. With proper working papers, I was privileged to join the summer camp's "Outdoor Crew," a proud, scruffy, tanned, can-do bunch. We liked to think we "made the place run," and took pride in that. The boss was a constant thinker, tinker and team leader, occasionally turbulent, always instructive. His name was Tom. Tom worked for the Camp's owners, Stan – WWII veteran – and wife Barbara; today, the famous Camp is run by their son Peter, and his wife Roberta.

From Tom, we learned – how to fix anything, build everything, pay close attention, own projects and get things done. We performed every maintenance task imaginable. As a group of six teenage boys, we got from Tom a survey course in plumbing and welding, carpentry and mechanical engineering, auto body and engine repair, landscaping and mowing, flooring and painting, roofing and sucking it up without complaining.

One of the town's World War II veterans, Tom taught lessons like "do it right the first time," "tear it down and start again," "no excuses" and "no job is too big." The word "cannot" was scrubbed from his lexicon, and soon from ours. When manuals ran out, he defaulted to imagination and persistence. Sometimes he began there, manuals be damned. Where he went, we followed.

Tom put more stock in grit than anybody I knew. His war service may be the cause. He was a turret gunner in a TBM Avenger, the legendary torpedo bomber that debuted in the Battle of Midway. Tom flew from the USS Hornet, deployed to the Pacific, although not at Midway. Notably, the Avenger's .50 caliber machine gun was mounted right beside the turret gunner's head. If Tom was action-oriented, edgy and impatient, you could understand why. Around the camp, he was in perpetual motion, always on a mission. Except for lunch, I do not recall Tom ever sitting. Deliberate or not, George Patton's shadow followed him.

Objectively, the head maintenance job was daunting. On Tom's back rested responsibility for keeping a large, unwieldy, high-end summer camp – literally hundreds of out-of-state kids and counselors – running flawlessly. Every day delivered unforeseen crises, as well as a chance to preempt the next one. Along the way, Tom managed to turn a bunch of mop-top teenage boys into hardened workers. His unspoken mantra was something like, "We will get it done." He reported to the owners; we reported to him.

Quickly, we learned that Tom was hard-bitten and hard to dissuade. He hated delays and indecision, preferring a commitment and mid-course corrections. No dawdling, no fretting. And he hated wafflers. What he wanted was regular, unbroken action, preferably pursued with a modicum of competence, confidence and reliability. That forced us to think harder than we ever had as teenagers, finish whatever we started, work as a team, and succeed – alone, if necessary.

Even as teens, we were entrusted with high levels of responsibility. Looking back, such things would be frowned on today – but we did more than survive; we thrived. We were all driving a stick shift, using power tools, building bunk houses and sinking nails in our early teens. Of necessity, we got resourceful. When we goofed up, we owned up. We might get an earful, but we also became resilient. The main mission: Never let people down. Like Old Man P, Tom taught by example, if not with a farmer's calm. Tom did not suffer fools, which meant some of us had to learn quickly. The focus was planning, follow-through and accountability. We set to.

The old turret gunner was also a man of heart. He hated to admit it. Why, I am not sure. Maybe he thought it was weakness. Like most of mankind, he was filled with contradictions. He could be hard as nails, then tell you to knock off early. He could set inordinately high expectations, but kept one eye out for your limits. By dead reckoning, we could do almost anything; on simple belief, he undertook huge projects – and we did with him. When some task grew overwhelming, he would recalibrate, intercede, and square the circle. Suddenly, we had backup. He wore a semi-permanent scowl, mostly for show I think, maybe out of habit. His penchant for sarcasm was keen, and kept us cautious. At the end of long days, he would usually nod in approval. From Tom, that was enough.

Over time, Tom's Crew built more and more, including a reputation for managing major projects. We built entire cottages, from footings and floors to walls and roofs. He led all these projects, including rebuilding the giant dining hall when it burned. He welded a thousand feet of floating dock together, assembling a massive, floating city of angle iron. His crew managed the camp's water supply, starting with a hilltop cistern and gravity fed piping. That went to 26 cottages and beyond. Maintenance projects were unceasing, as were creative undertakings.

Together, we constructed a winged stage for a playhouse, did engine and body work on camp cars, boats and the flatbed truck. We wired and brought up a camp radio station, long before CDs existed. It smelled of fresh pine, spun vinyl all day and half the night. We completed magnum opus projects, clearing land to build cedar fences, constructing a shooting range for .22 rifles, widening and maintaining baseball and soccer fields, building archery ranges, repairing and repainting totem poles. Tom imagined, we made it so. There is something unique about learning from such people, those who believe *anything* can be done. With them, the question is never *if,* only *how*. Working for Tom, we learned to think – not if, but how.

Tom's projects could be wild. Restore the body of a car with wire mesh, fiberglass, sandpaper and paint. Fell dozens of trees to fence enormous fields. Sand, repair and polyurethane wooden floors with the square footage of a school gymnasium. Build a cottage, nesting inside a photographic dark room. Each time we completed another one, our confidence grew. Tom was complex, but an educational boss. He could stir pride and instill fear. In one work day, he could encourage, fortify and mortify. The net result was a shared interest in not disappointing him.

To his credit, Tom did not give assignments and walk away. Most days, he showed us *how* the job was to be done, then expected us to complete it. He was suffused with tenacity, and some cussedness. He thrived on missions others thought impossible. He would undertake them; we would finish them. In that way, dozens of acres were sprayed for mosquitoes before that was common practice. Thickets were cleared, towers built, culverts laid, animals trapped, trees felled. Entry gates were built, rock walls restacked. Entire plumbing systems were replaced, yards of snarled piping snaked. To fix a truck engine, we looked under rocker arm covers and sanded spark plugs, dried distributor caps and removed radiators; belts were replaced, tanks patched, and metal welded. Then on to the next thing.

Under this sort of tutelage, we learned "stretch goals," with no books needed. We squeezed as much work into a day as fit. If Tom measured worth by sweat, we did too. If he never leaned on a shovel, we did not lean either, even in his absence. The last time I saw Tom, he was in his late 80s – stretched out to full length over an inboard engine, the engine nestled in a mahogany barrel back. He was adjusting for output. "You hear that?" he asked, smiling as he tinkered.

Tom's management style would make a case study at Harvard Business School. He upended norms, flew into storms, many of his own making. He was not about "quality circles," not soft, and not apologetic. He studied human nature, knew how to encourage and instruct, but rejected the notion that conflict and terse exchanges were to be avoided. Sardonic humor was just another tool, useful in leveraging boys from lunch to dig a septic or drainage ditch. He assumed fear had nothing to do with our performance, that we were animated by mission completion. That was part right, part wrong. Nevertheless, he instilled loyalty – among those that stayed.

Tom's temper popped the rivets on occasion, flapping before settling. If the damn thing got loose, it could be a wild cat, no subtlety. Sometimes outbursts spurred us to harder work, but mostly they did not. These moments were never taken personally. One sensed they reflected discontent with the past or unrealized potential, maybe something tied to upbringing or war. He was hardest on himself, hated to miss a goal. He could see a problem and solution, resented the distance between them, measured by time. If strident in such moments, his frustration was in the service of a worthy, unmet objective. His crew knew that. He cut us slack; we cut it back.

Over the years, I grew to believe that Tom saw something sublime in manual labor. Beyond accomplishment, it represented a kind of personal redemption or path to salvation, which justified allowing it to become all-consuming. None of us wanted to question the premise, as none of us were sure whether he was right or wrong. But his daily gait radiated purpose, and his crew tried to keep up. Maybe that was just a turret gunner on land.

We mowed more acres in a summer than the total township. We fiber-glassed countless boats, sanded and polyurethaned hundreds of board feet, poured cement footers, studded walls, re-roofed cottages. We scraped, sanded, primed and painted; grew handy with vice grips, pipe cutters, and clamps. We snaked shower drains, widened roads, tightened bolts, cut sheet metal, and burned beehives from rafters with propane torches. I personally cleaned or repaired more than a thousand toilets every summer.

We changed air and oil filters, rotated tires and washed cars. We moved giant freezers without losing toes, stained buildings (and ourselves) with enthusiasm, dropped branches to protect power lines. We lavished black tar creosote on wooden posts, surveyed woods, snapped chalk lines to lay planking. We got sticky with resins and hardeners, figured out chainsaws, and suffered push brooms. We built young muscles moving dirt and mulch, carried things here to there, back there from here. I cannot recall the term "core strengthening," but we did that. These things all needed doing. Five summers passed. I learned mission completion from the old gunner, even if we never agreed on politics.

For all this, his crew members owed Tom – they all did, and knew it. Before cancer took him, I let him know. His tutelage had been invaluable, patriotism an example. When I later wrestled "can we or can't we" in faraway places like Iraq, Afghanistan, Colombia and Kosovo, working for Colin Powell, Tom's can-do attitude flooded back. "Of course, we can." And then we did. If Tom was a lifelong Democrat, me a Republican, it made no difference. What he taught was never give up, never fear uncertainty, never duck responsibility, never shy from the "big thing," and always finish it!

Two events crystalize those five summers. One day, returning from bunk-line duty (toilet cleaning and repair), Tom intercepted me. His face was twisted in a big grimace. He nodded behind him. "We have a fiberglass job … see what you can do with it …" That was all he said. I had no idea what he was talking about, but knew enough not to ask. If he had more to say, he would. But nope, he just assumed I'd figure it out. "Ok, I'll get on it," I said.

What *was* behind him? Several hundred feet further, I stood in our crew's pine needle workspace. Before me lay two piles of crushed, purple fiberglass. Vaguely familiar, they looked like crumpled ice cream cones, covered in purple sequins. Mauled and mashed, they might have been motorcycle fenders, a psychedelic garbage can. I surveyed the piles. The shattered, twisted fiberglass was metallic. The prickly heaps glistened in the sun, slightly cylindrical. They might have been anything. They were, I realized, remains of a once pristine kayak – gone wrong.

The kayak, as it turned out, was crushed in whitewater, then dragged from the Allagash. For some reason, the pieces were back at camp. I wondered about the camper, but my job was obvious. Convert the glistening piles of fiberglass rubbish back into an operational kayak. The assignment was ridiculous, and mildly exciting. I wondered if it could be done, then began.

Recasting the crumpled kayak as an art project, I disentangled, flattened, sculpted, glued, sanded, and eventually smoothed out the fibers into something "all the king's horses and all the king's men" would have been proud of. The outcome was half science, half art. Tested for buoyancy and weight distribution, dabbed up with resin and hardener, it floated with a person in it. Not stylish, it never made another Allagash run, but worked on flat water. And there it was: Tom let me frame that problem, own and solve it. He could have tossed away the purple piles; instead he taught with them. Those who employ the young are always teachers, always. He got that.

Some mornings, Tom stormed the dining hall, graying hair on fire, coffee in a fist, brows bent and eyes fixed. That meant he had an assignment in mind. He was already working details, matching people to tasks, picturing completion. Other mornings, his temper was even, furrows shallower. "Ok boys, we are going to replace a septic," he might say. Or "Ok boys, time to pull docks," or "rebuild a rifle range," or just "come with me." Instantly, we were in motion.

Occasionally, he led with humor or, God forbid, politics. He and I sparred good-naturedly over politics – for 40 years. Even here, he taught. Consciously or not, he triggered thinking. He reminded me that national things mattered, even in small town Maine. Poking about for contrary opinions, he would joust with merriment; he would throw out some absurdity, then smile. Sometimes I responded; sometimes he got no takers. Either way, we were soon at work. I took this as respect. He never stopped pressing me on politics, but never fired me. Sometimes people just want to joust.

Tom's "theory of the firm" was elementary. "Do your job well, and be proud of what you do." Newcomers were given time; some blanched and left. His style was not for everyone. To me, the five summers were a chance to learn, prove myself, be independent and earn a paycheck. That was enough. Those who worked for Tom used what he taught. Some later became managers, marine engineers, auto mechanics; some high school teachers, others entrepreneurs. One camp hand became a Master Maine Guide, another joined the Peace Corps, and still others ended up wearing the nation's uniform, as he had. All learned from Tom to make a difference and complete the mission. Maybe this comes from small towns, maybe from good mentors.

A last story about Tom. The morning was unusual, oppressively hot. Morning heat signaled a blistering day. Tom banged into the dining room, already half on fire. We wiped sleep away and chugged coffee. He launched into the plan – no time for banter. "Today boys, we are going to build a cedar fence around the soccer field." That field, we all knew, was enormous and unfenced, a meadow with an 800-foot perimeter. Tom wanted it fenced in cedar, today. Ok. We had no cedar posts, cross bars, post holes, or blueprints. We had post-hole diggers. None of us had built a cedar fence. To Tom's view, that was irrelevant. He was empowering us.

We nodded, exchanged glances, and immediately began thinking. We were on our own, to meet Tom's expectations. Nobody shrank or asked anything. Tom pivoted and was gone. He had other things to do. Suddenly, we got bigger. We should be able to figure this out. We began plotting "how." We unpacked "impossible," broke it into pieces of "possible." We wasted no time. What would it take? We drew up a list, divvied tasks. There were six of us. Half would start digging post holes, the other half take the camp truck to the old Manter place, negotiate a price for his cedars, and start cutting. I was in the second group. Trees were a dollar each. I chuckled: One cedar apparently equaled ten rows of weeded peas.

We picked straight cedars, cut and limbed them with a chain saw, piled them on the truck, and got them back to Camp – tails wagging off the flat bed. Cutting cedars, we had to estimate how many trees we needed to encircle an 800-foot field, with posts and double rails. Dropping sweet conifers, shaving them of branches, piling them high and bouncing back to Camp was … fun.

Late day, multiple truckloads had been deposited. We began creating posts and rails, measuring twice, cutting once. Clay notwithstanding, two-foot holes ringed the sports field. Prep done, we got to planting posts, nailing rails. We formed a bucket brigade to soak post-bottoms in a petroleum preservative, which would keep moisture out for years. We saturated the freshly-cut posts, dropped them into holes, filled in behind, tamped until hard with crowbar and boots.

Eventually, we started driving spikes, pinning crossbars to vertical posts. This was the hardest part. By now, for all our efficiency, we were racing the sun. In one day, we had gotten far – but hardly finished. We knew this was a multi-day effort. We knew Tom's expectations were high. He never used words like results, accountability, or metrics – but he knew them. He expected things to get done. We aimed to show him we could. We would at least show progress. Some days, enthusiasm battled fatigue. This was one, and had to be. We pushed on.

For some reason, the green cedar hated us. These logs were knotty, grain tight and sticky. No mystery, really. In the forest, they were festooned with branches. The knottiness, plus fresh-cut and uneven grains, bent our twenty-penny nails, what we called spikes – every time. This was frustrating. We hammered a spike, and it bent. Then again. And again. We would flip the hammer, claw the spike, yank and try again. This took time, wasted time. Slam, bend, pull, straighten or toss, reposition, slam, straighten, slam flush – next. The process was not smooth.

Suddenly, who should show up? Sun at the horizon, there was Tom, coming to inspect. "How we doing boys?" came his tough, predictable inquiry. Nobody spoke. He could see – we were far from done. His voice reflected the day's strain, heat and frustration. He had worked long. We knew the mood. We had pulled for project completion, but not today. We had done our best. He would know that. Still, a bad last inning spoils the game; we were in the inning. Bent spikes were turning our final inning into a rout – for the spikes. Now here was Tom, descending. Team manager was headed for the mound, his head down.

We explained the spikes were bending in fresh, knotty cedar. "Well, let's see about that," said Tom. Complaints were suspect. This was a teaching moment. Tom wanted his crew to push through, "mind over matter," no excuses. As was his way, he would now *show us!* Knowing – as each of us did – the gnarly, uncooperative nature of this fresh cedar, we stepped back, gave him room. Good to give Tom room in these moments.

Tom's cocksure approach was about to sting him. To a crew member, we knew he would get his own. No one wanted to be here when he did, but here we were. No one wanted to tell him the hornet was circling; knotty green does not recognize rank. We knew these trees were contrary, no matter who swung the hammer. Never mind, Tom would show us.

His face became all determination, jaw tight, brow rutted. We knew the look. He picked up the hammer and reached for a spike. He looked at the pile of bent ones. "What's the matter boys, not able to get 'em to go?" he said tartly. His message was simple: *Try harder.* He began whacking with inimitable "let me show you how it's done" swings. His were giant, uncompromising, take-no-breath, drive-the-damn-thing-to-China swings. He leaned over, let loose power strokes.

In one blow, he had the spike half in. A second blow put it two-thirds down. The third – his moment of glory, the ultimate "I told you so" slam – bent it flat. Sideways, useless, flat. No one breathed. This was what we suspected would happen. We knew the cedar would frustrate him, as it had us. Fear extinguished the instinct to console or laugh. We all looked at our feet.

The moment was heavy. We were not sure what would happen next. We knew this was embarrassing. Tom had intended, in his way, to create a memorable "teaching moment." Instead, it had become something else. In any other situation, the word might be humbling. Even the instructor might laugh, and then we could. Not here. Not Tom's disposition. We were silent. The wood had foiled Tom, as it had us. Tom was purple with rage, holding it in – barely. Cedar logs were supposed to know better. Tom's third strike had made our point, better than words. His spike lay bowed, flat as a penny on rails after a train.

Suddenly, silence broke. Tom doubled down. He did not retreat, apologize or hesitate. Instead, sweat pouring off his agitated brow, he pressed leathery fingers into the wood, under that flat, insubordinate spike. We watched. This we had to see. Bent spikes do not budge with hammer claws, let alone fingers.

Tom heaved. The spike did not move – of course. It went nowhere; it was going nowhere. Spikes bent in green cedar are cement moorings on a lake bottom – stuck solid. Nevertheless, Tom sucked in another breath, plunged his fingers into the green wood. The spike did not move. The whole thing was becoming a farce. This was embarrassing, hard to watch.

Nobody liked seeing a crew member defeated. No one wanted Tom locked in a struggle he could not win, trying to make a point he need not make. The cedar was not his adversary, nor we. The adversary was somewhere else; best to acknowledge limits. Tom hated such moments.

So here we were, standing uncomfortably, watching him face-to-face with human frailty. An impossible task foiled his intent, forcing *can-do* into *cannot.* By now, Tom's lungs were heaving and hunting oxygen. His heart was pounding through a soaked shirt, veins popping from neck and arms. His legs, scarred by napalm from an accident aboard the carrier deck, were rock tense.

Tom seemed not to see us anymore. Nor could he see the inevitable. The spike was not bending to his will, nor would it. Tom would not concede nature's power to render humans powerless. Knotty, sappy cedar is irascible, cranky, impenetrable stuff, inscrutable and impossible. Spikes hate it. We hated it. But that was how it was. Spikes bend in it, slowing human progress.

Someone was about to say something. That was when it happened. Tom leaned in, pulsing veins writhing like hungry pythons, twisting down his temples, around his thick neck. He had brought the dead rivers of Mars back to life. They frothed and flowed with adrenaline. He was seething. He gave that bent spike one last, uncompromising heave, punctuated by a deep, guttural exhale. Agitated and resolved, his fingers turned the cedar to putty, doing what only hammer claws were supposed to. To our shock, he pulled the spike from deep in the cedar with his bare hand – transforming the world in which we stood.

His will was a scene-changing force. Bottom of the ninth, two outs, two strikes, and clutch. All-or-nothing, last chance. Tom hated to lose. He hated it more when making a public point – ironically, that we should all hate to lose. In such moments, his face became Mars. Improbable but true, the flat spike conceded itself from the cedar, came to rest in Tom's throbbing hand. Our jaws went slack. Tom had won. He did not say a word. He did not seem to notice us. He lifted the hammer, straightened the spike, and decisively slammed it home – in one go-to-Hades blow, right through the hole that moments earlier was his nemesis. The spike sank like a brick in freefall, gone.

Tom did not pause to wipe his flooding brow, rapids pouring down his face. He did not laugh. He did not break into conversation. He just said, "That's how it's done," drew a long breath, and finished with, "Ok, enough for one day, knock off … we'll finish this tomorrow." Then he returned to the car, and was gone. We looked after him. We looked at the spike, buried in the rail. Damned if he hadn't done it, after all.

Typical of Tom, this was just one point on the arc of life. I doubt he recalled it. Not the way we did. He set expectations, sometimes unrealistic, then pressed to meet them. His method was simple – set goal, take risk, strive hard, complete mission, do again. Over that spike, it was the same. He reared to height and won.

Heck of a way to live life, but Tom never quit, not that I saw. Not even when the cancer came. He battled it more than a decade, grit and courage to the last. Even there, he taught. Rise to the challenges you choose, and the ones you don't. Muster fire, sustain effort, get up when knocked down, forgive and forget, keep one eye on the finish.

Not really Patton, more the flavor of Churchill. Maybe the old Democrat and young Republican could agree on Churchill, maybe not.

Churchill's 1941 speech to British youth comes to mind. "Never give in, never give in, never, never; never, never – in nothing great or small, large or petty – never give in except to convictions of honor and good sense." Tom's spike pull, like Churchill's words, still echoes.

Young Tom Lane in uniform, WWII-era in Hawaii, headed for turret gunner in Pacific

Older Tom Lane, 1970s, tough boss and irreplaceable mentor

–Building Houses

Then … there was George, another boss. Like Richie, Old Man P, and Tom, George was a veteran of World War II. His service was in the Far East. George was another matter, altogether. Quiet, he loved building quality houses. With a shock of white hair worn in flattop, buck-tooth smile and easy manner, George was an uncompromising perfectionist. Whatever he built lasted. To him, hard work was measured by outcomes, as much as by sweat. I worked for him at age seventeen.

Under George's tutelage, I learned how to pound nails flush in two swings, create cement forms and mix, pour and rake wet cement; how to measure and cut boards – straight, no bows, nothing out of square; how to turn them vertical and stud up walls. I grew proficient at shingling, and learned to care about every step in building a house.

George made nothing of his past, not that I saw. You just had to know. It was something. He had been a signalman 2nd class, Pacific Theater, 1942 through 1944. Those were tough years. What he saw we never knew, since he preferred not to talk about himself – or the war. Whatever he saw, it infused him with resolve. He was consistent and unapologetically gentle. He toted a light heart and sound judgment. He paused and thought before speaking. Even then, he spoke only as needed. George started and concluded each day high energy, seemingly at peace about everything. To problems, he took a long view, but he always got to a solution. If he shared qualities like determination, perseverance and optimism with Richie, Old Man P and Tom, his style was unique. Through that unique style, he too taught.

Around George, people buzzed with intention – since he did. We worked about a house site as bees tend a hive, coming and going. Each had a job. Watching George, the team saw patience and precision, attention to detail, preoccupation with getting it right – whatever it was. George had vision and method. His ambitions were sensible, if a reach. He was always smiling, almost elfin by nature. No long strides, he made lots of short ones. He offered no controversial opinions, none I heard. He was firm, but never harsh. He could be whimsical, chortling over something until others saw it. He wanted projects completed, but understood things take time.

So, we got practice with hammer, skill saw, level and ladder. He gave assignments, made sure they were understood, and let us go. He was a study in having seen the world, and left its vast irrelevance behind. Sometimes adversity, especially combat, leaves a person troubled and doubting. Other times, it instills uncommon confidence and calm. George fell into the latter group. We were the beneficiaries.

For George, work did not seem salvation, just time spent with high purpose, serving others with his skills. It was about making an honest living, doing something he liked, and serving the community – people he knew and always would. Nothing lofty or preachy about George, nothing desperate or driven either. Career was a source of satisfaction. He planned, organized and built things – good things. He used "advanced lookout skills," that attention to detail required of a World War II Navy signalman in the Pacific. Puzzling shapes and functionality, he constructed three-story worlds in which little feet could safely run. That was George's contentment; he was meticulous. People called it "George's way."

Roofing for George, I spent time with another old timer, Harold. Harold was, by the time I knew him, a septuagenarian. That meant nothing to Harold, George, or me. Harold was a hammer-swinging member of George's team. He had experience, could work, and George had a need. Harold and I spent days shingling roofs. We passed time soaking up sun as it crossed, Harold cracking jokes between swings, offering wisdom in digestible doses to his young colleague.

During World War II, Harold worked in the town's famous crutch factory. The factory is gone, but it once stood beside the Mill Pond, near the Wayne General Store. Sadly, there was a special need for crutches. During World War II, while Richie, Tom, George, Ford, Vern and others served overseas, Harold and townspeople worked in the factory. Their work mattered; their work ethic was all-in. Lila, wife of Richie's brother, Waldo (better known as "Tink"), operated the crutch factory's drill press. When Tink returned home, he became Postmaster; Lila served as Town Clerk for more than 30 years. During World War II, Lila worked with the Red Cross, Aircraft Warning Service, and war-related Emergency Feeding Program. Everyone did his or her part.

From Harold, I learned how to cling to acute angles without falling, wear a carpenter's apron without losing nails, and keep a straight shingle line. Shingles not straight got ripped off and re-laid. My balance on ladders, shingles over one shoulder, improved. Harold tutored across a range of topics, including scaffold climbing, use of skill saw, picking straight two-by-fours, holding nails in one's teeth, gun-slinging from a hammer holster. I learned to be nimble on rafters and sink nails without scarring – all while not falling. Other days, I learned how to be quiet for hours. That skill was hard to retain, but essential on a hot roof – just like humor.

I learned that some combat vets, like George, are inherently calm. He did not "sweat small stuff." If I needed a good talking to, he would stiffen his jaw, say a few words, and that was it. When I decided to trust my eye for level, he corrected the mistake. It might have thrown the entire house off square. When I chose a bowed board, he spoke up. These mistakes were not made twice. George did not yell; his way was to smile and correct. When I let a shingle line drift, smudged hot shingles, or used too many nails – he set me right, no drama. Whether war had wrung emotion out of him or he saw no need for extremes, the result was the same. I liked that leadership style, expectant and motivational, instructional and forever calm.

Like other World War II vets around town, George lived with high purpose. He felt an obligation to get things accomplished, make the most of each day. He never said so, but seemed lifted by things well beyond himself. An early riser, his toothy grin testified to productivity. Embedded in each sunrise was a chance – to get something good done by sunset. All you had to do was use each hour well. He taught the attitude. Everyone liked working for him.

George had worn America's white "eagle wings," over signal flags and a red stripe, insignia of all Navy signalmen. He wore them with distinction. But by the time I worked for him, guns and warbirds were past. He was defined by building homes, and radiated irrepressible brightness. I cycled to work in those days. On rainy afternoons, he would throw my bike in the pickup and take me home. As William Wordsworth, the old English Lakes District poet, once observed: "That best portion of a man's life … little, nameless, unremembered acts of kindness and love." George was full of them, even if much was unsaid.

You will recall our Mill Pond, and the local dam. On Memorial Day, the wreath goes over that dam. The dam holds tons of upstream water, releasing it slowly into Androscoggin Lake. Beside the dam is a small plaque. It is there even today. It is easy to miss. The plaque honors our townsman, George. It does not honor his service in World War II, although it could. It does not honor his patience, judgment or carpentry skills. Not really. True to his nature, it is humbler. It honors his fidelity to the place he lived. It pays tribute to his personal commitment to supervising the rebuilding of our dam – being the person he always was, a friend to all.

If someday you stand over the plaque, you will see water curling to your right, crashing or trickling onto rocks below. You might see a loon behind you on the Mill Pond. Even now, one is often there. You might spy a heron on the rocks below, or eagle overhead. In these birds, you have the signalman's "wings," symbol of service. That was George, in every season. Last time I saw him, he was in his late 80s, at a Memorial Day parade, sporting his hallmark buckteeth and flat-top, cheerful as the day was long.

So, summers were about work, as much as fun. We learned as much in summer as in school. I spent another summer teaching kids to swim at a YMCA in Camden. I used lessons from Farmer P, Tom and George. I never quit on a child. I watched for details. I tried to model patience. I ran miles each morning, to smile all day. These kids came from an island off the Maine coast. Their fathers were all lobstermen – mostly unable to swim. That summer, all those kids became swimmers – which was good, since boats got passed down. When their turn came, they would be ready. Today, those kids are pulling traps, and probably teaching their kids to swim.

Over the years, we learned things – how to tell peas from weeds, fix broken kayaks, cut cedars, dig post holes and shingle roofs. I figured out that – despite the bad rap – hard work is a good time. Employers are educators. Self-worth resides in work well done, if you look for it. All you have to do is – start. Done right, work is much more than a means to ends; it is an end itself, a purpose worth rising for. Tutored by those who knew, town kids learned. Most never forgot.

Young George Richardson in uniform, WWII-era, headed for signalman in Pacific theater

Older George, 1980s, cheerfully building homes for local families, supervising dam reconstruction, gentle boss

16. *What if?*

Given time, kids dreamed. Without electronics, distractions were few. Once chores were done, we set to thinking. Some kids thought in practical terms, about summer jobs, baseball plays, tree houses, fishing lures, fixing a bicycle, harvests to come. Others thought impractically, about meandering runs, looking into constellations, girls, inventions, and flipping off sand banks at the dump. I thought about all of those, and more. Some days, a young mind flipped and flipped, tumbling into the world of "what if?" I did that.

Such days could lead nowhere, and everywhere. As Emerson wrote, "In the woods we return to reason and faith." And we did, thinking about the world – there in the woods. But his student, Thoreau, added a vital footnote. "It's not what you look at that matters, it's what you see." As we imagined, we saw more. Quiet towns allow that. Years on, I remain grateful.

Imagining started simple. What if … we tried to hang glide in a bedsheet? What if … we blew the lake's length on ice skates? What if … we launched a rocket sideways? What if …we designed our own balsa wood plane? What if … we put a sail on the wagon? What if … we tried to touch the tree's top? Built a trap for partridge from a slatted apple box? Made a new alphabet? Cycled an anniversary cake to friends, despite the rain? Tried "dead reckoning" to a friend's house through the woods? Counted stars, imagined being on the moon? Hunted spruce gum? Constructed a fort in the pines, then slept in it? Learned to bake bread, split big logs, saw faster, build a birdhouse, make Christmas ornaments, climb a tree to the roof, get back down, or fix a problem others thought unfixable?

As time passed, the "what ifs" changed. A kid's thinking shifted – to cars, girls, sports, earning money, getting his license, maybe a snowmobile. Some thoughts became focused – toward school and then, what lay beyond. The balance differed wildly by kid, but was there. For me, worry intruded on play. My "what ifs" slowly changed.

What if … I could run longer, slightly faster? At cross country practice, somebody mentioned a marathon. What was a marathon? What if … I got grades up, reached a little higher, thought about college? Scholarships were available; I would need them. Someone said college would help, if you got in. My father never went. My mother did – on scholarship. What if … I aimed higher? How did people get to faraway places, Washington, D.C.,

America's west coast, Europe, India, or the Middle East? I started running farther, on my own and out of season. I joined the debate team, competed with vigor, focused more on classes. Scouting and sports held interest, but I thought beyond "now," into the murk that was the future. What *was* possible?

Dreams took shape, and gradually things happened. For one thing, scholarships came – with effort. Little "what ifs" led to bigger "what ifs," and things started to move. Never a great athlete, sports scholarships were out. I thought about the military; that would have to wait. Love of the outdoors, ice fishing, smelting, waterskiing, camping and exploring, began to pay off. Building on school and scouting achievements, I mustered the courage to apply to an Ivy League school. My dream was Dartmouth. To do that, I had to address doubt. Maybe I was getting above myself. But "what if…?"

The gamble was taken. While others pursued dreams of work, military service, travel and education closer to home, even flying and starting a business, my focus stayed on Dartmouth. Why not? True, I had no family or friends with any links, no money, no legacy, and one parent who had never graduated, so what? This was America. If you didn't try, you would never know. As Robert Browning wrote, and I knew: "A man's reach should exceed his grasp, or what's a heaven for?" A kid's curiosity and hope should exceed apparent limits. What's childhood for?

The scholarship idea nagged. I would need one. I worked harder. To my shock, resulting in tears, laughter and sudden fear, I was admitted to Dartmouth. This was an inflection point, although that term was not known to me. This was literally "a dream come true," a "what if" that came to pass. But there was, frustratingly, a footnote. I was not given any money to attend. Since none existed in the family and my earnings were insufficient, the irony was acute. I had gotten in, but could not go. My academic efforts, debate team, distance running and hard work had paid off – now this.

I was not ready to give in, not yet. The old "what ifs" – and making some come true – met new ones. I asked my mother if I could borrow the family car. We had only one. This was a big ask. Dartmouth was five hours away. She knew exactly what hung in the balance. I guess she approved my tenacity, as she let me go. I headed for Hanover resolved. They had handed me a paradox – admitted me, yet denied me the chance to attend. They were not obligated of course; still, I kept my chin up. The goal of my trip was to point out this irony, the granting and withholding of a dream in one envelope.

I just hoped the powers that governed that great institution would listen. I wrote down "thirteen points," each point a reason why, from the college's perspective, I was a good bet. The meeting occurred, I presented my case – and nothing changed. The outcome remained indeterminate. Not immediately convinced, they allowed that they would review the file and let me know. True to their word, they did. Their review produced another miracle – within a week, they presented me with a package of scholarship grants, long-term loans and enough work to cover my first year bills. That was all I needed. I was ecstatic. Another "what if" … had come to pass.

Winding the clock ahead, every succeeding "what if" seemed more important. Early lessons – work hard, give your imagination room, let God take care of the rest – continued to deliver. From Dartmouth, scholarships took me to Oxford University for two years, then Columbia Law School, into jobs for a US Court of Appeals, two presidents, the US Congress, the Navy, eventually into my own business tied to national security. Along the way, I continued asking "what if?" The question was central. It has always been central. Even when disappointed, it was worth asking. Family, teachers and employers allowed me to ask it, so I did.

Then something else happened. Happily married, with two wonderful children, blessed to survive 9/11 despite losing Navy friends, plugging away at work, the phone rang. Another "what if" was on the other end. More accurately, it was a "would you like to?" The second Bush White House, namely Secretary of State Colin Powell, wanted to explore my interest in serving as an Assistant Secretary.

This job entailed running law enforcement and counter-narcotics programs worldwide, operations in 70 countries, a two-billion dollar budget. That was a mouthful to say, and to hear. It was a far cry from my early "what ifs." The job required establishing police training for Iraq and Afghanistan, next stages for post-war Kosovo, and everything tied to Plan Colombia. What could I say? What would you? Of course, yes.

This led, in many ways, to completion of that "what if" circle. Early "what ifs" presaged later "what ifs." All had been preparation. Learning to ask and to envision, while also working hard, proved invaluable. No longer concerned about partridges in slatted apple boxes or spruce gum, better ways to split wood or slam spikes, build houses or clean toilets, I had other concerns. We needed police up and running in Iraq and Afghanistan. This was the early 2000s. We needed to calm post-war waters in Kosovo, where riots threatened to undo NATO's work. We needed to roll back terrorism and drug trafficking in Colombia, give peace a chance.

So … "what if" America trained Iraqi police in *both* Baghdad and Jordan, established *seven* training centers in Afghanistan, inspired Kosovar Albanians to *redouble* their commitment to rule of law, ramped up support for peace in Colombia, helped *end* drug-funded terror? "What if" we pulled members of Congress from *both* parties behind these efforts? "What if" we worked to make what, in many ways, seemed impossible – *possible?*

There was another layer of 'what if' questions beyond this one. "What if …" we accelerated the police training facility in Jordan, to support Iraq? "What if" we built that center on the open desert, securing it with stand-off detection technology? "What if" we leveraged nine US Air Force C-130 transports to ferry 1500 Iraqi police recruits from Baghdad to Amman every four weeks, returning with 1500 fully-trained police cadets? "What if" we overlapped classes of 1500 for continuity? "What if" we ran them for eight weeks, training 3000 Iraqi police at any given time? "What if," with Secretary Powell's go-ahead, we sought buy-in from the White House, Congress and military brass? "What if," for housing Iraqi police in Jordan we tried something risky, putting hundreds of Sunnis, Shia, Christians, Kurds and Yazidis *together* in large, open-air housing units? Would it work? Might it set the tone for nationwide police cohesion later?

In Afghanistan, having met leadership and gotten buy-in, "what if" we worked to unpack similar problems? Security mattered in both places. It was the foundation of all else. "What if" we … tried unconventional ideas? In Kosovo, "what if" we used the police academy as a model, then advanced peace in and outside the Serb enclaves, turning down emotions with an appeal to rule of law and the international community of law enforcement? "What if" we could convince Albanian police officers to arrest Albanians for offenses against Serbs? Would that not give law the upper hand over sectarian violence?

In Colombia, "what if" regional counter-drug, counter-terrorism, and rule of law commitments were vectored toward peace? "What if" the Colombian National Police, US Congress and armed forces in both countries fashioned credible deterrence, and leveraged a peace accord? "What if" the two governments worked together to dismantle decades of terrorist violence? "What if?"

Sometimes just asking begins the process. That rural disposition for asking "what if" helped to leverage results. For reasons complex and simple, hopeful and perennially challenging, good things did occur. The Iraqi police were trained, tens of thousands of them. In another untold story, 3000 ethnically diverse recruits lived together – and at peace – for eight-week periods on the Jordanian desert, year in and year out, no attrition and no ethnic violence. If it could happen there, why not on a larger basis? Why not try, why not now? Just think "what if…?"

In Afghanistan, the confluence of overlapping regional and ideological conflicts, widespread illiteracy, endemic poverty and a frustrating disinterest in counter-narcotics by leaders undermined progress toward peace, but trained Afghan police did their part. Free elections occurred in the early 2000s, due to their courage. Why? Because the Afghans asked, "what if?"

In Kosovo, while ethnic tensions simmer and periodically boil over; while stability remains delicate and religious freedom tenuous, fenced and indefinite; while economic development encounters back steps, hope is nevertheless alive. In part, that is the product of a conscious and continuing, indigenous and assisted pressure for rule of law – having Albanian policemen, answering to conscience and training, arrest Albanian offenders for crimes against Serbs, and vice versa. When hoped-for events are intergenerational, hope can seem elusive. It is still there for those who keep asking "what if?"

In Colombia, the multi-decade effort to create deterrence, sustain political will, wring terrorism from the sprawling, ungoverned jungle, has also paid off. The focus on reducing transnational crime, addressing human rights and tackling rampant drug-funding of terror has been rewarded. American and Colombian resolve, millions of minds and voices asking "what if" combined to deliver an accord that, for now, has made peace possible. It began, as always, with "what if?"

As for me, the "what ifs" have led far from home, but not that far. I still ask "what if" on many occasions. Instead of flying in rural Maine and building balsa models, I have gotten a chance to fly in an F-16, enjoyed the "what if" of vertical flight, inverted and barrel rolls. Instead of blowing on skates down a frozen lake or sailing a wagon down the meadow, I have blown across the Middle East, cork-screwed into Baghdad, watched a moon rise over the Iraqi desert. I never used my alternate alphabet, but Navy Intelligence gave me "what ifs" in that realm. I never cycled a second anniversary cake to old friends, but we have stayed close. Dead reckoning lately has been through a wilderness of modern law and politics. As for running a marathon, I finally did.

Sometimes, the scent of pine, swing of an ax, a long run in Maine take me back. They return me to that question, "what if…?" In the end, the question is not just for children. It is a surrogate for hope in – and at – every age. It offers a certain timeless light. By that light, curious souls see further. As long as we continue asking, hope abounds.

Author left, in high school, with neighbor, Will. In rural Maine, we were encouraged to ask "what if" in activities like Boy Scouts, debate, running and football, circa 1977.

Author, sworn-in as Assistant Secretary of State (INL) to Colin Powell, with wife Marina

Author spending time with another old boss, Ronald Reagan.

17. Grand Idea

Sun spread across the quiet lake, Androscoggin. Herringbone clouds drifted in a cobalt sky. Today, was the grand test. No excuses. The Wrights, assembling their wares at Kitty Hawk, must have felt as I did. I was giddy. Not flying, my idea was "water walking" – nothing miraculous, just primitive engineering. How primitive, I would soon learn.

Days earlier, enjoying my fifteenth summer, I had stumbled on two slabs of Styrofoam. I considered them treasures. They were leftovers from a camp project, sadly destined for the dump. I rescued them. Each stood six feet tall, a foot thick. And they floated. To a teen boy, these were unconstructed rafts, aquaplanes, something. Finally, the "something" dawned on me.

Giant water shoes. This is what these slabs would become. If they held me on water, could be shaped, shod and stabilized, could be bound together front and rear, could be equipped with friction for locomotion … I could literally walk across the lake! Maybe I could run!

This was sure to be the "next big thing." Suddenly, I knew it. I would test them, then deliver my water-walking shoes to the world! They would revolutionize recreation, giving lake lovers everywhere a new sport. Kick-boards, life rings and safety bubbles were fine, but crooners could soon walk along the shoreline *on the water!* People could take morning runs and evening strolls on their favorite lakes, ponds and rivers. New sports might emerge – water-skating, water-dancing, water-football. Couples could dance by moonlight, *on the water!* Restaurants would grow up around these sports. They would be the rage, no boat needed. Now *that* was egalitarian!

Before long, I had fashioned two six-foot water-walking shoes from my porous foam finds. Each got neatly carved, triangular treads. Old sneakers were epoxied to their midsections. Buoyancy was tested, stabilizers added, balance checked, rope affixed front and back to prevent side-pulling. My water shoes were kept narrow, permitting back-and-forth steps. They were long, the price of buoyancy. Heck, snow skies were long, too. Besides length added stability. All I needed … was a test run. Water-walking was about to become *huge.* I just knew it.

At this point, readers with any inclination toward engineering, basic knowledge of friction and familiarity with water, will have some questions. I can hear you. What about waves, wind, and propulsion? How will those shoes move on water without a paddle, pole, wind or motor? If docks rest on water, they go nowhere, not usually. They are intended to go nowhere.

Yes, you are right. I missed these fine points. My mind was taking leaps; I was running lake laps.

On shore, I now stood watching the flat lake. Under each arm I held one magical six-foot water-walking shoe. At dock's end, I sat down, laced up and prepared to make history. This was innovation, my version of the light bulb, or a better mousetrap. Here began a new national pastime! Slowly, I leaned forward, turning sideways to accommodate my shoes' length. So far, so good. With relative ease, I stood up. I was standing *on the water!* This was exhilarating. Now, one thing remained … walking.

Looking out, my eyes fell on a float several hundred feet away. Goal in sight, I stepped forward. Nothing happened. Methodically, I raised one shoe, thrust it forward, and returned it to the water – right where it began. A minute more, and it hit me. Creating friction on water is harder than it looks. Actually, it is nearly impossible without an assist. Sneaking forward, stiffly striding, coyly wriggling, boldly bouncing and energetically jumping – left me right where I started.

Darned if I was going to be outdone by physics! Over the next half hour, I slogged, sloshed, twitched, slapped and slid on the water, arriving pooped, soggy and sore at the float. This, I knew, was a pyrrhic victory. I was sopping, breathless, insteps aching and muscles spent. After a long rest, I hazarded the return trip – looking to see if anyone was watching. Back on shore, my water-walking shoes were quietly placed on the dump pile, a grand idea – missing something. Four decades later, the popularity of paddle boarding suggests my bread just needed yeast. Sometimes "what if?" ended with "oh well." There was always tomorrow.

18. Another Grand Idea

In those days, water skiing was a regular source of summer horseplay. We performed modest tricks, slalom cuts and rooster tails, tried stacking people, used multiple ski lines, even parasailed, compliments of a wonderful local family, the Brooks clan. The Brooks kids were *bona fide* pros. They owned a 1959 mahogany Century named *Rebel.* That gorgeous boat kicked a monster wake, and had pulled skiers in the "waterski nationals," before finally retiring to Androscoggin. The Brooks clan – led by Dan, Byron and Lynda – taught half the lake to ski. Their circle included champion long jumpers, pyramid builders, tricksters and slalom winners. They made time for little folks, including me. They gave hours and taught love of the sport. Byron continued doing so when he returned from Vietman, and after he married Lynda's college roommate Terry.

One other town figure, another Mr. P, owned a mahogany boat, *Miss Andy.* Between *Rebel* and *Miss Andy*, every youngster in town who wished to ski, did. Mr. P collected gas money; that was it. On skis, we tested ourselves, learning to throw plumes, jump wide, perform dock starts, try 180s and 360s, hold a line with one foot, ski parallel, and cut like greased lightning. Skiing was a hamlet specialty, compliments of families Brooks and Mr. P.

But skiing was dependent on boats. One day, friends and I wondered if our 25-horse motor would allow for skiing. Swapping off as driver, spotter and skier, friends Mark, Karl and I took a second swipe at physics. Ignoring power to mass ratios, we tried to ski behind this putter boat. In our version of the sport, a "skier" grabbed the tow rope and leaned back, shouting "hit it." This was *just* like with the mahogany boats. Here similarities end. Our "skier" was dragged hundreds of feet, before muscling up behind that little engine, a coffee grinder chewing nails.

The spotter hung off the bow, as counter-weight. The driver worried the boat forward. The skier's feet flipped this way and that, arms sore as a rodeo rider, water rushing over and into him. This persisted the length of a football field – until the skier either rose or let go. Being "up" meant standing ankle deep in water. Putative skiers concentrated or sank. Today, experts might call this "dynamic exercise," "explosive power training," "crossover pulling," or "good for the core." We just called it a challenge, and "wicked fun."

You have to picture this devilish sport to understand why it never caught on. Water rushed about a skier's feet and ankles. Staying up was like walking a greased balance beam. The skier invariably wobbled, swiveled and swayed. His only aim was to stay vertical long enough to justify the struggle, a mission shared by driver and spotter. Crossing wakes was dicey, not advisable. The skier might get over, but suddenly stop the boat. This forced a restart, new slog.

Any attempt at swinging broadly was madness, in which we indulged occasionally. Centrifugal forces left the skier moving, boat dead, until skier stopped and sank. We credited ourselves with a new sport – and resolved to love it. Like "water walking shoes," it never caught on. Still, it filled time when mahoganies were quiet.

Perhaps the most daring and grandest idea on water skis belonged to Chris, whom you met earlier behind the town plow. He once skied behind a seaplane. In all events, hope sprang eternal, along with our ability to fail spectacularly, and start all over again.

Waterskiing behind "Rebel" 1960, Byron driving, his brother Dan skiing

Byron (left), future Vietnam veteran, with brother Dan, on Androscoggin Lake. They taught half the town to waterski.

Byron asked "what if"—then invented a new trick, ladder skiing

Brooks boat pulls six skiers, seventh joining from right, circa 1960

My sisters (left to right), Anita and Cynthia, on lake with Lynda Brooks, circa 1967

My mother Doris Anne (left), Aunt Neetie (right), with Ellie (Hyatt) Ault, circa 1945. Ellie married Richard (USMC), brother of Peter, whose Korean War service is profiled (Army). Neetie became a state skiing standout, later married the son of WWII veteran Vern, who ran the Wayne General Store.

19. Noble Ghosts of Androscoggin Island

This day was like no other. We climbed from canoe ribbing onto an abandoned island – stepping into a distinguished past and haunted present. We encountered what you might call noble ghosts. Here was Abenaki history, Maine's oldest summer camp for boys, and a vacancy that burdened the heart. How we got here, why and what we found that day, seems worth telling.

On this little-known island, celebrated playwright Steven Sondheim once played. With him, irreverent lyricist, mathematician and pianist Tom Lehrer spent early years. Here, World War II POW leader General Delmar Spivey once served as counselor. Here, dozens of famous figures ran freely, as children. And earlier, the island's first campers were Abenaki Indians.

Androscoggin, once dubbed Hog, later called San Souci, lies at the north end of Androscoggin Lake. The island, in this town we called home, has a singular and memorable history. Once a stopover for Abenaki tribesmen trekking to the ocean, it served boys for seventy years, through two world wars.

In 1906, Androscoggin Island became Maine's first "Summer Camp for Boys." Over the next seven decades, heart-warming tales were spun by campers and counselors. In June of each year, the entourage arrived from bustling cities along the eastern seaboard. The island became their temporary home. In time, this camp became well known – as did some who attended. Then very suddenly, it collapsed. Bubbling and bugling one day, it went bankrupt the next, and was abruptly abandoned. That was 1971.

For all intents and purposes, the island was forsaken. Lodgings went dark. Human activity ceased. In place of laughter and play, only silence. The place seemed suspended in time, suddenly uninviting, vaguely forbidding. From a distance, cabins looked forlorn and embankments became overgrown. The island seemed adrift on time, haunted.

Weather took a toll. Trees fell. The ballfield's backstop tipped. Shadows grew. Eventually, the place would pass into private hands, pass again and become a summer residence. All that happened much later. For a time, it just drifted. According to zoning laws, the island's tenure as a boys' camp was over. Perhaps that compounded the remorse.

Vital papers and film records – essential to understanding the camp's long run – fell to weather and to mice. No one rushed to save them. No one felt empowered to do so. Following bankruptcy and abandonment, the island turned ghost town. Silhouettes disappeared in gangly trees and hungry alders. Generations of campers and shoreline dwellers tried to shrug. But people do not forget.

It was in these years of limbo that some of us began to wonder: *What was out there? What had life been like in that summer paradise, in the early days? What was it like in its heyday? More, what had happened? What was left?* To kids, the island was a mystery, unexplained and spooky. Of course, mysteries attract youthful attention. The empty island did ours.

The sudden demise of such an iconic place seemed an unsolved crime. The island was an unfinished story. Its disappearance left people curious. Many reconciled themselves and carried on, or perhaps cared less than we kids. A few were nostalgic and told stories. Some looked over – and stayed curious. Those of us working at the shoreline successor camp fit that group.

In our lifetimes, nothing so key to town life had vanished so quickly. For almost three-quarters of a century, people had heard the camp's bugler – reveille, assembly, mess and taps, dawn and dusk, breakfast and supper, then for lights out. The island had been alive. Laughter, water sports, musical performances for townspeople, canoe flotillas, visits to the Wayne General Store – all part of our town fabric. Then the fabric was rent.

Rumors as to why circulated, without detail. They did not matter. More important was what had been, and drawing inspiration from the camp's legacy. On the island's southeastern side, a string of gray bunkhouses looked gloomily across the lake, square eyes unblinking. They had seen a lot, now saw little. Made one shiver. They stood in a row like medieval battlements, careworn parapets on a castle wall. The castle was empty, proceeding to ruin. They knew it.

From a passing canoe, the island's interior looked dark, even by day. Trees poked through the canopy like spires. Below, a tangle of wood and shadows. Shouts never came back; echoes were swallowed. The place was wasting, more mysterious each year. Whatever history it held, would soon be gone, unpreserved. *What would come of it?* The place drew people, but then pushed them away.

People circled in their canoes, but stayed a distance. Spits of land showed old trails, ending in darkness. The wooden backstop twisted and slunk. A winged playhouse peeked from among trunks. A flagpole implied duties performed, salutes, songs, parade ground. For a moment, one could imagine sleepyheads assembling. Paddlers paused and listened, trying to hear, paddled on.

A wineglass beach lay along the south side. Near the island's center, visible only from the east, stood a giant structure. From this imposing edifice, a solemn chimney climbed toward the sky. Its stones caught first light, the sun sneaking over Morrison Heights each morning. The old building seemed like a sentry, arms folded, neck extended, staring across grass to the lake. Intruders were on notice. The sentry caught every eye. This had been a hub, the dining hall.

We knew a little… but not enough. We knew the camp had grown from a dream, been built by an enterprising man – and his son. The man and son had bought with high purpose. As WWI approached, the young man's father died. In combat, his brother died. The son married an understanding lady, who adopted his dream. Together they made the place prosper. Indeed, they made it their life's work. They nurtured it, until half the world knew Camp Androscoggin.

In the process, they grew young men up. These young men, in turn, had dreams. They took a piece of the island with them, were lifted by it, and made their dreams real. Grown boys married, became fathers, sent their sons back, who sent their sons back. The place became an institution. More, those who went forth did so with confidence, creativity and comfort with risk. Some went to Broadway, others into journalism, law, medicine, business, education – and war.

Decades on, the founding son and his wife grew old. I remember them well. Time came to sell their institution, which they did. By that point, two summer camps existed – one on the island for older boys, another on the shore for younger. Both were called Camp Androscoggin, but the island was dubbed Senior, the shoreline Junior. Senior was the one sold. Not long after that, the wheels came off. Dreams are like that, hard to keep real. By the early 1970s, the island camp was a memory, shoreline taking older boys. That was where I worked, the shoreline camp.

Apparently, ambiguities in ownership clouded responsibilities for care; the island's dense emptiness only got denser. Nature conspired with indifference to keep erasing the past. As we watched from afar, time got the upper hand. What "had been" continued to slip away.

Of course, the island camp *had* a history. Winding the clock back, it radiated achievement, enrichment and empowerment. It had taught values and confidence, character and comradery. The place had been an island of hope, literally, in a distressed world. For the better part of the 20th century, it had offered an escape, venue for play, locus for adolescent growth. The place had an annual cadence. Migration started in June. Hundreds of boys piled onto trains in far-away places, especially New York City. They came to Maine with camping gear (often in a leather suitcase). They were filled with enthusiasm. Soon, they were learning from counselors, many former campers. Documents show the place buzzing with fun, intellectual and athletic.

Camp Androscoggin Senior thrived in a heady century. In 1906, the camp's founding year, Jack London wrote *White Fang,* French aviation was born (following the Wrights), along with Anne Morrow Lindbergh (writer par excellence and future wife of Charles). Theodore Roosevelt – who also loved Maine – was then president.

In time, the camp got through World War I, the Great Depression, World War II, Korea and Vietnam. Camp boys saw a dozen presidents come and go – TR, then Taft, Wilson, Harding, Coolidge and Hoover, followed by FDR, Truman, Ike, JFK, Johnson and Nixon. Having come to life three years after the Wright brothers' first flight, the camp closed three years after Neil Armstrong and Buzz Aldrin walked on the moon.

Parenthetically, Maine's oldest continuous summer camp was founded for girls in 1902, but Camp Androscoggin came along next – for boys, 1906. Today, the oldest continuous Maine camps date to 1908; there are two. This history may seem whimsical and irrelevant, but the camps were national models. They offered adventure, encouraged young imaginations to grow, taught self-reliance. If geography were literature, these camps would be a genre.

From the earliest, campers learned routines. Boys arrived on trains at Leeds, disembarked near Dead River and took a powerboat to the island in Wayne. Eventually, they came by bus to the Wayne Yacht Club (which had no yachts), and were ferried to the island. Once ashore, summer began. Friendships were rekindled, traditions celebrated, along with games and literary outpourings, sing-alongs and canoe trips. Abilities were discovered, bonfires built, fast friends made. Today, summer camps do this everywhere. Androscoggin was a pioneer, for 64 summers.

The word "Androscoggin" comes from the Abenaki language. Anthropologists string together syllables and suggest it means "fish coming in spring." From smelting on, we know they do. The Abenaki, known to English and French explorers from the 1500s, spoke Algonquian. That language was common around Maine. "Abenaki" itself meant "people of the dawn land" or "dawn people," which makes sense too. Maine gets the dawn before all America – and did before Maine was Maine, and America, America.

While there is no proof Abenaki lived on the island, they certainly frequented the lake. That much is well-established. Crossing the lake, they portaged to the south on their way to Merrymeeting Bay in the mouth of the Kennebec River. Notably, the Abenaki populated river floodplains. Dead River's double delta fits that definition – as does the island. Arrow heads are still found along the river. So, who knows, perhaps the island's first campers were Abenaki.

Now defunct, the old *Lewiston Journal,* in December 1928, wrote about "The Last of the Indians." In part, the article reads:

"[The Abenaki] always made two trips each year to the sea-coast. These were made for the purposes of visiting the graves of their fathers, to hunt sea-fowl, to buy and sell furs. Coming from up river, they always paddled into Dead River of Leeds, and up to the old camping place ..."

Could that have been Androscoggin Island? The article continues:

"After awaiting their friends here and performing certain religious ceremonies, they divided. Part went over to Wilson Pond, worked along its waters to Cobbosseecontee [Lake], thence to the Kennebec. The other followed the Androscoggin [River]. They reunited at Merrymeeting Bay [sic], hunted ducks, fished and dried their fish and fowl .... The last of these trips of record is in 1796 ... Later a number of Androscoggin Indians lived in [surrounding areas]...They dwelt in wigwams or shacks ... were friendly but aloof ... made baskets, fished, hunted, and raised a little garden-stuff."

Having painted an anthropological backdrop, I come back to the island of my youth. The founder's "son" was named Edward M. Healy. He was affectionately known around town – and on the island – as the "Chief." After his father's passing, Ed took over. And where did some of the campers and counselors end up? We know some places. These shed light on the rest.

Famous island campers include Harvard math lecturer, pianist and comic satirist, Tom Lehrer. His incisive, irreverent songs still entertain, as they did 70 years ago. Lehrer spent time on the island in the 1940s, first as a camper, then counselor. Can you imagine having Lehrer teach baseball or piano? He entered Harvard at 15, composed with wit, is legendary today. Notably, he also served in the US Army and later with the National Security Agency.

History unearthed for this essay offers a glimpse of young Lehrer. He was a "junior camper" in 1937, according to the "Androlog," a chronical of camp activities. He was known as Tommy then, and lived in "Hawk" cabin. By 10, he was Editor-in-Chief of the "Junior Androlog." In that year, he wrote four articles. One describes "Our trip up to Camp" (by train from New York), another "The Hiking Trip" (Mount Blue), a third "The Indian Council Fire," a fourth "On Our Bunk Day." There is nothing satirical about them. He does note, "We sang a lot," including Gilbert and Sullivan, and boys enjoyed a "traditional water pistol fight," as well as collecting shells at "the rifle range." Lehrer was a pistol for sure. Years later, he put lyrics to the music of Gilbert and Sullivan. Young Lehrer closed that year's magazine with a quote from Edna St. Vincent Millay: "I know only that summer sang in me a little while, and in me sings no more."

Then came Stephen Sondheim, legendary composer and lyricist. Sondheim spent time there in the 1940s. As an adult, he pocketed more awards than anyone in his field, an Academy, eight Tonys, eight Grammys, a Pulitzer and a Laurence Olivier. In 1937, Sondheim was just a "junior camper" – with Lehrer. Can you imagine? He was known as Steve, his cabin Eagle.

Hey, there was big news that year. Lehrer earned "four feathers" during "Carnival Week," while Sondheim took home seven. Sondheim excelled at 25-yard dash and broad jump, Lehrer took the baseball throw. Sondheim was part of the "summer tribe" named the "Caucamargomacs," Lehrer's loyalty was with the "Passamagormacs." Fireworks lit the lake that July 4th – as they still do. Heading to town, they sang songs like "Darktown Strutter's Ball," a jazz standard by Shelton Brooks, written in 1917. On July 6th that year, Lehrer found the camp's "lucky rabbit," Oswald, just at taps. History is silent on whether joker Tommy engineered his disappearance.

Junior campers visited the island for movies, baseball and tennis, as well as lectures, including one on Eskimos. Late that summer, Lehrer was playing a character named Wimpy on Amateur Night. Can you imagine, maybe Sondheim scripting? That year, Andro campers headed home September 3rd – and the rest, as they say, is history. In one funny footnote, older Tom Lehrer once tried to adapt "Sweeney Todd" as a Broadway musical, later observing: "Nothing ever came of it, and of course twenty years later Stephen Sondheim beat me to the punch." Oh boy, first Carnival Week, then Sweeney Todd!

Andro alumni turn up regularly in American history. Alan Jay Lerner, camper in the 1930s, won three Tony Awards and three Academy Awards. Roy Goodman, camper with Lehrer and Sondheim, became New York State Senator and a presidential appointee. Robert Bloch, interviewed for Sondheim's biography, actually recalled Camp Androscoggin. "The Camp emphasized athletics from dawn to dusk: archery, tennis, boating, swimming, basketball, soccer, gymnastics," and "each hour of the day was closely supervised." Of Sondheim, he notes: "Stephen was a member of the Milk Squad, comprised of children who were considered to need extra nutrition." Sondheim's biographer says, however, the composer "has only warm memories of five summers spent there ..."

At least one counselor from the late 1920s rose to prominence during World War II. Delmar Taft Spivey, who courted his wife Virginia Street by canoe and by riding camp horses around the lake, became America's highest-ranking officer shot down in World War II.

You may not recall him, but could know him second-hand. He led the American side of the prisoner of war camp featured in *The Great Escape,* starring Steve McQueen. According to some, he also inspired Bing Crosby's television production *Hogan's Heroes* – although Spivey was self-disciplined, intensely loyal to family, selflessly devoted to saving his men. That said, Spivey was notorious for digging long tunnels and corrupting camp guards, including one named Shultz. He kept hundreds of Americans alive while imprisoned in that Luftwaffe Stalag.

Before the war, Spivey finished West Point, married the girl he courted by canoe and horseback, Ginny. She was my grandmother's first cousin. To me, they were just Aunt Ginny and Uncle Del. As a child, I knew nothing of his past. In 1943, Spivey was shot down on a secret B-17 mission. Thereafter, he led the POW camp for two grueling years. That experience is codified in his posthumous *POW Odyssey.* After the War, Spivey led America's Strategic Air Command, eventually retiring to his lakeside cottage – from which he looked out on Androscoggin Island.

As history would have it, the island produced many veterans. General Spivey was one. Ed Healy also clocked combat time in Europe. One day in 1942, a letter arrived for the "Camp Boys" from the "Chief." He was deployed to Great Britain, training near where Spivey's B-17 left on its last flight. In that letter, Healy says he is "somewhere in England." Operational security was high. As told by local author Ed Kallop in *Golden Summertime,* the Chief offered campers an upbeat message: "Dear Gang, I wish I could tell you something about over here, what I am doing and what I have seen, but I can't. I've heard all summer of what a truly swell job you have been doing. You have given Androscoggin its greatest year – a year I could not share because I had to go away to make it possible. Be proud of yourselves as I am of you ... If there was a war, I wanted to be in it; and if I was in it, I wanted very much to be in the middle of it. I am. Yes, I miss you, but someday we'll be back together again – and there will be peace." Signed "Chief."

Not surprisingly, Ed Healy's sentiment was echoed by Spivey, in his memoir. "Regardless of what many people say about fighting, most of us are raring to get in it once our country is committed to war. I was no exception." Born of peace and good heart, both men were called away from home, from dangling feet on a dock to war in Europe. Both came home to their lake.

Other alumni were no less notable, including Federal Judge Louis F. Oberdorfer, a force in American jurisprudence, camper in the 1930s. He spent four years in the Army during World War II, then clerked for U.S. Supreme Court Justice Hugo Black, worked for future Justice Byron White and Attorney General Robert Kennedy. In the late 1970s, he joined the U.S. District Court in Washington, D.C. He died at 94, leaving warm words in a 2008 oral history:

"The camp I went to the longest was called Camp Androscoggin in Wayne, Maine. It was on an island in Lake Androscoggin. Beautiful spot. It was run by a guy named Edward Healy whose brother, Jefferson Healy, had been killed in World War I. The camp had a kind of a military aspect to it. For example, I remember one evening there was a flag raising. The campers formed three sides of a square around a flagpole. I was the bugler and I blew the colors. The military aspect was underscored by the presence amongst the counselors of two West Pointers every year, undergraduates or underclassmen, or whatever you call them. The two counselors were cousins; one's last name was Herman. I remember he had two brothers, and I can't remember. Dick Herman, I think, and the other was Orvil Dreyfoos, whose name you will see on the masthead of The New York Times. *He married a social worker and they were Dartmouth undergraduates. I went to Dartmouth by influence of them."*

Jefferson A. Healy was a brother of the Chief. Born in 1895, he was 19 when World War I broke out. The Chief was born in 1898, his other brother Charles in 1901, making them too young to serve. Orvil Dreyfoos, graduated Dartmouth along with Oberdorfer. He assumed leadership of *The New York Times* in 1957, became a trustee of Dartmouth College, the Rockefeller Foundation, and other institutions. Oberdorfer added: *"[W]e went on canoe trips and hikes ... Lots of softball every evening after dinner and it was a very competitive place in the way they gave awards. The highest award ... was the Jefferson A. Healy Memorial Trophy."*

So, between 1906 and 1971, innumerable future leaders passed the threshold of Camp Androscoggin's dining hall, that island sentry. Then the magnificent undertaking came to an unceremonious and anticlimactic close...which returns me to my insatiable curiosity.

That summer, the island was dark and silent. No one knew whether it would be repossessed, sold or forsaken. Mystery surrounded the island. As shoreline workers at Androscoggin Junior-Senior, our eyes drifted toward those tilting trees and shadows. General Spivey and Chief Healy were still alive. The island's silence must have intruded on their peace. I once stopped in on the Chief. He lived part way up Morrison Heights. While animated, he paused often, thinking.

By the second summer, things were downright shaggy and unkempt. The island had become a no man's land, unclaimed and uncared for, forbidden and forgotten. People looked out with nostalgia and curiosity, increasingly indifferent. No one was to blame, but the grandeur was gone. Grass was long, folded over, stayed uncut. Nothing moved. The place was Roanoke's lost colony, caught in a temporal undertow, drifting backwards toward oblivion. We wondered. *What was there?* Off-limits, it seemed without stewardship. To whom was it still important? Preserving it seemed no one's mission. Stories circulated, hauntings and cautions. The overarching sentiment: Leave her noble ghosts alone.

That was not satisfying to me. The Chief was still alive. Camp history must matter to him. Besides, if we were told not to explore, that made exploring imperative. Employees of the shoreline camp were cautioned: An island visit could mean firing. *But why?* No one lived there. The place was dark, day and night. *One harmless visit could not hurt* ... I began to plot. I needed a partner for this caper, so went to my good friend, Stefan. Stefan and his brother Thomas were both good friends, but I worked with Stefan. Together, we planned a secret walk-about. We would go one evening, keep it clandestine. If Raleigh could return to Roanoke, we could visit the island. The thing had to be done, carefully. Caught, it was our jobs.

Like me, Stefan was curious, an unapologetic explorer. Later, he would undertake daring global adventures. He would spend years in remotest Fiji with the Peace Corps. He would go abroad, returning to Maine and applying hallmark patience, humor and management to guide local towns. Older by one year, Stefan was probably wiser by five. Open to my whimsy, he was logical. He was also methodical. On the other hand, like me, he was curious. Neither of us knew what the place held, behind the alder entanglements and shadows. *How had things been left? Were there clues to the abandonment?* We might be fired, but that made it more interesting. We agreed to be co-conspirators, hatched a plan.

At the close of a work day, we would talk about the sunset, pick a canoe and paddle from the western shore to see it. Our stated goal would be rounding the peninsula for a view. Around the bend, we would shift course, making a beeline for the island. With most of camp at supper, we would have a shot at staying undetected. By the time we returned, it would be dark. Working against darkness, we could explore what lay out there, flashlights in hand.

On the appointed evening, we made tracks for the waterfront. No one seemed to think anything of it. We adhered to the rules, grabbed life jackets, gazed at the peninsula. We were conspicuously headed nowhere in particular. As we paddled, we talked – about the sunset. It was comical. We had to keep from laughing. For several minutes, we paddled through no man's land. Beyond line of sight, we cut and headed for the mystery. *What was on the island? What would we find? What did it look like? Anything left of glory days? We would find out!*

Ducking for the far side, we beached the canoe, pulled it out of sight, and began to prowl. What we expected to find, I am not sure. What we found was strange. In a sense, the island really *was* Roanoke – evincing signs of sudden abandonment, nothing well-planned, an unsettling sense that all had left mid-meal. Gathering darkness caused greater stealth, and growing uneasiness.

Working our way around the abandoned site, we closed on the center. A feeling crept over me that we were on some movie set – everything in order for a shoot, only missing crew, actors and walk-ons. What had been a buzzing metropolis, overrun with happy boys and counselors, was now eerie. It was real but not real, ready but empty, not a sound except cracking twigs, no hosts, just ghosts. I recall feeling a sense of disassociation, the sort that comes over you when you see yourself and ask what in God's name you are doing. We seemed to be walking back in time, slipping through a sliver of time, entering into another place.

We picked our way with care, eyes like lantern globes. We flicked on flashlights ahead of the darkness. Small cabins – each named for an animal – formed a little "Main Street." This Disney-like thoroughfare ran a wooded swath, crossing much of the island. Each cabin had once housed two or four boys, nothing like the large *Junior-Senior* cottages. Every mattress was in place, some beds still made, eerie. Initials and names were carved in overhead rafters, with readable dates. Most dates were older than we were, by a lot. Floorboards and roofs were sound, as if campers would soon arrive. They never would. A dank, sweet smell attached to cabins, not unpleasant, aging wood. They each smelled like a cupboard, without china.

For the most part, walking paths were navigable. The flagpole was straight, parade ground overgrown. Despite Nature's assault, most buildings seemed ready for business, just needing a sweep. In one place, an outer door swung wide to what must have been the photo shack. Dark room supplies spilled through an interior door, the work of animals, photo paper splayed across an open table. Otherwise the place was untouched. Pine dust, chewed edges, plentiful droppings suggested mice and squirrels. All was quiet.

A little administration building was also open. It contained manila folders, camp brochures, ruffled stacks of typing paper, everything warped by moisture but legible. Yellowing envelopes with camp insignia, useless now, were stacked near yellowing postcards. Scattered in piles, camp records were tinted brown, molding, nibbled. Here and there, something had tipped over a box, spreading papers across the floor. Winter lodgers' paws had come and gone.

The old playhouse had a stage, side tables, wings and costumes. No play would ever be performed there again. Curtains hung neatly on both sides, ready to be closed. There was no next act. The aliveness of something so dead was hard to process, no one to show us about. It was endearing and spooky. We felt as if we were walking back through some dark medium. Time melted, left us standing in a different world – minus the people.

The spookiness got spookier. As we entered the once animated dining hall, boards creaked under our feet. To one side, a stone fireplace became the towering chimney, the sentry. To another, stood an upright piano. Stefan plunked out a few notes. They echoed. The piano must have anchored sing-alongs, skits, rainy days. Did Sondheim or Lehrer play those keys? The giant hall, once known as the Bungalow and Lodge, seemed an extension of the piano. The ancient upright was probably the same described in a 1907 brochure: "Recreation room contained a piano and games …" Our eyes continued adjusting to the darkness.

History is strange, stranger when you can smell it. The place had a smell, of oldness. No books lay about, but it had the aroma of good times. *Whose?* You could almost feel them around you. *Who sat over there? Who came through that door? Who walked those stairs? Who played this piano?* Maybe it was our imagination playing tricks, or long anticipation of the secret visit, but the place seemed as full as it was empty. With each new step, the floor creaked. This building was not weathering well, although still sound. Looking around, there was more to the hall.

The structure extended in every direction, mostly up. There was a staircase. Agreeing we should not be deterred by sounds or the sinking sun, we committed to explore. We were here, after all. One more flight of stairs – even two or three – would not kill us. We pushed on. If there was someone on the upper floors, we were going to meet them. Besides, what could be up there? By appearances, no one had been here for ages. We clutched our flashlights. If needed, we could beat a hasty retreat. We headed up.

The old stairs, no surprise, creaked more than the hall floor. Upper floors seemed chiefly for storage. Again, we came face-to-face with a haunting sense that campers would soon arrive. Camp gear was spread widely. To block rodents, a matrix of floor-to-ceiling cages had been constructed. Each cage amounted to walk-in storage, baseball equipment, boat floats, non-perishable foodstuffs, random sports gear, and other unidentified paraphernalia. Most cages were locked and untouched. We left things where they were. They seemed ready for use, yet relics. They deserved to be untouched. Maybe I make more of it, but that is how we felt – respectful, wholly out of sync with time and place, edgy.

One pen stood open, as if never closed. Contents were spread willy-nilly, seemingly tossed or stacked in a hurry, last minute. Maybe we were seeing the effects of animals, but the pen was a mess. In that cage – a small room – lay a pile of clutter. To one side lay round, metal canisters, some opened and damaged, others sealed. *What were they? Why were some open?* The lot was weathering and warping, some rusting, all in shambles.

We looked closer. Some of the canisters had writing on them, and dates. *Each canister was filled – or had been – with a single film, apparently an historic recording of camp life.* From the dates, some went back to the century's early decades. Hand-written numbers were grease-penned on aging canisters. *Here was the heartbeat of the camp. Here was a time capsule! Here was the answer to our question "What had camp life been like?" What did it look like in the 1930s, before the Second World War?* Here was the answer, right here.

As we looked at the canisters, we mulled this reality scattered before us. Weather, animals, and disinterest had moved indoors. Together, they were reclaiming these priceless testimonials. Irreplaceable records, already half destroyed. The balance would soon be gone, victims of moisture and bacteria – the remorseless advance of time. It spared nothing. *How could records this intrinsic, at least nostalgic, be left to spoil? How allowed to succumb without a fight?*

In a sentimental way, as if silent voices spoke from these canisters, the discovery burdened us. It brought us up short. More than anything over which we had stumbled, this discovery was unexpected. The films seemed out of place, worthy of protection. Here we were, witness to their casual destruction, watching generations slip into obscurity. The canisters contained priceless history, gradually being sucked into what? *Oblivion.*

We looked over the deteriorating archive. Memories were important. They had value beyond the present. We knelt and looked closely. Reading dates, we understood. This was an extract of the camp. Wasting away were 60 years of recorded history, portions of summers memorialized. Each canister weighed five pounds. We stood for minutes, uneasy. Darkness was closing in.

We were face to face with it, drawn into it. There was something suffocating about the feeling. A burden was being placed on us, not one we came for. The canisters, the few remaining, looked askance. While silent, they demanded an answer: Were we thrill seekers or a lifeline? Like it or not, we stood over the past, watching it die – again. We found ourselves absorbed in the moment. *How did we stumble on such a thing? Why were we here anyhow?* All of a sudden, we were part of the legacy. The camera was rolling. In darkness, light. We stood stage center.

Who would care if we left them here, strewn and fading? No one. Only a thousand young faces, who believed in preserving time on film. For some, it might be of no importance, for others last proof they had existed. The faces wanted to know: What would we do? Like writers of notes stuffed in bottles and cast to sea, they waited. They hoped for discovery, knowing their bottles might never be found, or worse, found and never opened. They could not have known that the camp would go bankrupt, that they had cast their bottles on a dry sea. But we knew. We lived now, at the exact intersection of their hope in the future and oblivion. *What should we do?*

A moment more, we stared. The films were not ours. We could leave, should leave, and had to leave. We did not belong here. Or did we? *Who said that?* Who knows why God puts anyone anywhere? Only He does, I guess. He put us here, now. We felt the weight. *Decision time.*

Outside, tall grasses peeked through cabin decks, advanced on the parade ground. Branches littered trails. The place dissolving. It shook us, and let us go. The spell was broken, behind it a dull ache. We had to leave. The canisters were spoiling. A few remained intact. A single canister might – just one – be more valuable than all the words of good men. By the time anyone realized they were at risk, they would be gone, gummy emulsion and gelatin, sticky cellulose nitrite, garbage. Those memorialized would be gone too.

What would the Chief do? Was there any doubt? Rash sentimentalism shot through me. Stefan shared it. We reached down and picked up two canisters. I told myself, by way of justification, they were for the Chief. I hated seeing history die, could not be party to that. Perhaps we should have left them, let them vanish, allowed the elements to prevail. There was an argument for that. It is the argument for letting blow-downs linger and burn. If the elements are intent on destruction, who are we to resist? I never bought into that reasoning, too fatalistic. Do not believe in letting blow-downs burn either, taking half a mountain with them. If we can save a forest, why not? If we can save history, why not? We picked up two canisters.

Outside, we took a last look. Time was reclaiming what humanity had renounced, taking the photo shack, administrative offices, bunk houses, playhouse, and legendary dining hall. Nature was in charge, erasing the acetate, laying waste to this picture painted by mankind's halide salts. The mighty elements dipped their brushes, painting over them, blurring the face of the place. Everywhere, the untended acre was theirs. Perhaps it was meant to be. Still, walking away was hard. We had the canisters. Maybe we should have left them, maybe gotten more, hard to say. We made our way to the canoe, never looked back.

That surreal world, lovely and haunting, was not forgotten by either of us. Even in last light, darkness on the floodtide, the place was somehow transcendent. I do not recall what Stefan thought specifically, but to me it was Narnia. We might have met anything out there. We might have met Aslan, on sweet summer air. Who knows, maybe we did. When we found those canisters, we encountered something, just enough to pick them up.

Surrealism at close quarters is discomfiting. You witness an obvious clash between what should be and what is not – all in one place. Rather than meeting a vibrant summer camp or one wholly dead, we met a place prepared for life yet devoid of it, full but empty. Then rather ironically, we found missing lives in dead canisters. Fascinating and mind-bending. Contradictions force adjustments in thinking. There was a bit of *Alice in Wonderland* to our visit. Lewis Carroll put Alice in the company of the Mad Hatter and March Hare. They shared tea, but time stopped, the moment never passing, just repeating. They were destined to have tea forever at 6:00 – that nonsensical punishment by that nonsensical Queen of Hearts. The island seemed similarly caught, bound up in a time loop. Walking about, it was forever at 6:00. To make the point stick, that anonymous Queen of Hearts had pressed two canisters into our hands. In the canisters, it would always would be 6:00 – always teatime at the dining hall.

Back on the water, we paddled slowly. We talked sparingly. We helped each other digest what we had seen. It left an impression. We were oddly satisfied by the expedition, happy to have made the trip. That is my chief memory of the paddle back. We had wandered through some inner sanctum, absorbed it, and could now reflect on it. We had walked the island slowly, no hurry, no aim except exploring and absorbing. From afar, we had gazed on the place with curiosity; now we knew what we were gazing at. There was no way to go back in time, but stepping onto the island felt like it. The dare had been exhilarating. And we did not get fired.

My hope was to visit the Chief again. Unfortunately, his fading health and my slowness kept me from doing so. Decades passed. I lost the canisters. *Had I packed them away?* They did not come up in conversation – for a long time. Time moved on, as it does. A year or so after the fateful canoe visit, tragedy struck. The town watched from afar, as the historic dining hall mysteriously burned to the ground. Flames leaped into the night sky. The old sentry burned for hours, smoked for days. People could see the conflagration from around the lake. Stefan's family and mine watched from atop Morrison Heights.

Somewhere in this timeframe, just before or just after, another family bought the island. In the years ahead, they became good friends. Eventually, they resold it. Once or twice more, I visited. In daylight, things looked different. Gone was the dining hall, and all it contained. Eventually, new owners built a house and cottage. Today, the island is alive again – as a summer residence. People motor, kayak and canoe around it, exchanging waves. Life goes on. One of those with a cottage is an accomplished craftsman of wooden boats. He and his wife infuse the place with a smile. He rescues stranded sailors, and visitors adrift on the lake. They keep the lights on.

In later years, Stefan and I talked and laughed about that trip. We were glad to have seen the camp in its twilight. We could picture the piano, caged baseball gear and foodstuffs. We recalled the film pen. I looked hard for the missing canisters – to no avail. The loss seemed personal. Somehow, I felt I had not done my part, preserved what was entrusted to me. My mind periodically wandered to the missing artifacts.

Into those canisters, sealed in the 1930s before the outbreak of World War II, the island's noble ghosts had poured life's joy. They had poured a bit of pre-war life, a legacy.

I had lost it. How could I have done that? They had given me the chance to carry it forward, and I fumbled. With other canisters gone, those two seemed priceless, a rare window into the island's past. With them, we had a slice of pre-World War II island life. Without them, just a guess. Someday…

And then, it happened. Having looked for 40 years, I imagined them gone. Until one day the phone rang. My mother was cleaning her basement. "Do you know anything about this box with paper towels, a lumpy plastic bag, two metal tins?" *Hallelujah!* I knew exactly what the box contained. Inside, two 16 mm film canisters lay undamaged – after four more decades. I put them in the hands of a film expert. One canister was silver, date 1936. It opened easily. The other was flat black, undated, same vintage, harder to open. I asked the expert to treat them as one-of-a-kind. Before long, we were viewing spinning reels on an old projector, watching little figures bounce around the screen. One look confirmed what we always imagined – a fascinating find. I had them converted to DVD, and made copies – gave them to the town library.

In truth, the world has plenty of wartime films – men marching in uniform. They too were important, for different reasons. Professional films existed from before the war. But how many films showed everyday kids laughing, pre-war life? Not many – not in our neck of the woods.

The film expert transferred them perfectly. Before long, we were watching on computer. *What a find!* The first lasted 11 minutes and 58 seconds, black and white, focused on Junior and Senior. It opened up a window on camp life in the 1930s. It told a story, albeit silently, of how campers lived, carried themselves, and interacted pre-war. The second one was five minutes and 28 seconds, color. It focused on older campers and the island. Neither had audio; neither needed it. Pre-war life was cheerful, even without sound.

These pre-war DVDs highlighted many activities. Mostly, they contained happy faces. Kids played on the lake, island and local "desert" (which looks identical today). They splashed, ran, rowed, and were rambunctious. Here was circa 1936 Wayne, Maine. While most campers came from out of state, cameos included local farmers and horses, parents and counselors. Island, town and activities were indigenous. Young Mr. and Mrs. Healy made an appearance.

In the first film, we see kids and counselors playing shirtless baseball, no doubt without sunscreen. There is a "Soviet Day," replete with sports competitions, a "Horrible House" with games galore. On land, there is a mix of hard running and lounging, vigor and rest. On the lake, races in rowboats, swimming competitions, smiles and buckteeth, trim haircuts, lots of shoulder-held chicken fights, then footraces, wrestling, team canoeing in canvas canoes.

There are sandwiches on white bread, campers on white sand, and races up and down desert dunes, where we used to flip. Not a single overweight child or counselor in the group! Dozens of campers have feature roles, lots of self-effacing extras. Breezes blow, Camp Androscoggin is emblazoned on shirts. At Junior Camp, kids are riding horses, reading comic books, running with abandon. These are simpler times, free play, respect for others, organization and splash-fests. Everyone had fun. One imagines that there were no liability waivers, no one cared.

Not every camper got a ribbon, either. Ribbons were earned and displayed. Winners beamed for their times, distances, paddles and runs. Everyone participated in pig piles, chicken fights, riding horses. Sandcastles were created by unhurried young hands. Behind them, workhorses pulled plows. There was no discontinuity in the picture. Work and play, exertion and rest coexisted. While cultures differed, these were all Americans, pursuing their respective summer routines.

The second film jumps to life – in color. Here, canoes are tipped by older boys, and life includes pranks. Tomfoolery occurs on the water. Tug of war fills the baseball field. Tennis matches, canoeing and bunkhouses give the island character. Kids are allowed to write on bunkhouse doors, carve names on walls, and be boys. A parents' day shows mothers and fathers congregating, each in their own way. We return to campers, high jump competition, long jumping, sprinting. There is an early morning assembly. The camera captures sleepy informality, fidelity to the flag. Some young men are in uniform, all turned out for the bugle. The occasion is clear, raising of America's flag. While we cannot hear it, the bugle is surely playing. Camera zooms to the flag. Such occasions would soon have bigger meaning.

Finally, the second reel captures – with uncanny poignancy – end of season, boys and counselors departing for their winter homes. Boys proceed to boats from the island's high ground, dressed in suits and ties, reflecting fun and uncommon dignity. They are dressed for travel, if not for home, when people did that. These young men come with bags and rackets to waiting boats, some rowboats, others motorized. One wooden boat zooms past, an escort. Faces, even in this moment, are happy – not as happy as running, swimming or competing, but happy. And tanned. The trek is down Dead River again, where they will meet the train at North Leeds – head home.

The closing scene is rural North Leeds, the train station. Boys amble about on their own, few rules. They enjoy freedom. They are expected to make recourse to common sense, trusted to have judgment. Here was life lived at a reasonable pace, even among boys – a pace that permitted milling on railroad tracks. They banter and explore the rails, headed for civilization. This was a last bit of vacation – boys being boys, departure for the long trip home.

What a time, what a day, what a summer camp. What a slice of history, uncensored and clear. What a bunch of great games, good hearts, and window into old Maine. What good luck that, by some random chance, two Wayne kids decided to skirt modern rules and explore the old island camp, before she fell to ruin. What good luck the noble ghosts blew warm in our ears, and two canisters of film survived another forty years.

Wayne Yacht Club rocking chairs, looking toward Androscoggin Island

Androscoggin Island, north end of Androscoggin Lake, from Morrison Heights

Friend Stefan at work, circa mid-1970s

Older Stefan sailing, between managing Maine towns (Readfield and Hallowell)

General Delmar Taft Spivey, shot down in 1943, served as Senior American Officer, Center Compound, Stalag Luft III (1943-45). In his youth, he was a counselor at Camp Androscoggin. In old age, he settled back on Androscoggin, in family cottage of his wife, Virginia (nee' Street). General Spivey's son Delmar B. (Pete) Spivey, was a military officer; grandsons are Delmar Scott Spivey (former US Coast Guard) and Richard Edward Spivey.

20. Yankee Humor

He was a nice enough guy, this out-of-stater, respectful but quite the talker. A little self-satisfied, he wore horn-rimmed glasses, came from a city, liked to share opinions. He did not seem to be talking down, but not equal either. Mostly, he talked about us. He seemed to like locals. Nothing wrong with that. He was kind to give us his time. We had lots, he had less.

Anyway, he mostly stopped to look at the airplanes. We had two small ones, a hand-built J-3 Cub and an old Cessna 170. We flew both out of the side yard. Guess seeing planes beside a road that wiggles to nowhere and turns to dirt, was unusual. He was intrigued, quite intellectual and clearly out of his element, whether he knew it or not.

In fairness, bumping into planes out here was probably odd. Both could be seen from the road, coming from the right direction, which he obviously had. On this day, the sun was high. The visitor was full of ideas, wanting to let them loose in the country. Our stepfather was listening. He seemed to know this fellow from some attenuated link, or maybe not. The airplanes were his hobby, when he was not flying commercial.

The two men walked down the upper runway. That makes it sound glorified, which it was not. It was a grass strip, a rock-picked, well-cut meadow. The visitor reminded me of a seed spreader, spraying knowledge in all directions, somewhat indiscriminately. Still, it was exciting to witness. He was full of observations on the world, hard to slow down. He did not breathe a lot; he did not have time. Anyway, I tagged along, as kids will, wanting to learn a thing or two.

The upper runway had a grand view, and it took a while to walk. It looked out over Androscoggin Lake. You could even see Androscoggin Island. As the men walked, I listened. I was not expected to say anything, and did not. Once the visitor had lightened his load, conversation lagged. Below us, the lake glistened in the sun, stretching out like a lazy cat. We could see nearly the whole from our place. The day was pleasant, high pressure and no humidity, breeze and sun. Wind swept up the mountain, across the runway, petering into the woods. Down by the lake, air was cooler by a few degrees. On summer days, breezes were frequent and sustained.

All of a sudden, the erudite visitor pressed a question on us, well, not really on me. By the tone in his voice, the question was scientific and serious, a mystery. After a long lead in, filled with bits of science, his question tumbled out. "So, what is that long, broad streak across the lake there – that unsettled place between the island and shore?" I looked at the lake, saw the swath, water rippling in a southeast wind, running off one end of Norris Island, thinning as it approached the near shore. The lake was disturbed by wind in a uniform and continuous way, which happened when the island's lee sheltered a stretch, leaving the rest stirred.

Our stepfather looked out over the lake. In his thick Maine accent, perfect for deadpan, he said, "Oh, that's jest where they dragged logs 'cross the lake last wintah." No laugh or smile, nothing. The visitor listened hard, looking at him, his forehead crinkling up, puzzling for a moment, then he nodded. "Ah, I see," he said, as if learning something. "That's it, is it?" "Ayah," was the response. Instead of smiling, the visitor got more intense. "Leaves a mark out there then, on the water?" he asked, vaguely puzzled. "Ayah" came the monotone answer, no elaboration.

There was a long silence. I tried to understand this nonsense. *Nobody logged across the lake, or dragged logs of any kind across the ice in winter. Nothing got dragged out there at all, except maybe an icehouse. Besides, let's be real: After the ice went out, nothing would be left on open water. How could it be? It was water!* The answer given was ridiculous, totally absurd. I worked to suppress a smile. Surely, this visitor understood it was a joke. But no.

Instead of laughing, his brow was crunched together over his eyes. He was again nodding, horn rimmed glasses rising and falling as he did. Suddenly enlightened, although I could not imagine how, he just said "Wonder why that happens …" For another minute his eyes stayed locked on the scratchy patch of lake. "… where they pulled logs …," was all he said, studying the place. Nodding, he said, "interesting, so they pull them from the island to this side, or is it done the other way round?" "Pull 'em this way, usually" was all he got back. The conversation soon turned to something else. That was Maine humor, bold and clear. It came at you sideways and suddenly, could leave a visitor wondering until – at some point, it hit you. I assume it hit the visitor, at some point – but maybe not.

You may recall I worked with old-timers, including Harold – who manned the crutch factory during the war. Pushing 80, Harold was a wit. He taught with wit, too. He watched me carry bags of sand for foundations, create forms for cement, saw off boards, bang nails, and climb wobbly ladders with shingles. Together, we studded up walls for fledgling houses, in George's service. We balanced planks on sawhorses, nursed blisters into calluses, leveled and measured. He lightened each day with humor, found in simple things. He wore a half smile. He set jokes the way some people bait traps, with deliberation. Then he sprang them, impish and chuckling.

Harold was a privilege to work with. He paused between nail strikes to offer glimpses of the past or catch me up – give a tutorial – with humor. Frankly, that was about the only way to teach a headstrong teenager. Shingling was repetitive, as every shingle had to be set straight and tacked. Once you got the routine, any break in monotony was welcome, even at your own expense. Days were long, jokes welcome, and punchlines lingered. Everything reminded Harold of a story, so I learned about logging roads, history, farming, and what makes wit dry.

Not every nugget held light, but *how* he offered them did. Harold's tempo was slow and rolling. His observations had the tumble of an ocean swell, never fast. His tone was take-it-or-leave-it, but wisdom resided in his cast-off comments. "Ground comes up fast over there," he would say, without looking at me. *What?* I thought, then realized he meant the 50-foot drop-off. "First step's a long one," he chuckled. That was his way of saying "daredevil shingling" is a bad idea.

Up on a roof, Harold kept the atmosphere light. "One bundle at a time, don't wanna wear out the ladder." *Translation:* Before you throw two loads over your shoulders, use common sense. He had set jokes, but his best were of the teaching sort. I had to listen, because he was always right. "Bubble works best in the middle," he nudged, when I fumbled with a level. George did not build crooked houses. Harold knew the trade, conveyed it lightly, with humor.

One day, when I proposed to take a run in a meadow at lunch, Harold tossed me a live one. "Cows up there …" *What did I care about cows?* I was not deterred. "Might need watchin'…" *He knew that meadow – watching for what?* "Bull up there?" I asked. "Nope," nothing more. Then, "worth keepin' one eye out." He chuckled a knowing chuckle. Something was up. Finally, he let on. "Lot of meadow muffins up there …" Cows might be away, but they left sign. I ran the road.

Sometimes, an old timer was funny without intending to be. Tony was that fellow, swarthy, fit and cheerful, a spritely holdover from log drives, half leprechaun. He was a powerful worker, persuading trees down with elbow grease. Always tanned, he wore more a hide than skin. Wrinkled by time and weather, Tony was all muscle and sinew, slow to speak, quick to smile.

Over several years, Tony cut timber behind our house. He brought down trees and put up cordwood. He did both faster than anyone we knew. He preferred working alone, never asked for help, used no special tools, switched between hand and chain saw. He did not quit for 10 hours, coming early, leaving when light left. He slipped into the woods like an elf, cut, cleared and stumped. Eventually, the second grass runway took shape. His sawing and chopping got so regular they became part of the outdoors. He moved with method, just felling and stacking. The delicious smell of cut wood was on the air. Four-by-four-by-eight stacks slowly built up.

Sometimes, when he was gone, I wandered down there and looked around. The smell of pine pitch and freshly-cut trees was invigorating. On hot days, I was assigned to pick through the brush, over stumps and through raspberries, to deliver iced lemonade. Tony never turned it down, was always grateful. That made my return easy. Besides, the entangling brush was perfect for hideouts. Tony might be soaked to the hide, but he always liked to work.

What Tony displayed was discipline. He was single-minded, watched the sun, asked little and delivered much. He notched trees and turned the forest into cordwood like a sculptor. He must have had moments, but he never shouted or bellowed. I never heard him sigh. He was uncompromising and self-contained, inspirational. He was also honest, and lived without complaining. His real boss was himself – Tony was tough on Tony. He was the closest I ever saw to a real lumberjack, although he would have chuckled at that description. He lived somewhere in the woods around town, modest means, good heart. Who knew what he did with his hard-earned money?

One morning early, Tony showed up at our door – in distress. No humor, no signature calm, his forehead was beaded and bunched in storm clouds. "My money is gone," he blurted out. Before we could ask, his story came in pieces. "I keep it in a place, and it's done – all taken, gone!" This was a blow to hear, and a blow to him. We tried to understand what had happened, and how it had happened. We heard his grief. A couple of calls and people were at his abode in the woods, trying to puzzle where his money had gone.

Facts piled up fast, quicker than Tony stacked cordwood. He was more traditional than we thought. Industrious as a red squirrel, he was a saver. He was thrifty, to a fault. He had saved all he earned, not spent on anything unneeded. He defined "need" narrowly. One look about the cabin proved his frugality. He explained that he did not trust banks, so he "banked" his savings in a stone wall – literally.

To be specific, Tony had squirreled away $3000 in small bills, hidden in a nearby stone wall. Recounting the facts, he seemed heartbroken. That morning, having not checked for some time, he visited the stone wall. To his shock, the cash was gone, completely vanished. For a man of characteristic peace, he was devastated. On his behalf, we were too. Everyone took a deep breath.

Tony conceded that he did not check the spot often. Whatever had happened could have occurred months back. One thing was sure: the cash was gone. A comprehensive search ensued. Thoughtful adults deployed like a swat team, hunting Tony's treasure. They fanned out along the stone wall, foraged in the woods, searched for clues as to what had happened to $3000 in cash – formerly secreted in the wall. This was no joke. This was Tony's life savings. Hours passed, then a break. Whether by bull-headedness or luck, the team found Tony's cash.

Mid-afternoon, someone lifted a rock. A couple of hundred feet from where Tony thought he had stashed the cash, it reappeared. Tony's precious bills – all $3000 – lay there, only a little worse for wear. According to Tony, they were discovered *far* from his original hiding place! The bills were mustered, all present and accounted for. Only mystery, their strange migration …

Everyone was relieved, especially Tony. Through wrinkles, he beamed. Then, as if needing to put us right, he *explained* what *must* have happened. He surmised that industrious squirrels had removed the banded cash down the wall. He imagined the bandits had taken the bills for a nest. He surmised the clepto-critters had worked over a long period. He reminded us squirrels and mice do this with seeds. Everyone nodded, glad for resolution, and Tony's peace of mind.

On reflection, one had to wonder about the mighty Maine squirrels and mice. Even as a child, I thought the villains hard-pressed to carry fat bundles of banded bills, not dropping one. None nibbled. Why not leaves? The truth washed over me slowly, a different sort of humor, the sort we inflict on ourselves. Tony had outwitted himself, forgetting his hiding place. In any event, Tony was happy, and so were we.

Sometimes, Yankee humor is subtle, sometimes less so. Sometimes it rests in plain sight, like a cool breeze or bundle of bills. The other day, I looked up and saw skidder tracks across the sky, bright and white, someone hauling logs across the continent at 37,000 feet. Does the heart good to smile, once in a while.

21. *Different Sort of Courage*

The white convertible was a head-turner, complete with two girls in front and out-of-state plates. The machine moved slowly, like our heads. A cloud of dust billowed behind, breaking the spell. We did not see cars like that very often, even in summer, not in rural Maine. Turns out, those girls had some courage – of a different sort.

Like it or not, newness is suspect. Comes with the turf, no matter what turf that is. People are inclined to do things as they have, their own way. We tend to distrust change, instinctively consider it overrated. Fads pass and styles shift, while some things never change. Leaves turn each fall, snow drops each winter, blackflies bite in spring, tourists in summer. People get comfortable with these patterns. Small towns – even thoughtful ones – are hard to crack.

Put differently, small towns travel at their own pace. They have ways of doing things, and things they see no value in doing. Inertia is a force, as in physics. *Not* trying something new has the upper hand.

So imagine trying to bring the enthusiasm of Broadway – to a town of 500. That is what these two sisters aimed to do, or at least one of them, and successfully did. The older sister, a New York actress, angled to be a summertime director, her sister part of the act. Watching that breezy white convertible pass, we had no idea what lay in store, nor did they.

To direct a play – any play, anywhere – is an enormous undertaking. The process begins with deciding to risk a flop. After announcing one's intent, there is no going back. Like paragliding, once you jump – you are in flight. Where you land is anyone's guess, but you are not going back. Those who make the jump, embrace the risk. Doubters are encouraged, veterans reassuring, and things begin – when a director decides to lead. This is especially true in a small town, where anonymity is impossible. As Yoda once advised, "Do or do not, there is no try." Risk takers do. Maybe Sondheim and Lehrer learned it here.

A director's role is the hardest. Everything depends on her – vision, recruiting, understanding human nature, and sustaining energy. She must inspire commitment, and coach each paraglider to a safe landing. Of all the tasks, picking a cast is probably hardest. In a small town, enticing commitment takes persuasion. It can require cajoling, assurances of trust. Cast selection is one at a time, like picking apples and cutting trees.

If talent runs deep, the pool is often still. Cast members must be approached, coaxed, supported, and made happy in their roles. Then a director must inspire memorization, and move from idea to action, concept to animation. If the play is a musical, a director must get these amateur actors to learn music – and then sing. In short, a small-town director is up against it.

Generally, a director must imagine wildly, elicit earnestly, encourage risk and get people out of their comfort zones. To this, add arranging practices, coordinating schedules around other obligations, finding a player for the piano, rummaging up or making costumes, creating vestiges of a set, and then – once all that is done – putting on the play, and filling seats! Daunting, eh?

Now, imagine doing this where, until you declared your intent, no one had performed a "town play" in living memory. Imagine you hailed from New York City. Imagine the play was to happen in a reserved village, self-contained individuals, slow to sign-up for anything not generations in the making. In other words, your gambit is where recruits are few, acting novel, temperaments modest, and getting to finish uncertain. And this: You are a summer visitor, officially "from away," not a "year-rounder." You have only weeks to assemble the production, no idea where to start. That's it, pour a bucket of can-do into that acorn cap. Do you accept?

You do if … You are a New York actress who knows what she is doing. You have highly motivated siblings, including a younger sister who has agreed to act, brothers willing to watch. You are a never-know-'til-you-try personality, determined to finish what you start. You are used to beating odds, content with doubters. The passage is narrow, current fast, but you say "Go!"

That was roughly how things looked in 1976. An out-of-state actress named Benita (soon "Binky") and her younger sister Liz arrived "from away." Binky was intent on directing a musical at the Ladd Center, a special venue for town activities, itself born of inspiration and generosity, gift of two philanthropists named George and Helen, parents of World War II veteran Linc. But that is another story.

How I actually met Binky and Liz, I do not recall, but the town soon warmed to them. In a place this small, everyone bumps into everyone soon enough. If nowhere else, we crossed paths at the general store or the yacht club. First impressions do last, and Binky made one. That summer, she never stopped smiling. Her family was friendly. They knew Tom, my boss, the old turret gunner and spike-puller. They knew the owners of Camp Androscoggin Junior-Senior. Whether we met here or there, the introduction occurred. This set in motion fateful events.

One thing led to another. Before long I was invited into their orbit. Intrigued by their can-do and city-savvy, I got to know them, when not working. Besides, Liz was my age. Binky was no nonsense from the start – squarely focused on directing a local musical. Like a marine, she set to. I admired the spirit, but resolved to avoid this play – in any way.

"How would you like to be in a play?" was among her first lines. New Yorkers are gregarious, congenial and disarmingly direct. She was no exception. This was not the ordinary way of conversations. Binky was obviously under the mistaken impression that she had landed in Stratford-upon-Avon, town of similar size – on a completely different continent. She seemed to think that a kid with no voice, no acting experience, always studying his shoes wanted to be in her musical. Most assuredly – not.

She had it wrong, wrong, wrong. At fifteen, while curious, I was cautious – to the point of timid. I had no interest in being on a stage – anywhere, anytime, singing anything, especially here in my own hometown. The whole idea was worse than dubious and unworkable. It was ridiculous and terrifying. Nice to be asked, of course. But no way. My gut, demeanor and voice said it all – "*Are you kidding? Act in a play, the sort where people come and watch? Nuts.*"

Trying to be tactful, aware that she knew my boss, taken by her younger sister, I offered a vague, polite, non-committal response. The way I recall it, I said something like, "Well, I'm not sure I'd be much good at that," or "I'm not sure I'm cut out for that, not much of an actor." The only plays I knew were from high school, a handful of lines, no singing. Besides, those roles arrived when someone failed to show up. I was *not* an actor. Indeed, I was resolved never to do that sort of thing. I assured her that I would be in the audience, watching. I recall smiling.

Quick with advice, I suggested she needed *real* actors, the sort who knew what they were doing. I was upbeat and enthusiastic. We were taught not to tamp down inspiration. Her idea was endearing, confidentially somewhat crazy. Good manners said support her ambitions, whatever they were. What were they? She wanted to direct Charles Schultz's classic musical, "You're a Good Man, Charlie Brown." I mumbled something about that sounding like a nice play, if you were going to produce a play in our town.

Everybody knew Charlie Brown, Snoopy and the *Peanuts* gang. I told her I thought it was a wonderful idea. Binky did not need my vote, of course. She sounded like a one-person theater company, experienced at organizing people and getting them to act. I was happy to encourage, relieved not be tapped for stagecraft – as I had none. I was glad to support the two summer girls, and their white convertible.

Somehow, I got misunderstood. Maybe I was distracted. Maybe I presented my "no" as a "maybe." In any event, Binky took my "no" as a "yes." I was given a warm "thank you" for joining the cast. *What?* The play, she assured me, would be a big success – lots of fun. She had thought it over, told me I would make a great Linus. A natural, she said. *Linus?* Yes, she would hold the spot for me. I was overwhelmed.

What a compliment! Imagine being cast as Linus in a summertime play, right on stage – with everyone out there watching. "No thank you," I tried to say. But it was too late. *How did I get into this mess?* I goofed it completely. I did not *want* to be in the play. I was not an actor. Diplomatically I had declined, but somehow here I was – Linus. This is one of those life mysteries, I later concluded, that can be reviewed many times – and always ends up without a good answer. My indefinite "no" became a "maybe," which became a "yes," which became I was in. Next stop, memorizing lines. And I needed a blanket. *Good grief!*

My unlikely inclusion in this musical, sudden as it was, created a new urgency. There must be *other actors* who knew how to do this, people in whom I could confide ignorance. I could not sing. This was a musical! *Who to ask?* This was not New York. Several friends gave the sensible response. "Are you serious, *Charlie Brown*?" End of story. I might as well have asked them to go paragliding; I would have gotten more takers.

By way of consolation, I was happy that Binky's younger sister, Liz, was part of the program. She was the reason I did not back out immediately. Friendly, pretty and non-judgmental, she would make rehearsals bearable. If the play flopped, or I did, the enterprise might still be entertaining. Even with a grueling work schedule, I could squeeze in practices. The two sisters were funny, quick wits. This meant the cast would laugh. That brought me full circle, back to my starting point: *Who else might enjoy this lark?* As it turned out, that summer Stefan was also working for Tom. *Why not ask Stefan?* I suggested Binky ask Stefan.

Knowing the play needed a Snoopy, I pitched Stefan for the role, soft-shoeing the idea to him. He thought I was crazy, claimed no interest. I tried to project "not being crazy," and reasoned with him. He still thought I was crazy. Finally, I arranged for Binky to meet him in the vicinity of a piano. Working her magic, she convinced him that he would be a *superb Snoopy*. Under the spell of piano music, and maybe the white convertible – he was in. Before long, Stefan was reciting lines, enjoying a star role, being the long-eared dog in Binky's budding musical. Somehow, by week's end, she had corralled half a dozen others into the cast. Suddenly, we were part of something. The train was rolling, we were on it! A musical in front of the whole town … *Can you imagine?* I could not.

Day by day, week by week, Binky built our ragtag team into a dedicated troupe. She brought to the mission her New York acting experience, which was considerable. She infused technique, guidance on voice projection, care in choreography and – above all – *confidence.* How she did this in a town so far from Stratford-upon-Avon, I cannot say. But she did. What motivated her is another mystery. But she persisted. I guess if you have once stepped into the void, future jumps are easier. She believed we could act; we dared to believe her.

Binky never hinted there was any escape. She was a gunnery sergeant that way. We were going to perform. Expectations set, no exit, we fell into formation and drilled. *We would succeed.* That was how she saw everything, coming together. She saw the whole musical in her mind – lights up, players on by turns, applause erupting. We tried to see it, too. Liz became Lucy, Stefan became Snoopy, I became Linus, and others filled their roles as if second nature. We were suddenly creations of Charles Schultz.

When the curtain finally rose on our much-anticipated summer play, Binky was right. We had it in us. Charlie Brown resolved not to give up any more. "All I need is one more try, gotta get that kite to fly, and I'm not the kind of guy, who gives up easily …" Schroeder borrowed a page from Binky. "If you're wondering 'how do we start?' just blow the music 'til you know it by heart …." Stefan, as Snoopy, yelped and sang authentically at suppertime, celebrating the happy life of every dog. "Pleasant day, pretty sky, life goes on, here I lie. Not bad, not bad at all. Cozy home, board and bed, sturdy roof beneath my head – not bad, not bad at all." Linus, comfortable in his philosophical fog, reminded Lucy that little brothers are not all bad, adding that "a blanket is as important to a child as a hobby to an adult."

Pressed by Charlie Brown on what might happen tomorrow, Linus – summoning stuff he did not know he had – waxed lyrical. "In some parts of the world tomorrow is already today, and today is already yesterday, so if tomorrow is already today, Charlie Brown, there's no way that tomorrow could be better than today." Except that, sometimes it is.

Liz, as Lucy, offered priceless instruction to her little brother, advising Linus on life's bigger mysteries. "Do you see this tree? It is a fir tree. It is called a fir because it gives us fur for coats. It also gives us wool in the winter time." More. "And way up there, those are clouds, they make the wind blow ... The little stars and planets make the rain that often showers, and when it's cold and winter is upon us, the snow comes up! Just like the flowers." Then she came to what might have been the main point. "This thing here, it's called a hydrant. They grow all over and no one seems to know just how a little thing like that gets so much water. See that bird? It's called an eagle. Since it's little, it has another name, a sparrow. And on Christmas and Thanksgiving we eat them." I recall thinking, girls are so smart.

We did not have hydrants in Wayne, but the crowd roared. Binky filled the house, and every heart. We had our play. We soared – or so it seemed then. That year, the town got a little bigger, saw something new. New hearts arrived on the southern breeze, pulled up in that white convertible, brought a bit of New York to the Ladd Center. And what a breeze! On rare occasions, winds shift and everything goes with them. They did that summer.

For years after that, Binky – and others in her stead – inspired our town to perform a "summer play." New kids signed up, overcame stage fright, wrestled insecurities, and wrapped themselves – for a time – in the world of theater. They stepped into the void, forgot their fears, glided across the stage under bright lights. Binky brought and taught confidence with her gregarious, life-lifting assumptions. She made of us daring hearts, carried us along a glide path, and showed us courage of a different sort. Liz was right there with her, stalwart sister and sanguine. Even small towns crack, and learn from kind visitors. "Do or do not, there is no try."

Fall Festivities

"Autumn is a second spring, when every leaf is a flower."

–Albert Camus

22. Fall Running

One day, temperatures suddenly drop. The world fills with crimson maples and flaming oaks. Sunsets refract in millions of fluttering leaves, clinging to ten thousand trees. Fall runners shoot down this corridor of color, instantly happy. Some days, autumn is lime and strawberry, tangerine and cherry, sometimes the whole fruit bowl. Evening runs are iridescent trout, steamy lobster, green chard and pecan pie. Sometimes, it is all a blur.

Fall running is just glorious. Surrounded by crisp air, the pace quickens. Walkers know the feeling. Arms stiffen, go deeper in pockets, lungs come alive. The sun's angle drifts west to south. More light hits the earth, as leaves fall. With autumn comes a quick cadence, freshness of purpose. That was especially so for cross country runners, their feet on leafy, winding trails.

The fall runner felt winged. Or I did. Gone were those heavy summer legs, hills climbed in heat and humidity. In their place, limber limbs to carry me over the road's camber, into the distance, forgetting what distance was. Oxygen transfer got better, a runner's blood thinned. One felt the change in attitude as scenery and temperatures shifted. Fall running was different.

Suddenly, every day was nippy. Twigs crunched and broke under foot. Sumac trees turned to embers. The forest threw a party. Trees dressed for the occasion, some rose and violet, others yellow topped, ruby slippers. Alders shed their speckles slowly. White birches jumped to pear from jade. Beeches snapped to bronze, mountain ashes exchanged chartreuse for chiffon.

Mornings turned frosty, and meadows were dusted white. We expelled clouds. Sugar maples went from green to yellow, yellow to orange, orange to red – sometimes on one leaf. Red maples became hot lava, then cooled to pumice in evening light. Runners picked their way among these trees. No oil or watercolorist could top the grandeur.

Quaking aspens quivered in breezes, sequins shimmering up slender arms. What was that? What were they saying? They just giggled and tittered. Big-toothed aspens were quiet, fading to amber. They kept their own counsel, no whispering. Evergreens were unchanged, mile on mile.

Meantime, towering oaks chaperoned the dance, like Beefeaters assigned door duty. They scattered about the forest floor, tall, red and mum. Their shadows grew longer as days got shorter, suits moving from red to orange. Dropping temperatures had a magnificent effect, turning timbers to tigers, until they became coffee with a touch of cream. Tigers gone, oaks lost their growl. Then, winter was coming.

Fall tees were gradually swapped for sweats and windbreakers. Dusk came sooner. Less light put bounce to my step, sped me up. With less illumination, my stride became longer, turnover faster. Leaves finally fell. We could see through the woods. What had been opaque was clear and deep. The last leaves fluttered like confetti, then snowflakes. I pulled out a red bandana, used it around my nose. It warmed frozen air. Ball cap turned to a pullover hat and gloves.

As trees and seasons changed, so did I. Beyond the bandana, my hunters' orange came out. Cross country runners like the peace, pace and place. But running in the woods during hunting season meant being alert. Shots sounded occasionally, usually in the distance. Hunters were not interested in runners; they wanted a deer. That said, white tail can create confusion. To avoid mistakes, we never wore white. Locals had slow trigger fingers, but caution was always good.

I did not plan to be a runner, yet somehow became one. A summertime co-worker, a miler from New York, dragged me out. After one run, I felt dead. After a week, I was interested, but sore. In two weeks, I was hooked. By three, I was running on my own – and loving it. Freedom and leg drive went together, reinforcing each other. The more I ran, the more I heard the road. That is how it started, at fourteen. My legs were wheels, gradually wings. Long days were made short by evening runs. My new wings took me places, anywhere – running.

It was anyone's game, since cross country was about competing with yourself. I liked that, more as the years passed. The sport was unforgiving, but inclusive and fair. No one's shoes propelled them; it was individual commitment. There was no bench to sit. The clock never lied, although its honesty could be painful. There were no arguments, human judgments, or disputed line calls.

Distance running opened horizons, literally. The farther I went, the farther I imagined going. It was all about freedom. My stamina grew, and mental toughness with it. Concentration and patience improved over time. Unlike other sports, there were no thrown flags, dropped passes or missed slap shots. Distance running was easier and harder. It was inherently redemptive and fulfilling. I never regretted a run, even a hard one. I was adversary, referee and timekeeper. There was no hiding. When the sport was you against you, it was all you – win, lose or draw.

Holding pace was something that challenged me, and required training. I did that on roads and woods trails. I was not fast, but pushed. Over time, I learned to manage cramping, dehydration, muscle and joint soreness, the entire workout – and liked it. I learned to listen to my body, breathe better, find pace and dissociate. I figured out when to accept distraction, when to ignore it. Running distance in fall became fun. It was not for everyone, but fall running awoke me.

When high school turned to college, I shed team sport. I put in long runs. Sometimes, flashlight in hand, I crunched cold shoulders under moonlight and stars. By junior year, I had logged a thousand consecutive days of running. Some days, I wanted to run more than to sleep. Ten miles, then twenty. If battling the flu, I would shuffle a mile, return to bed. Never a sprinter, I just worked on my distance.

One January morning, I rose to arctic air. That day was also an inflection point. Everything was frozen. Birds must have been frozen mid-flight. At minus 32, not counting the wind, I hesitated. For the first time in a long time, the weather was oppressive. I asked myself, "Is this running thing sensible, sane?" My battery was low, engine spluttering. Fall was gone, winter here. Thirty years later, I still think about that day, as I recorded on my return. I wrote:

"The morning stings with the bitter cold of an arctic freeze. I am two steps out the door, no more, when my face begins to tighten. My nostrils fill with iciness. The prickle is uncomfortable. A chill rushes through me, penetrates me, sends its tingle up my spine. I cannot stop the shudder, nor the shiver. There are more shivers. I pause. Stop.

"On all winter mornings past, there has been no hesitation. Always, I have dressed, stretched, opened the door, and put my body in motion. In a trice, I am usually floating along, absorbed in reflection, lost in leg-drive, relaxing. I am studying the pattern of salt and gravel, watching the road. The stiff and creaky becomes smooth and fluid. I am then a runner at ease, at peace, enjoying my freedom. On any other morning, I would already be finding my pace, pulling my hat down over my ears and sucking in the cool, clean air that gives winter running a magic all its own.

"But this morning is different. The air is not cool, not inviting. It is threatening. It presses in upon me, surrounds me, envelopes me. It seeps into my cozy cotton, then deeper; it chills the bones and soul alike. It is a hungry, biting cold that cuts to the quick and devours the will. In token sunlight, it is a beastly 32 degrees below zero. As I stand, the powerful cold tightens its grip upon me. My frozen breath drifts gently upward, blocks my line of sight, is whisked away.

"Only a dozen paces to my rear, behind a waiting door, there burns a warm and soothing wood stove – a wood stove, I remind myself, which must be dutifully tended on mornings this bitter, an old pot-belly which radiates an uncommon kind of comfort, one that would surely ease the stiffness in my joints, one that beckons. I remind myself, too, that I am a master of justification; it is one of my greater personal weaknesses.

"I do not move. A twist of swirling powder lifts from nowhere, dances in the road, and dashes into the woods. From the stiff-limbed pines, there comes a creaking, a whine, a protest. Silence. For a time, the stillness lingers. Then the northwest winds again pour forth from the corners of the house. They rise and fall, as if to say they are furious with my indecision. In a rage, they scream at this wide-eyed creature who dares to advance on them, orange cap, mismatched mittens, and tattered sweats.

"In no uncertain terms, they deliver their message; they issue their challenge: Will you lower your head to the call of the road and gust of the wind, or turn and seek the warmth of your fire, certain that you could have done what you didn't?

"I am nearly frozen. The wind roars in my ears. My nostrils burn. My toes and fingers have numbed. The time for decision has come … and now, at last, I understand. The Great Northwest winds and the devilish cold are not taunting me; they are giving me the greatest gift a runner can know. They are granting me a chance to prove my conviction, to bury my doubts and revel in the love of my sport. They beg me to accept, and to realize in my acceptance that the challenge does not come from without; it is a challenge from within. I am barely able to contain myself. This is a challenge that glistens full and bright in the morning sun. It is a gift.

"How often do men get such a gift? How often is anyone given the occasion to meet his inner self, plumb the depths of will, strip himself of pretense, and struggle in the audience of nature for such contentment? As I think of the woodstove and day's work ahead, of the driving wind and bitter cold, the answer becomes clear. This gift is rare. It is the gift of self-discovery, of inner strength, of winter running.

"My feet are in motion. One crunch followed by the next. I am happy in the arctic freeze, with icy nostrils and a tingly spine. I accept my gift and crack a smile. I am privileged and humbled, smitten and inspired. I am a grateful member of the Northwoods, a quiet winter runner."

Of course, winter running was nuts, but what fun! Nature was for and against you, a fickle friend. Over time, I stretched out the training runs. Back then, my knees did not ache, no operations; weight was slight, heart strong. I began training for a marathon, Foxboro, Massachusetts – a test.

The idea of running 26.2 miles was pure theory. I had never done it. It was just a number. Boston's Billy Rogers made it look easy, but everyone knew it was hard. Frank Shorter won gold in 1972, silver in 1976, but he was a star. Maine's Joan Benoit was setting records, her gold out in the distance. Who knew what a marathon was? Back then, few.

Injuries were my worry. I did not want to train, then miss the start. I stayed on familiar routes, regulated mileage. Ironically, academics got easier, as time had to be managed. Logging miles helped sleep, which aided concentration. Distance running, it turned out, spurred a virtuous cycle. Running helped me study harder; harder studies forced shake-it-off-runs.

Soon, I warmed to night training. It was unscheduled time. Nights came with no distractions, little traffic, no classes or unbreakable commitments. Nights were also exhilarating. Something primordial awoke, quickening my stride. Maybe our ancestors hunted or were hunted at night; maybe those were their best runs, too. In any event, as others slept, I took to running – and liked it. If most of us are programmed to sleep at night, runners sometimes just stretch and go.

Darkness heightened the senses. Alert to each foot plant, flashlight in hand, one focused on breathing. Night runs were about *feel* more than seeing. Moonbeams created moonscapes, giving the runner space without horizon. My only hazard was wet leaves. Night air cooled hard-working lungs. The absence of reference points was freeing. I was my only spectator.

As race day neared, intensity and caution attached to preparation. I watched for loose gravel, tried not to roll an ankle, and iced my knees. If stockpiling sleep was impossible, I still tried. To run a marathon seemed like advancing to some final round, no second chances, no double eliminations, and no more time outs. Once the gun sounded, it was all or nothing. Oddly, I liked that. The bigness and oneness of a marathon made me focus. Perhaps that was true of everyone.

Race day, when it came mid-fall 1980, was sunny. I toed the line, my one goal – finish. I aimed for a steady pace; that was challenge enough. I had never run this distance, not even in practice. Suddenly, bang and we were off. I recall starting far too fast. I knew it, even then. I could not slow. Carbohydrate loading made throttling back harder than expected. I sailed out over the flats, leaned into grades, downshifted on slopes, and kept reaffirming my commitment to finish.

I was finally here, uncompromisingly, frighteningly, all-in here. I kept reminding myself this was THE day, so use myself up. Doubt dissolved, aches were forgotten. I strived for simple cadence, something to carry me, not sure what the right timing really was.

My overarching fear was the much-ballyhooed "wall" – a thing marathoners glibly talk about, often in dubious, dark and mumbling tones, a thing you "hit" near the end of a race. I was told to expect it, together with waves of exhaustion, sometime between miles 22 and 26. I dreaded that wall all race long, even as I wondered and anticipated hitting it, the way a high diver anticipates water contact. When it came, I would be ready.

The idea of such a long test, pitting myself against myself on a bright and brisk, slightly breezy, inordinately sunny New England day, must have delivered more adrenaline than usual. Maybe the training was, as they say, adequate. Maybe the pace was too slow. But somehow unnoticed, I slipped or squished, plodded or padded through the great wall of marathoning. I missed it.

Ironically, missing the wall was mildly disappointing, as I had nothing to talk about when people mentioned that part of the experience. My legs became plenty heavy, quads sore (more the next few days), and breathing labored – but no epiphany. I completed that first marathon in 3:10:17, nothing radical but a good return on my investment. I was left a dishrag, but finished. I recall stumbling around after the race, so happy that pain was a punctuation point on my happiness, not a detriment; it was confirmation that I had completed the mission, became part of a good memory.

Over the next 35 years, I kept running, ran thousands of miles – and another eleven marathons. None was more exhilarating than the first. At 7:15 a mile over 26.2 miles, that one put me on course for lifetime running. Today, I still shuffle, happiest on a dirt road in fall. As leaves begin to turn, the magic of fall running stirs. I open the door, drink in crisp air, and look for those crimson maples and flaming oaks, ready to shoot down that corridor once again.

23. Wood Stacking

Mainers love wood stoves, almost as much as the French love their wine. We certainly did. We had two small top-feeders, one cast iron monster. They rattled and wheezed through three seasons, starting each fall. New stoves are tidy, crackle and huff less, but ours were just fine. They were reliable friends, and made good company on cold nights.

Like good friends everywhere, our friends needed sustenance, humoring, and special attention now and then. Growing up in a house heated by wood, we knew the needs and rituals, followed them closely. We took to the woods each fall, looking two years ahead. We cut the best wood, then methodically stacked it, allowing enough time for seasoning. Wood stacking was key. As the French would tell you, it's not all in the grapes.

Green wood, by definition, was wet. By wet, I mean sopping, dishcloth wet. In the forest, water was constantly flowing up tree trunks from roots to the canopy, turning to sugar up there in the leaves, then flowing back down. Live trees were tubular sponges, only held vertical by a wrap of xylem and phloem, mostly wet. Thrown on a fire or into a stove, green wood just hissed and bubbled. So we gave it time. We stacked green wood with care in the open air, let it dry.

Seasoning, which depended on proper stacking, had a proud history. Actually, some authorities say Mainers invented the best drying method for wet wood – the wood pile. After picking, cutting, and hauling, came stacking. Adults and kids participated in this ritual, which wore kids out for good sleeping and gave adults peaceful evenings. Our woodpile doubled as windbreak, sound barrier, and good place for leaving garden tools, or setting down a coffee mug.

A well-stacked pile, neatly fashioned from green sticks, was the only way to vintage logs. Vintage logs burned reliably, thoroughly and evenly. But proper stacking was essential. That meant planning, patience, and the elegant, unhurried pursuit of ancient art. A "cozy wood stove," fed by seasoned wood, started with high fidelity stacking. You will not find that fact in books, or not until this one.

Proper stacking relied on passed-down skills, what you might call unwritten rules. Styles varied, but the fundamentals never changed. Putting up good wood had core principles, like putting up a memorable wine. There was a right way, and every other way. Besides, proper stacking warmed Mainers twice, once putting up, once burning. Come to think of it, our piles even looked like wine racks.

The preliminaries, everyone knew. Pick the best trees, just like vintners pull the best grapes – with care and from the right hillside, lots of sun and not too much water. We did this with a chainsaw, aiming for hardwood and soft. Trees, if not too big, were sawed into two-foot lengths, sometimes four and then re-cut. Eventually, sticks were heaved onto the wagon, pulled to the woodshed, readied for stacking. All this was prelude. Once dried, wood was quartered with a maul and sledge, lugged and fed to the stoves. But first, came the stacking.

Across Maine, woodstoves trumped fireplaces. That may sound odd, given the beauty of a fireplace. But stoves hold heat behind a damper; fireplaces vent their woody goodness up the chimney. So, to make a woodpile last, minimizing labor and maximizing trees, stoves had an edge over fireplaces, at least in fall and winter. Heat retention.

Softwoods were porous, disappearing fast. Hardwoods matured slowly. They were dense, so heavier. Once lit, they burned slowly. Our woodshed contained both, like a wine cellar has red and white, I suppose. Softwoods included evergreens, especially cedar (which popped nicely), hemlock (not the Socrates sort), white pines, then blue, black and white spruce (prickly). We had some tamarack (what Canadians call hackmatack), which drops needles each year. Tamarack was slender, and liked mucky bogs. Cedar, hemlock, pine and spruce liked rich, dark soil, made from fallen trees. Parts of grape-growing Alsace have similar soil, which probably explains the elegant, complex aroma of Maine softwoods.

If wood was too light, it could not to be trusted. Sumac, alder and fibrous bushes fell into that miserable category, what we called – useless. They took up more space than they were worth, consumed more energy than they gave back. We torched them in piles, not stacks. Hardwoods, on the other hand, were slow to mature, long on finish, nice bouquet. Like premium wines, they were worth searching for and savoring.

Hardwoods shone best in deep winter. They burned from midnight to dawn. We could throw sticks on late and have coals at five, when our stoves were re-loaded. Among reliable hardwoods, some took the prize. White oak and ash burned especially well, with silver and red maple. Black walnut and cherry were finds. Coming in from a run or chore, the chimney often wafted of hardwood smoke. That smoke had a fruity, nutty nose, like full-bodied Cabernet Sauvignon, the earthy, pepper-scent of a Grenache from schist-rock France. I will not go so far as to say hardwoods were supple or smooth-textured, but they made nice wood smoke – for sure.

White, gray and yellow birch were regular go-to trees. We had to be careful with birches. If they got rained on, they went to pieces like crepe paper, just turned to mush. You might say they had delicate skins, or oxidation happened quickly. Anyway, no fun burning wood that squished like old grapes. By contrast, quaking aspen – with leaves that shivered in light wind – were easy to identify and burned very slowly. They had a recognizable bark, like beech and ironwood.

Unfortunately, elms were already rare in my youth, victims of Dutch elm disease. Once, they lined our town's Main Street, like glorious horse-chestnuts along the Champs Elysees, but no more. When one died, they all went. That was it. By the time I got to college, they just lived in postcards. That said, science is always advancing. Elms may reappear, if someone conjures up a hearty hybrid. After all, diseased wine vines survived abroad, then got imported back to France.

Old-timers explained the difference between soft and hard woods by reference to the sun. They surmised that a tree contains as much heat as sun accumulated over its lifetime. Simplistic, but could be something to the theory. Hardwoods grew slower, denser, had compressed rings. They burned longer, too. Softwoods got big fast, but burned lickety-split. They spent fewer years soaking up sun for the same gauge. Put differently, old-timers thought logs gave back what they got from the sun, more or less. Elegant theory. Sun in, heat out – hardwoods were better vaults.

As years went by, we felled and stacked, felled and stacked. Like Tony in the backfields, we cut wood by the cord. We stacked it in woodshed and breezeway. To the uninitiated, stacking – like stomping grapes – must seem pedestrian. To the urban dweller, it may seem like shoveling dirt or raking leaves. *But nothing could be further from the truth.* Stacking wood – like putting up fine wine – involves artistry. It sets up the aging process, brings out the tannins.

Nor was stacking an abstract art. Refined for centuries, college degrees might be earned in this discipline. Like bottled wine, no two woodpiles were the same. They got put up with care, each one unique. Wood stackers watched their lines, sought vintage crops worthy of conversation.

For starters, no one tolerated a leaning pile, let alone a pile threatening to topple. Rule one. As vintners labor over stages and sugar structure, wood stackers labor to segregate their sticks, letting big ones drift to the bottom. Airflow affects the aging. Piles were built under cover, if possible.

As fine wines age best in big vats, promising wood sticks prefer broad cover.

Similarly, no one wanted to see a sloppy woodpile, any more than drink vinegar. Stick ends had to be flush to the out-facing side. A stack was part puzzle. Pieces had to be fitted, gaps minimized. Presentation mattered, and affected substance. Looked at from any perspective, a woodpile should not be off-kilter; no waves, weaves, tips or wobbles. Like good wines at their peak, the good woodpile could not be lopsided, had to be balanced. With a vintner's precision, wood stackers used their trained eyes. And as wineries piled tasty bottles with aplomb, stackers plumbed their mottled piles – with taste.

Other rules governed. To stack right, logs had to be right-sized, then ordered for stability. Two-footers were common, but girth varied. Logs from old trees ran along the bottom, younger ones across the top. A good stacker laid sticks like a mason lays bricks, one atop the next with consideration, deliberation and precision. But a stacker – quite obviously – had the tougher job. Bricks were uniform, sticks irregular. Sticks were tubular, non-conforming, misshapen and covered in stubs; they had unsightly knots, tapers and twists, cracks, bends and wishbones.

Even a wine sommelier gets to use symmetrical cylinders; wood stackers had to stack anomalies by eye and feel. They had to build with imagination. A good stacker took care to fit and place, juxtapose gaps to knots, fats and tapers, stubs with stubs, bends to bows. There was a premium on creativity. With all due deference, masons and sommeliers do not have these problems. Like building stonewalls, choices had to be made. Boulders before pebbles, trunks before sticks.

So, you thought I was kidding, right? Thought this was just some parody, tongue-in-cheek essay. Hardly! Stacking is big stuff. As assayer Fleming Stephenson once said, making Mark Twain famous: "There's gold in them thar hills." And there is also in proper stacking. Takes thoughtful eyes, to be done right. Begins at the tree, alluvial, loam or silty origins. Then straight cuts, even lengths, neat shaving of stubs and suckers. Finally wishbones to brace the base, diameters shrinking as she rises, balanced assemblage of hard to soft, plentiful aeration over multiple seasons, and all the aggressive aromas mature to delicate woodshed bouquets.

In the process, the stacker creates a winter-warming combination, sticks that are alternately beefy, brawny and delicate, like the finest French wines. As French decant their fine wines in decanters, we decant our fine woods in woodstoves. And remember, the best woodpiles end with that flush finish – just like this tale. Once the wood is stacked, raise a glass – to the greatness of stackers and vintners!

24. Lugging

Just a few passing words about lugging, wood that is – filling your arms with seasoned sticks. By contrast to stacking, lugging is hardly an art. Not even close, so perish the thought. Lugging has no resemblance to winemaking. Growing up, we all lugged, especially me. In time, I bequeathed the task to my brother. Still, goodness resided in lugging, like in pomace, the leftover seeds and skins, after fine wine is made.

For a time, our house was wholly heated by wood. Stoves always needed stoking. Days were short, nights long, both cold. Accordingly, this chore never slipped. Decades later, ruminating on it, maybe there was something for appreciating. In youth, lugging made us stronger, better at balancing sticks anyway. We probably brought in ten loads a day, between my brother and me. But every trip was different, as bored minds wander, now and then cursing splinters.

Muscle memory took over the chore, with automatic assessments of balance, heft, volume and proportion. Across Maine, young people developed this lugging instinct. Without looking, they came to know the height of their woodpile, even as it shrank. They knew how to pull with care, carry with confidence, walk without dropping, set and return – blindfolded, if needed.

So, there was nothing special about lugging – really. Mainers did it in three seasons. Still, there was something strangely relaxing about this task, mentally freeing. Lugging allowed a body and mind to part ways, one toting by rote, the other exploring. The task was tactile, but offered a chance to think, like mowing, raking, cutting brush, shoveling snow. We got a workout, got something done, and got uninterrupted time for pondering.

Of course, lugging was devoid of creativity. Had to be. We became human metronomes, pendula traipsing back and forth, woodpile to stove, stove to woodpile. But as the body fell into a cadence, the mind took leave. In consequence of the chore's simplicity, no harm done.

To the uninitiated, lugging seems tedious, dirty and distasteful. True, we did have to brush sawdust off now and then. We did have to lean, heave and lift, straining the lower back, quads and forearms. Non-initiates can be forgiven for thinking this would be "no fun." But in practice, it was nearly a sport. If we were not pressed for time or racing a storm, lugging could be contenting. It held consolations known only to those who lug.

Like splitting softwood and watching pieces fly, lugging returned a boy's investment. Piles grew, and forearms too. But lugging was where anyone could go for peace. The task, like weeding peas or running, was fair to a fault. Close to home, it permitted distraction, no worry about farmers or cars. Lugging had a peace about it, not exactly fishing, but freeing. We could dream of things big and small, finding an emerald, hammering up a treehouse, jobs, college, snowmobiles, travel and girls. That is what made lugging fun, the escape.

Sometimes, song lyrics got stuck in my head, usually the Beatles. Sometimes, I did homework assignments, organized an essay, identified and worried out a problem. Sometimes lugging allowed for high purpose, saying a prayer or reviewing my – generally awful – time management. Call me a rube, but that's why – for all its simplicity – I liked lugging. Someone had to do it, and that someone was me. Better to like it, than suffer. Hard to get one's arms around, but something good resides in lugging. Did then, and still does.

Some days the old Beatle lyrics come back. "Don't carry the world upon your shoulders." "There are places I remember all my life, though some have changed." "You say I am a dreamer, but I'm not the only one." "It's been a hard day's night, and I been working like a dog; it's been a hard day's night, I should be sleeping like a log." Ah, the joy of lugging wood!

25. Secret Order

Now listen, keep this one quiet. It's technically part of history, but a mystery. It has got to stay that way, see? A cadre of young woodsmen exists, not well known. Funny, since they've been around a hundred years. Anyway, fleet of feet, big on tradition, they are like Indians of yore, leave no footprints. High-spirited mountain stampers, these are idealists. *Shhhhhh!*

Ok, here's the skinny. In Maine and across America, these kids are still around, a persistent lot. Devoted to adventure and others' wellbeing, comfortable on less traveled paths, they are members of a secret order. The Order celebrates America's pioneering past, see? Members – if they pass the Order's Ordeal – pledge themselves, believe it or not, to "cheerful service." *Shhhhhh!*

Look, these folks are not typical environmentalists, biologists or tree huggers. They fell, limb, chop and stack trees. They are anglers and oarsmen, hikers and scholars. They do love the forest and her lore. They get culled each year from the ranks of scouting. That's right – from Boy Scouts of America, those with a special penchant for survival. The Order has this Ordeal …

Soft walkers, the Order is not much interested in publicity. On many things, members are sworn to secrecy. But they do celebrate competence and can-do, productive motion over self-promotion. Eschewing ease, they actively hunt the unexpected. They disdain inertia, always pushing outward – and pushing themselves. They cultivate equanimity, tranquility in every storm, pockets of purposeful peace. Emerson would hew to their self-reliance, Thoreau to their can-do. Beverley Hills would not understand them at all.

Their coin is resourcefulness. In some ways, the Order is a proxy for America's past. They learn to be at home in the night's quiet and woods' wordless ways. They sleep by ones, in open air, under a canopy of stars. They are fine with cold, wind, rain, and damp. They labor in teams by day. They talk little, by design, no room for electronic distractions.

This lot has compass, inner and outer, or they learn it along the way. They teach care with care. Rudyard Kipling might smile. "If you can keep your head, when those about you are losing theirs … you will be a man my son." He would approve. They know the forest as home, respect it, themselves and each other. They read weather closely, no complaints. They are about goals.

A few granite facts. Candidates for the Order are not chosen by adults. They are chosen by peers. The tradition dates to 1915. In that year, Dr. E. Urner Goodman and Carroll A. Edson tested a group of Scouts in upper echelon skills. The Order … was born. Beyond camping, hiking, canoeing, orienteering, and pioneering; beyond swimming and lifesaving; beyond archery, rifles, fishing and first-aid, there was always … the Order.

Today, little is said of it – about the Order's tests of survival and temperament. No surprise, it came to life just before America entered World War I. Europe was consumed, all attention on survival, endurance, undivided purpose. Scouting was new, brainchild of Britain's Baden Powell, a standing challenge to young men of good heart. Eagle rank was arduous, about skills, principles, leadership and stick-to-it-ness. By design, there were ranks, badges and long odds on Eagle. Public service produced personal development, and vice versa. The Order added to that. It was short tests, one Ordeal, and then back to the long climb.

Scouts, as a rule, might be up at dawn and down at nightfall. They learned to make and break a camp, weather stiff winds, peg down tents, cook over fires, and lash up flagpoles, as well as towers and bridges. They were seasoned in paddling canvas, finding food in the forest, fishing, cresting mountains and climbing hand-over-hand up fire towers. They knew steep trails, tight passes, tall trees, and could whittle sticks for toasting marshmallows. They swamped canoes, forded streams, and shot fast water. They were up for adventure.

The Order added a new test. Scouting was journey and destination, a six-year trail to manhood, fun that produced strength – physical, mental, emotional and spiritual. That enterprise cultivated dedication to others and high purpose. Trust, teamwork, fidelity and singlemindedness. Scouts learned how to manage uncertainty, pick a trail and go. Scouting turned dependence to independence to interdependence, all while lashing ladders, tying knots, and practicing rescues.

In sum, scouting was the long trail. It was the way to leadership, figuring out the balance between risk and reward, action and inaction, joust and judgment. By negotiating those rapids, boys learned to be strategic and fruitfully stubborn, collaborative and compassionate, connected. The result was transformative. The Order just tested that alloy's temper.

All scouts pledged to aspire. The aim was to be "trustworthy, loyal, helpful, friendly, courteous, kind, obedient, cheerful, thrifty, brave, clean and reverent." No coincidence many have touched inconceivable heights. Eagle Scout Neil Armstrong commanded Apollo 11 and was the first man on the Moon. Eagle Jim Lovell commanded the miraculous Apollo 13 mission. Eagle Gerald Ford was a president known for peace, poise and confidence; he calmed a nation consumed in self-doubt. Others have populated government, business, education and science.

If scouting were a river, the Order – for all its mystique – would be an eddy. Still, it is an interesting eddy. Founded at Treasure Island near Philadelphia, when Theodore Roosevelt was still active, the Order centered on spirit, endurance, and "cheerful service." It tested a scout, while pressing higher aspirations. Some called it a "National Honor Society" for scouting, but the truth was simpler. The Order simply sought good hearts, unbroken smiles and those with stamina to traverse more wilderness. Inevitably, membership turned on surviving the Ordeal.

Officially, the Ordeal requires "maintaining silence, receiving small amounts of food, working on camp improvement projects, and sleeping apart from other campers." That is half of it. Inspiration attended every Ordeal. As a long-ago candidate, I here confess nostalgia for the thing. I can do that, as it has been a while. True to the Order's low profile, I shall leave most unsaid. I will just give a taste, a flavor to be savored.

I awoke on the second day soaked and tired, in a word, bedraggled. Having slept with no cover in drubbing rain and fickle winds, I was groggy. Everyone was. From my troop, just a friend named Scott and I were here. By design as much as circumstance, no one got shuteye. This night had been particularly long. Some ended up on rock walls, others in a bog. Some were put in brambles, others on soggy moss. A few scored granite, a luxury. By morning, we were wringing our socks, but resolved to carry on. Temperatures hung in the forties, barely. For comparison, just imagine sleeping in a cold shower, fan on your face. One of *those* days.

The Order, we soon learned, had some standards. They were high. We had to pass certain tests, or it was no-go. So we soldiered on. Sounds strange, but we liked the idea – at least the idea – of surmounting obstacles. On the other hand, things were gray getting grayer. Instructions now came fast. *Rule One:* No second chances. *Rule Two:* Fire must burn tall enough to cook a breakfast. *Rule Three*: Order does not tolerate excuses, including a sopping forest. *Rule Four:* Candidates get *one match* – no more, pass or fail.

Something about that last bit made me choke. In the warmth of home, no pressure, starting a good fire was easy. Dry match turned to flame on any dry rock, pant leg, zipper or eye tooth. The operable word was *dry.* Using a dry match on any dry day to light dry tinder is easy. Today was not dry.

Today, the world was drenched, squalls and puffs everywhere, a buffeting wind. Had been for hours. Lighting a fire here would be hard enough, but no second match? That defined challenge. Light or do not. Make it work or plan to go home. I received my match, grateful, excited and worried. With the match, I received an egg, paper cup and piece of bread. It was the match and me now, against the universe. Induction depended on us. I quickly put match in cup, cup in pocket. I put the egg down, and went to search birch. Soon, I had the oily magic.

Next problem: Fires are not made of birch bark alone; they also need wood. Wet wood, as you will recall, does not burn. The same conundrum faced each candidate, and each approached it differently. Nature was arrayed against us. Ground was saturated, branches dripping, kindling all soaked. Still, no one panicked. They just thought. Before long, scouts were hunting tinder in chipmunk holes and under big rocks, beneath fanning branches. Some went for pitchy pine and spruce; others snapped off dead branches. Some cut clefts, created feather sticks; others whittled for interior wood.

My strategy was simple. Under my slicker, I whittled a handful of shavings, put them into bark, and shielded the little pile. To this, I added whittled strips of interior. But would my match catch the bark, or just go out? Would my bark ignite the shavings? Would my shavings catch the twigs, twigs feed the branches? Rain and wind kept up. I needed a fire – to cook the egg and toast. I braced myself for the big match drag, then held my breath – and pulled.

Whoa, indiscretion has overcome me! What am I doing, telling you the Order's inner secrets! Already, I have said too much. I must say no more! Got to keep quiet. As you know, induction depended on bringing that little fire to life! It also imposed secrecy! You understand why I can say no more?

Well, here it is then. Whether my dry match caught bark or shavings; whether dry shavings sprang to flame; whether small twigs smoldered into a full flicker; whether they ignited quarter-inch, then half-inch, finally full-inch sticks; and whether a hot rock doubles well as a frying pan, sided by bread crust – I cannot divulge. Not even hint.

What I can say is this: The Order does things the hard way. Ordeals include meals, and those must be cooked, eaten hot. The Order, like scouting, teaches patience. It tolerates eggs prepared any which way, including *la pierre chaude,* if you will. Acceptable eggs include those sunny-side up, garnished with toasted crusts, washed down with rainwater. Scott may tell you more, but never me. Twist my arm, toss me on a stone wall, drench me, dress me down, throw me in the briar patch – but not a word from me, not about the Secret Order.

26. What a Hoot!

Who's afraid of the dark? Not me. That's what I always said. Walked miles in the dark, years in the dark, endless woods and ribbons of tar in the dark. Top of our mountain to bottom, bottom to top, into town, outa town, anywhere in the dark.

Street lights were not many, so kids got used to walking by moonlight, bouncing lumens and a day's ambient afterglow. That is how we found the ground. We walked at dusk, peacefully in darkness. We made our way home from fishing the narrows near Wilson and Dexter Ponds, playing baseball for Coach Ed, waterskiing and beach bumming; after exploring mountain caves, shooting soda bottles, playing football and meandering from a friend's home. Perambulation occurred in any light, or none at all. That was rural Maine, rural everywhere.

Some days, I cycled home at night, chasing a shaft of light that started on my handlebars and bounced everywhere. A wheel-mounted generator gave light, in proportion to how hard I pedaled. Some nights I pedaled fast, others middling. Summer evenings regularly found me rounding the lake and climbing our hill in darkness, confident as boys get, moisture condensing across my face. I would pedal past Grace's house, now nearly 100, who at age eight went to see Charles Lindbergh take off on his trans-Atlantic flight, even attended his ticker-tape parade on return. I would pedal past my aunt's home, with every light out.

In every season, I ran by fractions of moon, half, quarter, fingernail. I would carry a flashlight in one hand for cars, then out again. Darkness was my friend, as Paul Simon liked to say. Not in a bad way, either. "Hello darkness my old friend …" he crooned in the time. Animals were active in the darkness, too. Deer, squirrels and songbirds had settled, but others started to prowl. They were nocturnal friends. They headed out on their rounds, raccoons and skunks, flying squirrels and bats. For them night was day, or better.

For me, and I suspect others, asphalt and dirt were a cinch to find in the darkness. They did not get up and move. They did not change where they had been by day. Moonbeams, stars and lingering candela squeezed through crystal-rich cirrostratus clouds and brightened the road's shoulders. Scuffed pebbles popped. That sort of thing helped me stay centered on a dark road, spring, summer and fall. In winter, Chris's plow kept the road obvious, snug between embankments. Under a full moon, blue snowbanks rose on either side of the road, hemming in the tar. I could not get lost if I wanted to. There was no place to go, just the frozen corridor. Even in darkness, snowbanks loomed.

Back in springtime, sounds followed evening walkers. Water trickled, snow melted, creeks and gullies filled, all headed for local lakes. Summer nights were companionable. Breezes broke the humidity, crickets chirped and bullfrogs bellyached. Gnats came out, but soon vanished, eaten by swooping bats.

Come fall, moonlight penetrated leafless branches, making geometric shapes on the road. A big moon lit the woods white, diffused everywhere. Fall light was gentle, waves losing amplitude as they tapered, scattering freely about the forest. We would get a harvest moon. It rolled over the horizon like a fireball, making silhouettes of distant firs. The fireball shrank as it climbed, rung over rung, across the wide sky's ecliptic.

On other nights, the moon might stay half hidden, or just a sliver. It would play peek-a-boo with passing clouds, take a runner back in time, maybe far ahead. Imagination and endorphins flowed. As the moon rode the monthly cycle, I pedaled my own up and down the mountain. Or I walked. Either way, I got home. I did not worry about next steps. Night walking, like night running, was peaceful. Besides, all roads led home, under Jimmy Stewart's moon. I never worried anything.

Except on a *moonless* night. Those nights were different. They could be odd, no light at all. On such head-in-bag nights, I floated on an inky sea, not lost but surrounded. Navigating the inkiness required caution. Late fall, winter and early spring, these nights were silent – no frogs or bugs. They were otherworldly, something else – lifeless. I had to walk slowly, feel my way home, pawing through black velvet curtains. On some nights, even stars vanished.

By late fall, the leaves had all pulled their ripcords, floated to the road. Nights were getting chilly, some cold. No moon, no noise, just crunching feet. I walked with focus. Lovely as they were, these nights brought navigation to a higher level, called on different senses. Gone were smell, sight and sound, since frozen has no scent and does not move. Stars were a consolation, sometimes. Other times, they called their shafts home, a million snails pulling antennae in, gone. I was alone.

On such nights, I felt like a spacewalker, dangling out at the end of an invisible tether. These nights were peculiar and fun, no reference points. They were exhilarating, but could make adrenaline flow. Filled with emptiness, they rang. For better or worse, lightless nights were uncommon. When they came, I pawed home. Late fall and winter brought them, just deep space.

That is the sort of night it was, the night it occurred – cold, black and silent. It was perfect for space walking, but I was down here and on a road. I walked with care, comforting myself with happy imaginings. I fenced out misgivings, no thought of headless horsemen tonight. Forcibly, I tried to enjoy the walk. I might have been anywhere, spinning in orbit, plodding a canyon floor, far side of the moon. My fingertips tingled, strange. I scuffed the frozen road, able to see nothing. I kept pushing my way through chocolate pudding. That was a nice, happy thought.

It was late, later than usual. Near midnight. I was coming back from visiting a buddy, Will, and his father, Peter. We talked too late. Their home was half a mile beyond mine, nothing between. We had been talking of politics or town, coin collecting, debate team or scouting, maybe the world – beside their crackling fire. I cannot remember what we had been talking about, but time got away. Suddenly, I needed to get home. I bid farewell, and started walking. Midnight was here. Time was not consequential, except Mom would worry. I did not want her to worry, picked up the pace. *Wow, it was dark!*

Behind me, the little circle of light vanished, swallowed by hill and blackness. I knew rough distances, but tonight's blackness was blacker than usual. Silence was intense; it rang. Without sight and sound, I still had other senses. That was the good news. Bad news was, they picked up nothing. Smell was moribund. I did feel road beneath me, cold around me. I was oddly disconnected.

In truth, this night should have felt familiar. Many nights I just crunched home. I should have brought a flashlight, but forgot. It should have been ho-hum, unmemorable. The trek was normally ten minutes, fifteen tops. Tonight, my stride was slow and plodding, even trying to quicken it. I moved as if through syrup. My mind was nowhere, focused on my feet. *Boy, was it black!*

I eased over the mountain's brow. An archer's bow defined the road, I could feel it. On the downside now. Stone walls were somewhere in the blackness, lining this stretch. My boots crunched ice. That was the only sound. My fingers went deep in my pockets. I pulled my shoulders around my neck, pushed my chin down. Cold and dark. Dark and cold. They competed for attention. On I walked, into nothingness. The silence was an old friend, but a stranger too.

For situational awareness, I lifted one side of my hat, thought I heard a car, but no – nothing. I could hear cars a mile off. They did not come this way often. I kept my one ear out. If ears were cold anyway, best to use them. In this way, I marched toward home, through the emptiness, eyes watering, ears straining, frozen road under me.

When I passed the old maple, the "Suzie Tree," I would be halfway home. I could not see it. I would not have seen the Washington Monument if it were beside me. Mildly frustrating. In daylight, the tree overhung the road. It stood halfway between Will's house and mine. The old tree was a good reference. Will's dad made maple syrup from its sap annually. The Suzie Tree, named for whom I never learned, towered beside the road, commanding walls in two directions like royalty. She was the midpoint. Yet everything remained invisible, including her majesty. She was a solitary tree and strong. As Churchill said, "solitary trees, if they grow at all, grow strong." She had. Only I could not see her.

I squinted hard for the tree. The road was leveling, still *no tree.* Somewhere in the blinding crowd, she was elbowing the darkness toward me. Had to be. Amazing how dark darkness got. No moon, no visibility, no ambient anything, no nothing. I was in a burlap bag. *Where was the Suzie Tree, anyway? Somewhere. Boy, was it black! Was that a phone pole?* Could not tell. *Crunch, crunch.* I stopped. Not for any reason, but to be sure the crunch was mine. *Yup, mine.* I kept walking. *I would soon be home. Where was the Suzie Tree?* Finally, a shape. Not a phone pole, too fat. Here was my bearing, the tree. I crunched slowly toward that coal dark shadow. I looked up. *Suzie Tree or imagination? Relief, here she was! HERE was the tree! Halfway home!*

For whatever reason, my heart was beating fast. My courage was, I realized, somewhere back in the circle of light. What should have been a simple stroll had been a trek through Mordor, or across Doyle's Yorkshire moors. At last, I was halfway home! I had hacked my way through the darkness, slayed the dragon, would soon be in bed. *Silly,* I said to myself, drawing a breath. I remember that breath. It was the last thing I remember. That was when it *happened.*

I stepped out from under the Suzie Tree, assuming that step would be unremarkable. On any other night, it might have been. On this night, it was not. I shall never forget what happened next. For no reason, a chill ran the length of my spine. I knew something was up – then my ears exploded.

From feet above me, came the most deep-throated *"HOOOOOOOT!"* I had ever heard – ever have heard. It exploded over my head, like an air horn in the lowest branch. A traumatizing, untamed bellow pierced both my ears, reverberated about my skull. From a full and feathered chest, I got the "*WHOO-HOOT!*" of an unrepentant, nocturnal joker – the Great Horned Owl! He sent me into orbit, straight up the tree like a cartoon character. There, I exited my skin, hit the top like a bell clapper, and settled down to earth like a wad of spent firework paper, in a horrible heap.

When I finally dared to get up and reassemble myself, I was quite loose. Whatever fear I had before was expelled. Many things I have encountered, but nothing quite like that, before or since. I had ambled under Maine's loudest owl. He had impeccable timing, and a ruthless sense of humor. Unlike the barred owl's deference, the king used an exclamation point! He gave me his best, full-tilt tug blast, held nothing back, no sense of decorum. I got it – every decibel.

An older man might have left his dentures right there, or called it quits. I was younger. I admit, I was – yes – momentarily gripped by fear. However, I took consolation. I was no longer alone. There were now two of us, in this impenetrable darkness. And we had gotten to know each other, to a degree. I was home in a jiff, and slept like a baby. *What a hoot!*

27. Peter

My friend Will's father, was Peter. Only years on did I learn more about his past. Worth knowing, he was one of ten kids, irrepressibly cheerful, a constant guidepost, along with Will's mother, Lois. Peter, after finishing Bates College, saw action in the Korean War, an experience he shared only when asked.

Peter is a quiet fellow, father, grandfather, veteran, realist with an appreciation for timing and whimsy. For the better part of a century, he has worn a smile, letting it spread to townsmen, friends and visitors. Unassuming, he tends his mountaintop home, overlooking Androscoggin Lake, as ours did. Peter sees as far as the Earth's curvature will allow, which is a fair amount on a clear day. He must have collected ten thousand sunsets by now.

On a lazy afternoon, when the birds are fed, including goldfinches and wild turkeys, chores all done, he likes to look back over family and town – and to look forward. He never stops looking forward. Now approaching his 90s, he is a treasure trove of information.

While I have come to talk about his service in Korea, disembarkation at Inchon, movement of American troops north and south, he is content to begin with family history, now that we are on history. And so, I am also.

In time, we will return to his service in Korea. Of the ten children in his family, six were boys, four girls. All six boys signed up for the United States military, John and Richard in the US Marines, Robert and David in the Navy, Peter and Jimmy in the Army. Sisters Mary, Jane, Ruthie and Sarah served on the home front. Ruth, for context, is the mother of my friend Stefan.

Peter downplays my admiration for his family's service, noting that the nation of his youth faced different pressures, different urgency and expectations. Besides, while most volunteered – some for World War II, some later – they would all have been drafted had they not volunteered.

I am not dissuaded in my admiration. John was the oldest son. He served aboard the *USS San Jacinto,* Pacific Theater, in World War II. Carrier's name sounds familiar, so I start to ask. Peter is ahead of me. "Yes, you know, that was the carrier George H.W. Bush served on." I had not remembered, but he gives me credit. Now I do. The older George Bush was once America's youngest naval aviator, postponed college to train and fly a torpedo bomber, an Avenger, off the deck of the *USS San Jacinto.*

The older Bush flew – and older brother John served – during some of *San Jacinto*'s roughest action. Bush flew in the Battle of the Philippines, which ended Japan's capacity to mount carrier operations. Famously, before that, Bush flew from the *San Jacinto* against Chichijima, where his torpedo bomber got hit by anti-aircraft fire and burst into flames. Engine on fire, the elder Bush managed to deliver his payload from the burning plane, hitting key targets before nursing it back to sea and ditching. Bush and one crew member bailed. Bush's chute opened. His crew mate's did not. Bush was picked up by the *USS Finback*, a submarine. He was flying again from *San Jacinto*'s deck a month later.

Peter's oldest brother, John, ended up seeing action in Wake, Marcus, Saipan, Rota, Guam, Chichi, Haha and Iwo Jima. He was at Okinawa, Formosa, Luzon, Manila Bay and Leyte. He was there for dogfights over Tokyo. When I express amazement, Peter smiles and says John described himself as responsible for "ammunition, big shells, that's all."

Soon, we have worked through other brothers. Richard, with whom Peter worked at a logging site in northern Maine as kids, served in the US Marine Corps. Robert, Jimmy and David, all served post-World War II, David attending the US Naval Academy. Peter recalls visiting US Senator Margaret Chase Smith's office to see if the necessary Academy letter had been sent for David. It must have, as David got in. He wanted to fly, but medical kept him from the air. That said, David became a state legislator and town moderator. His niece, Wendy, followed him as State Representative.

Finally, after cheerful words about his sisters, we return to Korea – his service. He recalls when the announcement came of the attack by communist North Korea, rolling across the 38th parallel with Soviet support, invading South Korea. He knew his time had come, and was soon drafted into the Army.

No big deal, says Peter. Lots of training before getting to Inchon. Korea had been a Japanese colony. After World War II, it was divided, administered by the United Nations in the South, which meant by the US military, and by the Soviet Union to the North. By 1948, this division had hardened. On June 25th 1950, 67 years to the day of my typing, the Soviet-supported North invaded the South.

Peter described the run-up to his arrival at Inchon … Beginning in Maine, he was shipped south, then west, eventually readied for Inchon. While the big picture and how Peter fits into it interests me, little things stir him to muse, opine and occasionally chuckle. "They would ask what we did when we got to each training location – you know, whether we were a carpenter, or had some other skills. When they got to me, I would say I was a student. They would ask, 'Can you write? Can you type?' When I said 'yes,' they would pull me out of line, put me over in processing, typing. That happened a lot." Peter wanted, as his brother John had done, to go where the action was. Nevertheless, he learned to roll with the pulls and punches.

Asked what specialty he wanted, after he got to Korea, he did not know what to say. Given a choice between working "wheeled or flying" equipment, he figured he knew more about "wheeled" things. That turned him into a truck driver and Army soldier dedicated to repairing anything that rolled, short of tanks. "Those who chose flying things, ended up training to fly helicopters."

To Peter, the mechanic's lot seemed a mixed blessing. While he did not get to fly helicopters, he did get to work on lots of military equipment, putting skills to use in Korea beyond soldiering. Dryly, he notes "a lot of the helicopters got shot down."

He is right, of course. The Korean conflict was one of the bloodiest in modern history. America lost more than 36,000 men, suffered 103,000 wounded. The civilian toll ran into the millions. Even in 2017, some 7,747 American service members remained unaccounted for. Helicopters were, for the first time, used extensively. Vulnerable to ground fire, many were lost. In time, pilots became agile, heroic evacuations commonplace. In 1951, US Army helicopters ferried over 5,000 wounded. By mid-1953, US helos were carrying 1,200 wounded per month.

Nor were Army trucks, of the sort Peter drove and repaired, unimportant. They were critical in defending the Pusan perimeter, where he ended up. This was a small pocket in southeast Korea, into which United Nations and allied troops got pushed. Again, Peter's crisp memory is tied more to the nitty-gritty, seeing pockets of dislodged and aggrieved humanity.

Arriving at Inchon with a later wave, he was directed – with his skills – south to Pusan, while others were directed north. Along the way, he recalls seeing war's destruction, including things that linger, like an overturned locomotive, things destroyed. His voice trails off. He is not prone, I know, to drama. He makes clear that he was a late-comer, somehow secondary, not so much important. He switches to what he learned, fixing "wheeled" things.

Before long, Peter is talking again about family, his father and mother, their resilience through the Great Depression, what siblings did and are doing. We talk of making maple syrup, which he used to do, fixing old cars, which he still does. We talk of the beautiful view from his front room, how he plans to trim the trees. We talk of dahlias, goldfinches and wild turkeys.

In closing, since I do not want to overstay my welcome and sun is low, he notes that he has old wartime letters to and from siblings. I tell him I would love to go through them with him, or read a few. He is agreeable. He says he will try to locate the box, then talks of wall pictures. Peter's children are Will and George. Sister Ruthie is mother to friends Stefan, Thomas, Marek and Lisa. His brother Richard is father to friends David, Wendy, Charley and Linda. Peter's brother David is father to friends Kathy, Leslie and Chris. And so it goes. Small town, large families, really just one large family. I had never asked about Korea, or about John, despite having been Peter's neighbor forty-five years ago. Now, I know a little more.

His whimsical smile is now back in place. Peter walks me to the door, musing brightly about his late wife Lois, how she used to ride horses and taught him to ride, about his brother Richard and Richard's wife Ellie, all of whom have now passed on. Somehow, to him – and to me – they are still alive, recalled in these photos, stories, echoing voices, and outdoor flowers. Peter has served on every board, committee and governing body in town during the past 50 years; in 2014, he was honored by the Maine Municipal Association for 49 years of 'continuous service' – always smiling. Peter closes, "We old folks like to talk about the past, so come over any time." He chuckles, taking in the view. He knows I will be back.

Peter Ault in uniform, Korean War-era photo

Peter working on military trucks, Korean War

Ault family, left to right/top to bottom - Father Charles, baby David (future Navy), held by sister Jane, mother Ruth (with bow), oldest brother John (future USMC, shipmate of GHW Bush), Robert (Navy), Richard (USMC), Jimmy (Army), Ruth (Stefan's mother), Peter (Army). Absent: Sarah (unborn), Mary (married)

Peter today, sporting his wry sense of humor, still working on antique cars atop Morrison Heights. (Photo credit Andy Molloy, Kennebec Journal)

28. *What Do Pigs Not Eat?*

Half a mile south of home, opposite direction from Will's house, lived another set of neighbors. They lived around two bends, and over a long stretch of dirt. To my delight, they owned – for a while – two personable pigs. Having pigs down the road was cheering, for reasons hard to describe. Knowing they lived nearby was a source of wonder and curiosity. You see, pigs are genial by nature, friendly when you give them a chance, smart and unexpectedly entertaining. They also love visitors. So, I visited often.

Having a peccary outpost so close was enchanting, especially since I thought I wanted to be a veterinarian. No fault of the pigs, I parted with that notion in college. For me, these neighbors seemed relatives of Charlotte's Wilbur. Most days, I had no reason to visit. They had no reason to expect me. My visits were random and infrequent, if always fun. We would chat, then I would go.

One day that changed. The family that owned these pigs stopped by. They had a favor to ask. Might I want to tend the pigs, in their absence? They were going away for two weeks. This was the height of exciting. For all the work it might entail, the pigs would be mine for two weeks. The idea was electrifying. I would be responsible for them. I would be *tending pigs! Why not?* The pigs were affable. The job would allow me to earn pocket change. Our neighbors would get time off – from their pigs. I let them know, with my mother's consent, I was happy to tend their pigs. I was actually thrilled! Not yet a veterinarian, this was close – it had to be.

The truth was, of course, I knew nothing about tending pigs. Cats, dogs, even rabbits, yes – but pigs, no. Our neighbors assured me it was all very simple. Pen keeping, pig watering and other obligations and cautions were described and reviewed. Seemed pretty easy. "All you need to do beyond that is … feed them."

On my walk-through, I was told the details. "There is dried food right over here in this barrel. Once or twice a day should do it." They reviewed portions and the process. On parting, only one question occurred to me. "Could I bring down some other foods, greens, spare tomatoes, peelings, if we have some extra?" I asked. "Oh sure, you're free to feed them anything they'll eat, cuttings, corn husks, tomatoes … They will eat it all – Heck, they'll eat almost anything!" That seemed like the most important thing to know. Other details were colorless; this one was colorful. The pigs would eat "almost anything."

How and what to feed these big-bellied bruisers, how to keep them happy, had been my chief concern. I had a good start. Pigs needed room to gobble, so I would feed them in a trough. I would give them the feed our neighbors left. I was glad I could also experiment with our throw-away greens, when we had extras. This, at least, was my plan.

In no time at all, I discovered that pigs loved all kinds of fresh things. They could never get enough. We grew lots of vegetables. I would pile a bucket high with meal scraps, plus other things we were not going to eat, bruised, fading or wilted vegetables. I would pedal the bucket down to the pigs each day on my bicycle. My bucket always had something interesting in it.

Over the period, it held corn husks, moist cobs, beet greens, carrot tops, radish leaves, apple peelings and cores, peach skins, strawberry caps, overripe cauliflower, broccoli, lettuce, blue hubbard squash, butternut squash, pumpkins, blueberries, zucchini, cucumbers, cabbage and tomatoes. In varying portions, these disposables made their way to the pig pen. Since we grew all of those vegetables, we had plenty to share with the pigs.

Even before I had fed them for the first time, I had the sense this would be an education – for them, if not for me. It was both. During the first week, we got to know one another well. Pigs are smart, as I said. So, we talked. We would share important thoughts – in our respective languages.

They would let me know how much they liked the food, especially the scraps. We conversed about living in the big woods, impending weather, even politics. We snuffled to one another about the state of the world, the economy, baseball and other important things – always, including food. As long as I brought food, they were happy to talk. My sense was that these two pigs enjoyed our daily conversations, our shared commiserations, bemoaning national leadership and discussing the Red Sox, while reviewing the state of celery tops.

I could tell right away they liked me – and our regular talks, whether about politics, economics or baseball, because as soon as I got near their pen, they came running. They would come right up to the edge to greet me! All at once, they would start talking, snorting and sniffling. Soon, they were huffing and digging about in the dirt, asking me what I thought of current mud-slinging – inquiring, always inquiring, about what was in my bucket.

During this first week, foodstuffs varied. The variety steadily grew. I marveled at the pigs' capacity for consumption. They would eat anything and everything that I brought. Then, once done, they would nose about to see if they had missed anything, or if I were hiding anything from them. Once or twice I did, just to give it to them afterwards. Sometimes I would hold back a couple of celery sticks, a handful of beet greens, just to give them a surprise desert. They liked that. But they were never full, never so satisfied they backed off, rolled over or sat down to preen. They were unlike cats, or even rabbits. They were always hungry.

I began to feel rather bad for them. They were plainly not being fed enough to keep them fit. I was supposed to be keeping them well-fed, in fighting form, or at least healthy enough to look satisfied. But they never looked satisfied. All this talk of politics, stagflation and Red Sox baseball was obviously wearing them down. They needed to feed their highly active minds. They needed more food.

As week two got underway, I made a point of cycling down their road with two big buckets of anything organic I could find, one slung over each side of my cycle's handlebars. In these buckets, on top of the other goodies from our garden, were some things we did not grow. I threw in banana peels, orange peels, lemon rinds, turnip and celery butts, onion skins, garlic gloves, and – since I really felt these pigs were not getting their full share – some fresh tomatoes, apples and cucumbers. I knew my mother would not understand the pigs' nutritional peril, so I sneaked the tomatoes and cucumbers from our garden, apples from the refrigerator.

The pigs enjoyed the new fare, but still seemed insatiable. They would eat vigorously, mumbling responses to my opinions, snorting at some observations, but then – always – ended up hungry. I was not properly gauging how much they really needed, and so had to rethink my options.

As the second week progressed, I began to realize there was another problem. I was unable to keep the flow of disposable greenery and organic extras coming at the rate needed. I could get one bucket, but not two, of snuck tomatoes, cucumbers, onions, celery, lettuce and apples from home. More began to look peculiar – in the garden and refrigerator. I began to replenish the second bucket somewhere else.

As I cycled from our house to pen one day, a new idea occurred to me. Wild food abounded. It was everywhere. I stopped near the pigs' quarters and filled my second bucket with fresh-pulled wild grasses. Inedible to humans, my hope was the pigs could enjoy them. They did. By the time I had mixed the grasses with healthy slop, the grass smelled just like tomato-onion-apple goo. They ate every bite – and looked around for more. Once again, I had failed to make them happy.

The state of the world being what it was, I took their focus off world events. Instead, I put it on new types of food. This went down well. I picked all the grass around their pen – out to a radius of two hundred feet. I found wild chives and clover. On the day of my Grass-Is-Pig-Food epiphany, I cycled home thinking, thinking and thinking. What else could I feed them? At least, I had gotten them *closer* to being full. They had eaten every blade picked. Then, they had talked among themselves. The new food seemed of interest, but they would have liked more.

The next day, I expanded their horizons again. I branched into tender wood ferns and deciduous leafy fodder. I topped off the second bucket, now half full of organic refuse and fresh grass (including every blade in their glen), with a huge clump of tasty green ferns and handfuls of maple and oak leaves. Interesting! That seemed to sum up their reactions. The two pigs ate every bite of grass, fern and leaf. I watched them. Maybe they would be full today? Nope. They then looked around for anything missed. They were still hungry. We were nearing the end of week two. I felt pressure to get them fully fed now, each and every day.

On my last day of pig feeding and pig tending, I resolved they would be satisfied. Somehow, they would be satisfied. I would feed them so much that they would, literally, stop eating. In this way, I would have fulfilled my duty to keep them sated. This day would top off a long two-week period. Satisfying them after this would be up to the family that owned them. They were delightful, conversational and utterly insatiable peccaries.

On this day, I plied my talkative, famished friends with as much organic veggie refuse as two heaping buckets would hold. I supplemented my offerings with two huge bunches of fresh grass, picked from our own yard, before coming. I added to this combination a giant collection of premier green leaves – every last leaf in sight, actually. Then, I stood there and watched.

I liked my friends. Pigs are generally friendly, and these two were enthusiasts. They were expectant, but not unreasonable. They ate heartily and seemed appreciative, even if they wandered about looking for more. I was reminded of Winston Churchill's assessment of these unusual, and entertaining, creatures. He said: "I like pigs. Dogs look up to us. Cats look down on us. Pigs treat us as equals." Whether his comment was really about pigs, it worked for me. These two knew I had their best interests at heart, and I really did. I knew they had their best interests at heart, and they did. We understood each other perfectly.

In a scant four or five minutes, every last carrot peel, lettuce leaf, beet green, corn husk, onion skin, grass root and luscious turtle-green leaf – was gone. I turned to my stand-by, ferns. I knew they grew along the roadside, ran and started picking. I dashed back with a heaping armful of the delicate greens, and dumped them over the side of the pen. The pigs ate as fast as a child chewing candy, probably faster. Done, they looked around. More candy? I went back for more ferns, again and again, until I had stripped the roadside of ferns, an eighth of a mile in both directions. My friends were still hungry.

What else could I feed them? I had no more organic goodies to give away, no veggies, no more grass, leaves or sweet ferns. I looked around. Outside their pen, I had now uprooted virtually everything. Gone were dandelions and fiddleheads, crabgrass and every sort of weed. Inside their pen, they had done the same. There was nothing left, nothing left outside their pen, except pine needles – of which there was an ample supply. I surveyed the whole lot. There were no more options.

Wait a minute, I thought, *why not try pine needles? I had never tried pine needles. If these two pigs are really hungry, if they eat grass, ferns and leaves, dandelions, fiddleheads and weeds, why not give pine needles a try?* There was the vaguest semblance of logic to my thinking, since the two pigs had eaten absolutely everything I had offered to them. In a two-week period, they had refused nothing. Their pen was no more than mud and roots, so they had no pine needles, just as they had no ferns or grass. I decided that, if they were really hungry, they would eat this flat, pliable, tasteless leaf – so to speak – of a pine tree.

I gathered the freshest pile, including the most delicate selection of pine needles I could find. I made sure there were no twigs, no sticks hidden in the pile. I favored moist pine needles, since they were the closest to ferns and grass. Then, I dumped my entire lot into their pen. The two pigs rushed over to the pile of pine needles, as if dashing to consume beet greens, apple cores and fresh corn husks. They stuck their happy, flat noses straight into the middle of my big pile. They snorted and cooed, and then – they stopped.

They did not eat them. They did not seem to like what they were sniffing at, or else they were not hungry. True, they might have eaten fresh tomatoes. Our refrigerator's vegetable bin was, however, empty. They might have eaten succulent ferns, but there were no more to pick. They suddenly took what seemed an intellectual view of this old exercise, eating. They were all at once discerning, almost Parisian in their disposition toward food. My generous pile of pine needles sat there, untouched. They wagged their curly tails a little, then meandered away, nosing along the ground for neglected nibbles.

For me, I was also satisfied. We had not resolved any of the topics discussed – from leadership to economic growth, Red Sox batting order to celery production, but we had made progress on this front. We had moved one topic ahead, one that seemed to matter to all three of us: How to satisfy a pig's constant craving for everything, that is, how to fill them up.

Whether pine needles represented the limit for any discerning peccary palette, or were just inedible, they served a wonderful purpose. They capped a two-week feeding bonanza, leading my two piggy friends to an uncharacteristic display of good taste or self-control, and giving me the satisfaction of rendering them, if not full, seemingly full. I cycled away, quite happy. As I did, they prowled their pen and continued to discuss matters between themselves. They may have been cursing me, or bemoaning the degree to which I misunderstood the world, but I prefer to think they were murmuring on my endless generosity or their own sense of culinary taste and discernment, if not satisfaction.

29. Fallen Brother

Well, you know Richie. And Tom and George. You know Peter, and his siblings. You have heard about others, including Richie's three brothers, who all went to war, all came home. You recall Tink, our longtime postmaster, one of Richie's brothers, and how he married Lila, our longtime town manager. You read about Vern, who ran the Wayne General Store, and his brother Harold, who worked in the crutch factory. You recall Linc, who taught me English. In association with the island camp, you may recall General Spivey and, of course, the "Chief."

Our lives were touched by these veterans, shaped by that generation's selfless service – to America and to us. They were all tested, somewhere. Most came home, but … not all. One who did not, was Priscilla's brother, Ford. Priscilla was mother of Chris, who drove the snow plow. Chris, you recall, had five brothers, Doug, Ford, Craig, John and David. No coincidence that one of Priscilla's children was named Ford, another Doug, for her husband – who served in WWII.

I knocked, no answer. So, I pressed the screen door and went in. We do that in Maine. "Hello, anyone home?" Apparently, not. I put down the blueberry pie. I looked around for a notepad. Finding one, I scratched a message and stuck it under the pie. "Priscilla, sorry to have missed you …" I was just turning away, when a friend appeared from within. "Are you looking for Priscilla?" "Well, yes …" I said. "She is in the living room, let me just tell her you are here!" I thanked her, and made my way around several corners. Maine farmhouses are like that, big in all directions.

There she was, Priscilla herself. She sat comfortably in a high-backed chair, attentive, unassuming, and happy for company. She looked more at ease in her living room than most people do asleep. Nevertheless, she was alert, a kingfisher on her branch. What had she not seen? She had seen it all. Perhaps more true to nature, she was another eagle, comfortable in her nest. A widow now, she had raised six boys. With poise, she sat well-dressed, eyes quick and clear. Her voice had no quaver, her eyes no hesitation, even at the age of 97. In 2017, a persistent quick wit, she turned 100.

Before long, we were talking. That is why I had come, to talk with her. We do that too in Maine, just drop by and talk. Only today, I had come with higher purpose. I had come to talk – or listen – on a specific topic. I had come to meet her brother. Not literally, but figuratively. I was not quite sure how I was going to start this conversation, maybe like any other. But it was different, difficult. I wished I had started it years before, knew or felt I should have. He was one of those names etched in granite, on the memorial to our fallen, there beside the Mill Pond. His name was Joseph Ford Berry. He was her only brother. He had died in World War II.

I had girded myself for this conversation, assuming it might be emotional. One of her sons had encouraged me to visit, see if she would talk about him. I imagined a slow dialogue, filled with difficult and important memories, maybe teary eyes, certainly some long pauses, questions gently asked and answers carefully formulated. I was in no hurry. Still, the emotional side I was not looking forward to.

On the other hand, her recollections would be precious. She was the only one left who had really known him. I thought it might be cathartic to speak about him. I hoped it would. I imagined that this consolation might compensate for the intrusion I was making on her time and peace. I wondered to myself: *When was the last time she did talk about him? It could have been decades.* Still, her brother was, like she was, a piece of town history. So, the conversation was important – even if it would be sad, conducted in soft tones, could ebb and flow, and might not flow at all. She might not want to speak about him. If not, we would enjoy talking about the weather, friends, relatives and blueberry pie.

Boy, was I wrong. Within seconds, I was diagonally across from her in a slightly lower chair, answering a barrage of well-formulated questions. *Wow,* I thought, *is this upside down!* I had come to interview her, living pillar of the town, and now she was interviewing me. Closing on her first century, mother of those six strapping sons, grandmother and great-grandmother, she still managed her own labyrinthine house and gorgeous hillside farm. I should have guessed she had not gone from eagle to sparrow so soon. What was more, she did these things – and was asking incisive questions of me – as if all 97-year-olds did the same.

My last drop-in had been when she was 94. Not much had changed. At that time, I had walked in and found her cooking vigorously in her farm kitchen, by herself, no one else assisting. She had several pots bubbling and was in the process of making stew from scratch. The stew's savory scent filled the house. I laughed aloud, could not help it. Why, I had asked, all the food? Oh, she was making supper for a friend. The friend had fallen from a ladder working on her house, and broken several ribs. The friend was another lady in town, herself pushing into her 80s! The friend was Lois, whose husband was Peter and son Will, my friend. I laughed again. Then – and now – the thought occurred to me: *Where does America get these women, these unbreakable, unstoppable, un-self-pitying pioneers, these quiet pillars among us?*

On that first visit, I had told her I could not believe she did all this, and without complaint. She scoffed. "Age! What is age? Just a number. I think people ought to forget about the numbers. It does not matter. What matters is what you do, how you feel, what you make of the day after you get up. Age is not important." All this she said with absolute conviction, cutting vegetables, cutting meat, stirring them into the stew. She confounded expectations, making me wonder if she was not right. That had been three years ago. And here she was still, marching bravely on.

Now, I sat again with her, this crackerjack personality, confident and irrepressible, indomitable, cheerful and ready for any impromptu visitors – at 97. All of a sudden, I was caught in a windstorm, unexpectedly subject to her *tour de force.* Those great wings flapped slowly, but consciously. Her questions were sensitive but pointed, like the tip of a feather. She lifted the conversation, guided it and helped it glide topic to topic, no drag. Priscilla had known me – and my mother, grandmother, aunt, cousins, and siblings – all her life, and we her. But one thing was instantly clear: I had not stopped by *often enough.* And there was penance to pay for my oversight. I was getting the royal treatment, a string of polite and sociable questions, each one thoughtful, but posed systematically and expectantly, each deserving of a good answer.

Like my mother, grandmother and aunt – with whom she had worked – Priscilla was a former school teacher. Two of my siblings are teachers. You know about school teachers, right? They see the world as a classroom. An enormous blackboard – or today white board – follows them everywhere. All moments are intended for teaching or learning. They are most comfortable with chalk in hand, perhaps these days an electronic teaching implement. And they are good with questions. They never run out. So, there I sat – in the presence of a seasoned teacher, answering questions. This was not bad, just not what I had expected. The questions tumbled out, one upon the other, dice from a Yahtzee cup. I tried to keep up, giving complete answers in full sentences, without extra adverbs, hoping not to boldly go where every student does, and split my infinitives.

Her intent was all goodness and light, and she was right, I was lazy. Or at least tardy. So, Priscilla wanted to know about my kids, where were they at school? One already in college? Where was that? What was he studying? And my other child? And where was she? And what was she studying? And about the job, a company? What did my company do? And what did I do for the company? And how about my schedule, while back in town? And for how long was I back? And when would I return? Ah, that was nice. Each question spot on, kindly but clear, thoughtful, useful in filling gaps left by my tardiness. The windstorm was a product of my poor visiting record. She gave me time to answer, then on to the next topic.

This was funny, very funny. After all, I was the one who had come with pointed questions. Or that is what I had thought. Yet here she was, conducting the interview. That was Priscilla, inquiring and engaged. Age was irrelevant. She was interested in others, interested in the world, and unintimidated by either. She was the quintessential mother, grandmother, great-grandmother, teacher, leader and daughter. She was also, as I was soon to learn, a quintessential sister, admiring, independent, thoughtful, inextricably tied to memories of her brother. Eventually, we came back around to that topic, her brother.

She suggested, as I prepared for my little interview, we get pieces of blueberry pie. I tried to demur, but she would have none of it. My excuses were unavailing, as if I were blaming my undone homework on a dog. She noted that it was nearly lunch time, and that she loved blueberry pie. So, up she popped and after her I followed. We were soon relocated in the three-season room, a large porch overlooking her whole farm and adjoining lands, under the watchful gaze of an enormous moose. The moose's rack expanded into the room from the wall. He beautified the room, like meandering branches of a live oak, or perhaps of an old Main Street elm. Here, she invited me to have a seat, have some pie, and ask away with my questions. "So, what can I tell you?"

I started by noting that, with an interest in history and town, I had recently visited the granite memorial again, stopping to read the names. I did not have to tell her what the memorial looked like. She knew. How many times she had stopped, if ever, I do not know. But the memorial had been there all of my life, probably more than half of hers. And she had lived her entire life – up to this point – in Wayne. In a flat spot, the granite reads: "Wayne Memorial Park. In memory of the veterans of Wayne who served in all our wars. Dedicated May 30, 1949." Below these words: "To those who made the supreme sacrifice in World Wars I and II. World War I – 1914-1918. Benjamin P. Bradford. Leland Gordan. World War II – 1941-1945. *Joseph Ford Berry.* George E. Dodge. Paul W. Manter." The whole thing stands no more than elbow high, four feet wide. Behind it, water.

After a little background, I came to the point. I hoped she would help me bridge the gap in time – and get to know her brother. Well, yes, she could do that. She responded with no hesitation, perhaps a twinge of curiosity, but nothing worth further questions. She had obviously not been asked much about him, or not in a very long time. She was happy to oblige, almost eager.

To me, Joseph Ford Berry, was a fallen eagle. He was a patriot from our town who had not come home. He deserved more than a few inches of granite, precious as they were. She might help me bring him back to life for a time and in a way. I wanted to get to know him, that far away spirit so close to home.

To her, the exercise was very different. He was, after all, her brother. He was, by definition, a patriot, yes of course. But first and foremost, he was her brother – and more than that. He was not her soldier brother, not her warrior or patriot brother, not her hero or dead brother, but her beloved brother, a brother to whom she was still very close, if only in memory. If he had prematurely taken leave, if it had been assigned before he wished, he was still in many ways here. At least for her, he was still here. That was the impression with which one was left.

To most questions, she gave ready and vivid answers. Sometimes, if I asked a particular question, she paused to collect the details before answering. Her answers were given in complete sentences, and seemed to come from a complete picture. Her mind seemed to see into the past with clarity. She just had to check on the picture. On one or two occasions, with no undue emotion and a slight apology, she would say, "It was a long time ago, you know …" And I would nod. Then she would resume. She would continue looking back into the past with her quick, clear eyes, and relaying to me what she saw there. It really was like that, as if she were looking at him again, seeing him distinctly through a key hole in time's locked door, yet completely – as if she could touch him through a crack in mortality's impenetrable wall, and then tell me again the feeling. This was what I had so hoped she might do, and she did it.

She was looking in on herself, too – which must have been funny. She saw herself first as a girl intent on helping her mother, since "girls did that." Then, she was the admiring sister, before becoming a young lady, eventually a newlywed. The fog of time cleared for her, as I had hoped it would. She was an eagle riding her own thermal, vanquishing time as she rose above it. With a strong mind and memory, she took me to a place above it all, from which we could both look back. It was a stretch rich and saturated with lively events, cooled only slightly by forgetting. Fog gone, she spoke plainly of her youth – and his. What she saw, surprised me.

I had been prepared for emotion, but not the emotions I encountered. What she saw was not sadness, not even articulated regret, although these two emotions lingered somewhere off stage. I imagined that they were stored in a dusty trunk, one with which she was all too familiar. Instead, most of what she saw and relayed was genuinely joyous, at times amusing to her, whimsical when placed in modern context, a reason for quiet laughter. I was slow to ask and careful not to interrupt once I did. But this time, she let me do the asking. She flipped roles, and offered answers.

Slowly, her answers became more complete, her focus grew better. I became peripheral. Her range finder locked onto subjects far away in time – and brought them closer. Her field of vision expanded, giving her wider latitude for comment – which she used. She took the visual images that came to her, that only she possessed, and shared them. I had hoped she would. It was a great privilege to be able to listen. And in this way, she helped me to meet her brother, another great privilege. I was stuck in time, sitting here at the table, over my blueberry pie, under the vigilant moose, but she was out there, back there, far away. Still, I tried to see what she saw, and slowly he emerged as more real. He was, as I knew he would be, far more than a name, even thoughtfully immortalized, in granite. He was real.

"You know, he was a regular guy, a man's man, just a regular guy. He loved athletics, especially baseball. He did play football, but he loved baseball. We did not get a lot of spare time, not on a farm. He worked with my father a lot, cleaning the barn, with the cows…" I could not see the farm the way she saw it, but I could conjure a good guess. I could imagine chores before sunup, muscles built lifting and hauling – happily reconditioned to fielding hard-hit balls, swinging a big bat at a distant fence, or no fence at all.

"He had an interest in forestry. When the time came for college, he went off to college in New Hampshire, University of New Hampshire. He won a scholarship. He was on an ROTC scholarship …." So there was one important fact. Her brother had not necessarily been an enthusiast for war. He had been an athlete and a scholar, hard worker, trained to duty. As a college graduate, his eyes had been on forestry. Yet he ended up at war, and fought with valor. Why? Perhaps by choice, perhaps by obligation. He had risen to fulfill his ROTC scholarship commitment. True enough, he had chosen ROTC. But what other scholarship options were there in that day? Strange, too, it washed over me. The first boy to fall in *All Quiet on the Western Front,* epic World War I novel by Erich Paul Remarque, was 19-year-old Franz Kemmerich, who on his deathbed confesses, "I wanted to become a head forester once."

"Once he left for the war, he did write letters home, mostly to my mother. He was a good brother and a good son. I do not know what happened to those letters … He was named Joseph, but was always called Ford. You see, my great-grandfather was named Peleg Ford Pike. My father wanted to name him Peleg, but my mother put her foot down. She said no to Peleg." Priscilla laughed out loud here. "Peleg, you know, that would have been a tough name …" I could see her point, but there was history in that name, too. She seemed glad he had ended up Ford, not Peleg. She named one of her six sons Ford. None of them, so far as I know, was given the name Peleg. Certainly none of them was ever known by that name.

"We all went to school in a horse and wagon, in winter a horse and sleigh. It was a two or three seat pung, we used to call it. It was pulled by one horse. It would take us down to the school and home each day. The school was where the library is now …." She paused and seemed to see the school, describing it as small. She noted that "the kids had to bundle up" for rides down to school in the sleigh. "It was a long ride." A little research helped me see the pung more clearly. As she had described it, the pung was a one-horse box sleigh, with several seats. Interestingly, the word is derived from an Algonquin word for something similar. The Algonquin is "tom-pung," source also for the word toboggan. Priscilla turned back to describing her brother.

Was he good with guns? "Well, yes, he hunted once or twice, but that was enough. He preferred fishing. He would catch perch, pickerel and trout. He liked the woods and liked the lake. He could fish for hours. At home, we sometimes played a card game called Flinch. We also played checkers. He liked checkers." So here was more important information. He was handy with firearms, but preferred fishing. Yes, he could shoot, but it did not light his fire. He was more a fisherman and baseball player, enjoying Flinch and checkers at home with his sister. He must have been patient to have made time – after chores, baseball and fishing – to play cards and checkers with his sister. And he had left her with the impression, perhaps entirely true, but important enough to be remembered by her, that he liked playing checkers *with her*. As for Flinch, some modest research reveals that it was a card game, yes. It was invented in 1901 by another farming family. It used its own peculiar cards, and centered on the importance of stockpiling, always important for a farm family. Here then was leisure with a lesson.

Priscilla went on. "He was very good in school, too … and I was proud of him. He was well-rounded, an intellectual, but not too musical. He liked to read adventures, and that included the Horatio Alger series. And he just loved to play baseball … He played in high school and in college … not as fond of football. The family did not want him to play football." So here I mused again on a young man who was, at once, an intellectual and loved baseball, but who played football and probably demurred to assuage a mother's concerns about safety. In those days, Knute Rockne was coaching Notre Dame, but the game was filled with injuries. Leather helmets were used into the 1930s. Concussions (or worse) were common. Perhaps he liked football, but gave it up for family peace of mind. Or perhaps he really did not like football, but gave it a try. In all events, he loved baseball.

As for the Horatio Alger series, that was not likely assigned by school teachers. The series centered on inspirational themes, including heroism and entrepreneurship. While popular, the books had been out for decades before Ford read them. They featured boys or young men who rose from relative poverty through hard work and common decency to various definitions of success. They almost always involved acts of bravery, which were later recognized. The principles illustrated were sound, books engaging, but stories all fiction. One does wonder to what extent, if any, they motivated the actions or sustained the soul of a young, college-educated soldier grown up in a farming family.

Priscilla had certain memories that spoke volumes. "He always came home for Christmas … He would come through Augusta, Winthrop, Leeds or East Livermore … He always came home." Yes, that part mattered enough to be stored away, the coming home times. Christmas must have been special fun, times of special peace. As we worked through various smaller questions, she would occasionally stop me and go back to add a missing detail, or add something new. At one point, she went back to scholarship, to the fact that he was an intellectual, but had not thrilled to play music. She corrected herself. He had "played the trumpet, although he generally did not like playing music." And what more needed to be said about that? There are those who have musical talent, and those – like me – who have considerably less. He was fully able, but preferred reading, fishing and baseball. Nevertheless, he obviously had taken time to learn.

He could read music and play the trumpet, an instrument difficult to master. One wonders if he ever used that skill in uniform, perhaps as a bugler.

I asked her about her own interests in girlhood, or at the time her older brother was playing the trumpet, baseball and fishing. She had clear memories here, too. "I played the flute as a girl, and played the piano. I did not like the piano, however, as much as the flute. I liked the flute. Mother was a musician. She had a number of piano students. She could play the organ, too. She would play the organ in church." I thought about the time required to master those two instruments, and wondered where that time came from – if this little girl was also helping her mother with the chores. There must have been, in town and across the country, heavy emphasis on self-discipline – or perhaps just on discipline. Kids, especially farm kids, learned to use time well, not to waste it.

Priscilla explained that her parents had sent both her brother and herself to college. She had ended up in Boston, after Farmington, not in New Hampshire. She had finished at Boston University. Her interest had always been teaching. She had gone to college hoping to teach. Her brother had finished college, and so had she. He had aimed to go into forestry, and she into teaching. They *each* had their dreams. While her brother knew farming and had "helped father" cleaning the barn and with cows, he had also helped with plowing, and "the plow was pulled with a horse, no tractor." Still, he had gone to college; he had other plans. And their parents seemed to want them each to realize their dreams.

For a moment, hearing this, I was thrown back to another memory – those two 16 mm tapes from Androscoggin Island, the ones we had accidentally rescued, both of which were filmed in the 1930s. Why? Because in the background of those tapes, as camp boys played games, Wayne farmers – and they were *Wayne farmers* – had guided farm horses across open land near the camp. The horses had each been pulling a plow. What is more intriguing, these camp games – or some of them – were actually filmed on the "Wayne Desert," land that adjoined a farm owned by the Berry family. And this was Priscilla's maiden name, Berry. Was it possible that the farmer or farmers in those tapes, the ones near the Wayne Desert and guiding horses with plows, included either Priscilla's father or brother? I could not say, and in all likelihood neither could she. Still, with their distinctive hats and postures, build and movements, one wondered if it might be possible to figure out their identities. To date, this remains an unsolved mystery, but one is given to wonder ….

As Priscilla described heading off to college, aspiring to teach and becoming trained to teach, there was just a faint sense that this expectation might have been positively influenced by someone other than her determined parents, possibly by someone who preceded her. Could she have felt empowered, encouraged to head for college – at a time when women did not often do so from a farming life – by her brother? What had she said several times? "He was a very good brother." She did travel in circles with him outside the home, too. At least a little. That is how she recalls meeting her husband, who hailed from out of state and showed up in Wayne during summers. "Ford was a baseball player in high school and college, but also on the town team each summer… I helped mother in the kitchen and gardening, played piano, but also went to Ford's baseball games. He could play different positions. He was very good. That is how I met my husband, for the first time … either at one of those baseball games that Ford played in or at the yacht club at a dance." So Ford had been a "very good brother," accompanying his younger sister to local dances in summer; and she had been a very good sister, accompanying him to the baseball field.

How funny life is. Two children, bound to each other by the timeless force of brotherhood, sisterhood, and strong family; defined in their own eyes and each other's by work and play, farm chores and fishing, music and sport; held tight in youth through sibling protection and reliance, an unspoken two-way adoration, since it must have been two-way; knowing one another's stamina and worries, resolve and life ambitions, hoping with and for each other; bound through hours bundled in a winter sleigh and that common transition to college from the farm – yet also by laughter of checkers jumping one another, cards played, and Christmases shared; as dear as any family bond could be … suddenly cut from each other, tragically and irreversibly, without recourse or even consolation. "You sink into a hole … it is devastating." Priscilla paused on that reality, but only briefly. That singular fact, his young death, was less consequential than all that preceded it. Life triumphs over death, she seemed to be saying. Positive memories triumph over the evil that robbed her of more.

Her late husband Douglas, affectionately known as "TDO" (for his initials), was himself a living legend, a lifetime teacher, community leader and avid sailor. Overflowing with life knowledge, unselfconscious enthusiasm, quick wit and playful exhortation, he loomed large behind that broad, all-knowing smile.

TDO had stories to tell, left mostly untold. As part of the 49th Brigade, he landed on Omaha Beach, White Dog sector, Normandy invasion, at 'D plus 6 hours.' Day One, he was promoted to captain, on the beach. His commanding general strode the beach fearlessly, rallying the men. That said, TDO seldom spoke of war.

The impression left was that TDO felt World War I had been much ballyhooed, encouraging young Americans to sign up for World War II lightly. He would not be party to making war romantic. Perhaps there was something more. If TDO was introduced to his wife by her brother, TDO knew him too. The loss of a fallen soldier is felt widely.

Fast forward to this very minute with me, 80 years later. Here I sit, with Priscilla. Here she sits with me, one of those two devoted siblings, bringing the other back to life. Her tone is not defeatist or discouraged. It is triumphant, resolved to convey the happiness she found in being the sister of a brother she adored. "He did not talk a lot, he was quiet … You know, he liked to fish. But he was a good brother … and he always came home at Christmas. When he went away, he wrote letters to Mother. He was an intellectual, and he loved baseball. He was just a regular guy." In that brief stanza, she summed up the conversation.

Yes, perhaps, he was "just a regular guy." Or maybe not. Maybe Joseph Ford Berry was much more than a regular guy. Maybe he was a son that reached upward for his parents and his sister, as well as himself, setting his eyes on a career in forestry – making a commitment to his country, through ROTC. Maybe he was a son who steered clear of football, to put his mother's mind at ease. Maybe he was a brother who made sure there was time for checkers and cards with his sister, even after barn chores, bringing in the cows, plowing behind that workhorse, baseball games, trumpet practice and studies that would get him into college. Maybe he was the sort of good brother who made sure his little sister was bundled tight in the sleigh to and from school, just as he watched over her at local dances, including the one where she met her future husband.

Maybe all these things came naturally to Ford, as naturally as fishing and fielding, and so maybe his highest aspiration – when all was said and done, had he known what lay in store, would not have been to be recalled a dead war hero for posterity, but something very different: To be remembered in a lively, liberating way as "just a regular guy" by his sister, and by all those he loved the most, including the town for which he fought. Maybe, after all, some part of Ford's aspiration has been and can be still fulfilled.

His exceptionalism, distilled 80 years on, might be remembered in the humble appellation, just the way he has been remembered by his sister – as "a regular guy." I put it to you, what is better – a few inches on a granite block for eternity, or being loved and remembered as "just a regular guy?" Such a man was Priscilla's brother, Joseph Ford Berry. And how many other young men, patriots for sure, but sons, husbands, fathers and brothers, are more alive today if we remember them as national heroes second, members of their loving families first?

These eagles, after all, did not come from a void, and should not disappear into one. Whether they made the return flight or not, they hailed from nests in which they learned love, wisdom and commitment. They gave because they knew what giving was. We honor them by remembering that they were and are, each and every one, more than heroes etched in stone. They are men who, more often than not, loved much and were much loved; who were exceptional for having died to preserve freedom, but in other ways, too. Their exceptionalism is personified in Joseph Ford Berry, a "very good brother" who still inspires love after 80 years, "just a regular guy."

Postscript – In mid-2018, I sat down again with Priscilla, this time with her son Ford. She was bright-eyed, full of conversation, soon turning 101. Her son Doug had just run the 2018 Memorial Day ceremony, flawlessly. Her sons Ford and John had recently gone to Italy, one mission: Find their uncle's grave and battle site. They did.

Here is what I learned: Joseph Ford Berry, Priscilla's brother, that "regular guy," was actually more than a "regular guy." For his actions during World War II, he was awarded the Distinguished Service Cross. His citation reads, in part: "For extraordinary heroism … in action against enemy forces on 11 July 1943, in Sicily."

More explicitly: "When the enemy hurled an attack of 30 or 40 tanks against the recently established beachhead, Captain Berry … fearlessly left a concealed position and made his way over hundreds of yards of heavily shelled terrain in the path of the approaching tanks to reach an abandoned anti-tank gun."

More: "Captain Berry engaged the enemy armor at almost point-blank range and continued to fire even after a tank had encircled his position. Captain Berry remained at this position engaging the enemy until he was mortally wounded."

His citation's conclusion: "Captain Berry's courage and heroism, resulting in loss of his life, materially contributed to the eventual defeat of the enemy. His inspiring leadership, personal bravery and zealous devotion to duty at the cost of his life, exemplify the highest traditions of the military forces of the United States and reflect great credit upon himself, the 1st Infantry Division, and the United States Army."

This is what really happened when Priscilla's brother, that "regular guy" from a small Maine town, felt compelled to save others, at enormous risk to himself. He knew the risk. He did not flinch. He did not think of himself. He gave everything – his life. For such extraordinary Americans, we can only be brought to silence and enduringly grateful. That is why it is worth remembering, as Priscilla still does, her fallen brother.

Priscilla's brother, Joseph Ford Berry, pre-war photo

Joseph Ford Berry, WWII-era photo, killed in action, 11 July 1943, Sicily. Awarded Distinguished Service Cross for heroism in combat.

Priscilla's husband TDO (Doug Stevenson), WWII-era, probably in France after D-Day invasion. TDO participated in Normandy invasion, June 6, 1944, storming Omaha Beach under fire, at "D-plus 6 hours"

Circa early 1970s, young Priscilla and TDO with family (left to right, back row to front), Doug, Ford, Craig, Chris, then David, mother Priscilla, father TDO (Doug), and John.

Priscilla in her older years, now approaching 101 in 2018

30. Mike's Century

Not all of the Greatest Generation went to war. Some served at home, like Harold. They too were beacons. They influenced our lives as much as those who went. One of the big influences on my life was Mike. Mike is not who you think.

In 1908, things were good in America and Maine. No wars. A boy with fond memories of Maine was president of the United States. Theodore Roosevelt, true to his enthusiasms, was busy preserving parks and spreading "peace through strength." One of his dictums described the times. "Keep your eyes on the stars, and your feet on the ground." He did that, and so did most Americans. They aimed high, worked hard, stayed inspired, and were realistic. Inventiveness and daring were a happy pairing – both were on a rip.

The first "around the world" race, New York to Paris, occurred in February, 1908. France, Italy and Germany put in a good showing. America won. The Americans drove a Thomas Flyer 22,000 miles. Only transit to Alaska and crossing the Pacific required a boat; the Bering Strait was unpassable. TR hosted them at the summer White House. Fitting, as he was the first president to ride in a car – and in an airplane. "Can do" was his motto, and all America's.

What a year! In May, "Mother's Day" was celebrated for the first time. By September, Henry Ford was rolling out his Model T. In October, the Chicago Cubs won the World Series – second in a row, last for 108 years! Banner year for Hollywood, too. Born were Jimmy Stewart, Bette Davis, Milton Berle and Carole Lombard. Politics got a bumper crop, with Lyndon Johnson, Harry Blackmun, and Adam Clayton Powell, Jr. Meantime, science got John Bardeen, future Nobel winner in physics, twice – once for the transistor, again for superconductivity. The first gave us electronics, telephones, and computers. The second gave us lifesaving MRI technology.

One other thing happened in 1908 – in rural Maine. Not as publicized as the car race, five days before Christmas, a little girl was born. Many missed it. TR had other things to wrestle. The Wright brothers were distracted, another flight. Maine's Joshua Chamberlain, Civil War hero and Bowdoin professor, was alive – but likely giving speeches. Winston Churchill, then a budding 24-year-old, was getting married. Nevertheless, in South Gardner, one family got an early gift. Her name was Marguerite Rand. She would grow up nicknamed Mike.

Mike was married at 22, and had three children, Joan and twins, Jean and John (Jack). She was a nurse by 30, widow at 60, remarried and was widowed again at 74. Midstream, she moved to a little town – our town. Standing less than five feet tall, she was a giant, in church and civic life. Over time, Mike spent 32 years as a Girl Scout leader, served the town library, led groups devoted to senior citizens. Early on, she made house calls with doctors, back when those were done. She was a Maine guide of another sort, never preachy. She and Jean helped local kids learn the service ethic, concern first for others. They lived the ethic, turning Sunday sermons real.

Whether organizing Christmas caroling, teaching unruly boys to be acolytes, or lifting all spirits as a Sunday greeter, Mike – and then Jeanie – guided and grounded us. In time, Mike taught us to be confident when *we* welcomed people to church. She taught us how to escort people to a pew, make them at home. By actions, she taught the unblinking standard.

Mike never spoke about deep thinking. She never lectured on faith. She never judged youth's failings. When I arrived in sneakers or a crumpled suit; when I dropped candles and missed cues, her counsel was firm but kind. She picked words carefully, just the right number, not too many. We knew, without her saying so, her eyes were on the stars, feet on ground. She had done plenty of learning, suffering and smiling before we came along.

She taught in subtle ways. Words of the Bible mattered; so did people. She was exceptional at listening and watching. Mother of a young child got an aisle seat, close to the back. Parishioner hard of hearing was second to the front. Unless requested, no one was forced into the front row. Longtime devotees of a window got it. Those shy about being there could sit to the rear. Those friendly with another found themselves nearby. She seemed to understand what lay behind words. In time, watching her, we started to understand – and listen better.

Mike modeled authority, almost silently. Now, there is a lost art! Hers was the presence that radiated respect for others, and made respect kind of catchy. She was understanding of restless families, reluctant altar boys, choir members, and anguished visitors hunting an invisible pew. She was at ease with long-haired teens (of whom I was one) and stout hearts in fragile bodies. She had seen it all. Mike was there for them – each.

As a nurse, she had a bit of Clara Barton about her, but the dry wit was more Barbara Stanwyck. Her aptitude and attitude, grace and height defied comparison. She was herself. As innumerable New England mothers, grandmothers, great-grandmothers – or in her case, great-great-grandmothers – she was tough and gentle, resolved and expectant, endlessly forgiving. Town boys stood proudly in church, beside her 60 inches. Like Clara Barton, alive when Mike was born – our local nurse was unsung and thoughtful.

The church's white steeple pointed to heaven, and the bell reminded us to look up. Mike's hair was white like the steeple. Her voice told, as the bell tolled, of important things to come. The bell was rung at her direction. When it rang, stragglers quickened their pace, even if there was *always* room. Late or early, people were glad they came. Mike was part of that. She stood in the back mostly, ushers and acolytes nearby. If the door but quivered, Mike was up – nodding to us. Smiles were exchanged and seats found. Sometimes the late family was ours.

At Christmas, Mike radiated the season's joy. One arm squeeze said, "Glad you are here." That made us want to return. High school football players and cross-country runners fell into formation for Mike. Her step was light. She was physically fragile, spiritually strong. If angels ever grow old, they must look like Mike.

How many decades Mike mentored and greeted, I cannot say. How many young people she guided, I don't know. We all grew up, many moved away, at least for a while. I would come back, but never enough. One year, although "away," she and Jeanie asked if I might usher at Christmas. That was high honor. When things got quiet, Mike took my elbow. "You've done well, Bobby," she nodded. The words meant everything, coming from her.

I visited Mike, for what was our last real time, in 2010. As usual, we enjoyed a leisurely chat. She was happy as ever. Glad for the visit, she was still quick of wit. At home with Jeanie, comfortable beside the Mill Pond, she sat on her couch. She had been watching reruns of *The Lawrence Welk Show*. Jeanie laughed and told me she always "dreamed of … taking care of Mom when she got old," now she had her wish! Mike's laugh also rang out, like the church bell. She was then 101 years old. How did she do it?

I introduced her to my teenage son, and his friend. I am sure she imagined they were good parishioners, which they were. In a way, removed by a generation, she was part of his life, too. We talked of the old days – and new. We talked of how things had changed – and not much. I was graying, hair thinner. Mike's was unchanged, her old self. She radiated dignity, just as if in church. These days, she had 16 great-grandchildren, six great-great-grandchildren! Not bad.

In 2012, I saw her again near the post office, with Jeanie. Both laughed and smiled. Mike gave her hallmark wave, she saw me before I saw her. In September of 2012 – at the age of 103, two months shy of 104 – she returned to her Lord. He never keeps us beyond our time. She was a beacon, that girl born in 1908, five days before Christmas. Grown old, she went home. Having greeted others, she was now to be greeted.

To think about Mike and her generation, is to think about America at its best, giving and confident, duty and service, content with what lies ahead, grateful for what came before. Their century was America's century. Born when TR strode the White House, Mike arrived to a world with no cars, never mind highways. No air travel, just whooping cranes in the sky. Two World Wars lay ahead, unimaginable. Undiscovered still were telephones, microphones, and gramophones. Ahead lay Lindbergh's crossing of the Atlantic. Further still, a rocket engine, then Saturn Five, America's triumphant walks on the moon. Not imagined yet were battleships and submarines, computers and Internet, cell phones and cellular research, nuclear power and radiological medicine. No antibiotics, avionics, radio or television. The vast majority of what surrounds us today – simply did not exist. She weathered it all, with unblinking faith.

At her memorial service, three Psalms got read. She asked for them, specifically. The 23rd, 46th and 121st – and their first lines are telling: "The Lord is my Shepherd …," "God is our refuge and strength," and "I lift up my eyes to the hills …" She lived the Psalms, taught by doing, took comfort in the promise, and lifted her eyes to the hills. Stefan – my pal from youth – was asked by Mike to sing a song at the memorial. Like many Mainers, he was musical. Unlike many, he had a remarkable, resonant voice. She might have asked him to sing any popular song. She did not. She asked humbler fare. Stefan returned to her a portion of the kindness she gave to others, singing "You'll never walk alone." She never did. And because of that, we never did.

Wayne Church, our town's unchanging centerpiece

Mike, lifetime friend and mentor, was vigorous to 103

Winter Thrills

"I wonder if the snow loves the trees and fields, that it kisses them so gently? And then it covers them up snug, you know, with a white quilt; and perhaps it says 'Go to sleep, darlings, till the summer comes again.'"

–Lewis Carroll

31. Winter Fury

Some winters sneaked up on us, others arrived like crashing cymbals. There were signs. Barometric pressure slowly falling – that meant a big storm was coming. We felt it, too. When one finally pounced, everything was in motion, and white overnight. Snow piled up fast, and kept on piling. Mobility was an instant challenge. We retreated indoors, to wait it out. Soon, Chris would be around with the plow.

When a whopper hit, the thing aped a marauding army, wave after wave of snow – veritable storm troopers, an unending assault. That kind of fury was hard to repulse. Sometimes these waves took out lights, tore off siding and shingles, and downed surrounding trees. In a dozen ways, winter's fury changed the routine. Swirling white, these marauders came on.

In the lead up, wind shifted and the sky changed. Temperatures dropped, as pressure slid. My job, of course, was to pile wood high by the stoves, and more the better. Getting ready was rather exciting. Stoves burned bright, long before snow flew. We stocked the woodshed for these occasions. The potbellies whistled, harmonizing with rising noise beyond the door. Front and woodshed doors shivered on their hinges, stood firm. Outside, the vengeance mounted.

Soon, siege was laid on us. Passing brigades of troopers slammed and rattled our door handles, poked indignant heads down the chimney, dashed away. In wolf packs, they prowled and howled under the eaves, throwing up a siren song. Drafts came and went. The onslaught lasted and lasted, successive bands of rabble hooting and ranting like hooligans, then chortling off.

As the storm bore down, we made more runs to the woodshed, brought in more wood. Mom was stocked with staples, knowing we would need them. That included candles and matches. You never knew about the electricity. It might be off half a month or half an hour; weeks, days or minutes, then back on, then gone again. We did not have high technology to tell us.

Through frosted windows, we watched the galloping madness! Invisible forces shook the towering pines. They never gave ground, or not much, but weren't stoic either. They winced and whined, creaked and groaned, like unoiled hinges or bad knees. They exercised free speech, and registered loud objections. At the pinnacle, these sentries might reel and recoil. Once in a while, they took a crack at the onslaught, dropped a branch. Sometimes, a trunk. Throughout the melee, branches slashed the air, pushing back against this Arctic intrusion.

Strong storms came from the northeast. They gathered over the Atlantic, then pounded the state's interior. Unforgiving torrents surged around homes, barns and woodsheds. Withering winds encircled the church and library. Snow plastered outbuildings and at least one side of the steeple. It drifted high about the townhouse, a vestige of the 1840s. Every storm swept down Main Street, up side roads, climbed Morrison Heights and blanketed our mountain.

A Nor'easter spared no one. It shellacked the Wayne General Store, whitewashed windows at the post office, covered the hand-painted "Firehouse" sign, and pushed into every nook and corner of the elementary school. A typical blizzard created rivers of snow, wriggling and writhing along empty streets, burying uncovered cars, trucks, tractors and wagons. Loose flowerpots, canvas tarps, buckets and farm tools were goners until spring.

Storm winds shook window panes, making them clink. Big winds were ubiquitous, not to be quarreled with, not gone into. A storm would spit flakes into half-moons on windowsills, daring anyone to clear them. No one did. Indignant, the snow troopers recognized no authority. They slapped shingles and doors, pouring between attic boards, descended through cracks. Now and then, a tide ebbed, but not for long. Things got quiet, then resumed.

Winter storms were unruly, undisciplined and insatiable. Inland, they swallowed mailboxes and doghouses, woodpiles and pump houses, took colossal bites. They snatched and grabbed, spun things about, got into everything. They chewed on house corners, got between logs of a woodpile, and missed no chance to knock over shovels, rakes and brooms, anything left out.

For all the fuss, they were also – I must admit – entrancing, enchanting. They knew how to hold attention. Beyond getting us out of school, they changed how the world looked. We liked that. They woke people up, brought the world outside to life. They delivered sledding, skiing, snowmen and forts.

A good blizzard focused the mind and animated the soul. For all the rage, they never beat us. We knew how to keep our stoves hot. Inside, we stayed comfortable. The town weathered storms with regularity, mostly with patience. Over a long one, irritability might surface, but it got tamped down with grace. At the height, woodstoves kept half the town warm.

And then things tapered. Fast as the barometric pressure had fallen, it rose. Flailing branches settled on their encrusted trunks. Tinkling windows stopped their shivering and jangling. Rowdy troopers retreated, winds receded. Calm filled in behind. As the thrashing stopped, peace returned. Storms came in giant, unwieldy turns, and left the same way. Like a teapot coming off the stove, they simmered and then stopped.

Brigades of arctic air would flee into the woods, speed over far hills. We could hear them for a while, then no more. Occasionally, a band of snow would tack back, then dash away. We imagined them catching up with the main storm, headed somewhere. Off they galloped, scattered flute and drum corps, exhausted and congregating beyond the horizon.

As their retreat became complete, we poked our own heads out. We surveyed what was left behind. Millions of flakes had fallen. The world had changed – until spring. Like art, snow curled around every stump and protrusion, painted the sides of trees. Impassable roads awaited the plow, and frost-heaves finally perked up.

For my part, there was shoveling to be done. If I did not snowshoe, that got me outdoors. Like stacking and lugging, it was a job. It gave the mailman the mailbox, connected the garage to the road. After shoveling, wet stuff – coat, gloves and hat – were draped over a chair or upright log, near a stove. I would stand dazed, palms out, soaking up the glorious heat.

Then, post-blizzard fun. For a while, ground squalls played hide-and-seek, circling on the wind. Flake spouts rose and fell along the road, winter magic. Pillars spun to life, danced off tipsy. Pint-sized funnel clouds glistened with a thousand crystals. Backdrafts were short-lived, but pretty, an epilogue. Silvery cones stood on point, then scattered. Clumps of powder were cajoled off the ground, took center stage, were dismissed into the wings, and settled back to earth. Powdered snow mimicked dandelion fuzz, tufts on gusts. Storms came. Storms went.

As a child, we saw storms – and loved them. We were all eyes – then feet, legs, mittens and sliding. We had a big hill. It called us out until we came. If storms kept us bottled up, the cork finally popped. We were like champagne, out without hesitation. Freezing rain was different. It left everything glassy, like Baccarat crystal. For sliding, that was grand; for driving, ice was miserable. On the plus side, it meant more time off from school.

Ice storms were especially heavy. Ice weighed on young trees, especially birches. They bowed homage, became hunchbacks. Too deep a bow, and birches snapped. Snow on lake ice displaced millions of gallons of water. The displaced water would rush around the edges and up through cracks, spreading over the ice, sometimes making a lake impassable or unsafe. These were small things, more often coming by degrees than at once.

Mostly, the world lay quiet after a blizzard, the battlefield transformed into a fairy tale. We found ourselves in a new storybook, empowered to explore. What lay outside had only a passing resemblance to what had been. Swells and rollers were mid-curl, all over the meadow. Waves stretched out to the horizon, bending and wrinkling. Ridges collided with each other, made accommodations, rippled here and hollowed out there. Wind scooped ice cream, left massive divots. Everything was reset.

Studying this vastness, we imagined an ocean, desert, mountain range, meringue pie. Little Alps and Rockies abounded where rabbit hutches had been, a Triple Divide where the chimney lived. Outdoor passages and doorframes were cupped in cols, curvaceous mountain passes. Beyond the dooryard, evergreens wore gowns, upper branches white sleeves. Pines were surrounded by foothills. The whole thing took your breath away. Different every time, only God had the blueprint for each storm. In aftermath, Creation was sanded smooth, sawdust blown free.

Best of all, everyone and everything was at peace. Chipmunks and chickadees hunkered down in their clefts and nests. Squirrels and raccoons snuggled into holes thick with milkweed fleece and woodchips. Snowshoe rabbits holed-up in insulated burrows, linked by subterranean tunnels. Deer bedded down, flat against the pine needles. Black bears snoozed, content in their solstice slumber. Most animals would soon wake, but first they slept. The world slept.

Cracking the door to morning light, we were always transformed. Time just stood still. We blinked into the light, scanning the blanket, the beauty and newness. To me, that newness was magic. This was a moment of pure wonder. The coming and going of a winter storm, that was all. That was enough.

32. Into the Aftermath

Maine kids threw themselves into the aftermath. They slid, scrambled, built forts and erected snowmen. Some promptly headed for the ski slope, while others shoveled and skated. On rare days, I did something different. I rose early and walked the great white on snowshoes.

Opening our front door, snow tumbled in. Of course, it did not belong there, not on the wood floors. And I did not belong in pajamas. Still, I drank in the freshness, held it and listened to the silence. The aftermath was transcendent. The world was muffled. The universe stood still. These magical mornings were *made* for snowshoes.

Mainers know this, too. Most New Englanders do. Even visitors appreciate the magic of an aftermath. President Theodore Roosevelt, in his teens, wrote to his mother after awaking to a Maine storm: "I have never seen a grander or more beautiful sight than the northern woods in winter ... The evergreens laden with snow make the most beautiful contrast of green and white, and when it freezes after a rain all the trees look as though they were made of crystal." Blizzards are not always crystal, but TR's words say it all. An aftermath is timeless.

Quickly, I dressed. Then I found my long-forgotten friends – unassuming leather and wood snowshoes. These friends were antique, which was part of their charm. They lived high on the woodshed wall. Today, I own a different pair. But like my old friends, my new ones have yellow webbing, leather bindings, wood frames. They are not gaudy, just practical.

These days, you can buy much lighter, streamlined, durable and computer-designed snowshoes. You can buy them of tough plastic, composite and hybrid frames. Not for me. I am happy on older ones. Being on their webs takes me back in time. Strapping them on, in my youth, connected me with a more distant past. Authenticity always trumped convenience. Besides, my friends were reliable. Most of the year, they hung unnoticed. In winter, they came down.

That pair went back to lumberjacks and woodsmen. They were plain, no paint or trim, no fancy anything. That was their beauty. They embodied exploration, tied me to people unknown. Wearing them brought me closer to old-timers, who I imagined walked their worlds of white. On those weathered webs, other feet and eyes had probed the aftermath of distant blizzards. Like me, maybe they were enchanted by what they saw, or just doing chores. On them, maybe they assessed tree damage or lake level, hunted deer or chased missing animals. Maybe they ranged closer to barn or wood pile. In any event, I walked on the same webs – so back in time.

Those old snowshoes opened a door normally kept locked. They turned the tumblers and through I went. Behind the door lay fun on unscarred, untraveled snow – and somehow the suspension of time. Most seasons, the door was bolted tight. But not on these mornings. Curiosity pushed it open. Suddenly, I was on frozen waves of snow and time.

Even then, snowshoes came in different shapes. Some were long and sleek, others big and gangly, teardrops with tails. My friends were stubby. They were pudgy, rounded in the front, no tail. They looked like hamsters or ostrich eggs, not elegant. But they worked. That was all that mattered. They held me above the snow. They did not win races, but they moved a teenage boy over the white. Who needed more?

Resting one end on our woodshed floor, my friends stood knee high. Later, I learned people called them bear paws. I liked the name. It got to their "go anywhere" reliability. What mattered in the moment was their ability to hoodwink gravity. They whisked me over meadows and stumps, brambles and granite, no complaints. On these snowshoes, I wandered among whitewashed oaks, crossed bogs, picked paths, went where I could not in other seasons.

My bear paws took me everywhere – even over stone walls. Undulating piles of continental crust, Maine's stone walls went back centuries. Once for keeping cattle and making "good neighbors," they just divided trees from trees now. But surely they could tell stories. On aftermath mornings, they seemed to.

Most stone walls appeared when my great-grandmother's great-grandmother was a little girl. That's been a while. The stones were laid on open grass, acres and acres of it. They were surrounded by grass. Farmers cut the grass with sickle and scythe. But in time, trees seeded, grew to wave over them. That past was gone. The forest took charge, but here the walls lay. They still commanded a little soil.

My great-grandmother's great-grandmother – wherever she lived – might not have imagined her great-great-great-great-grandson out in an aftermath, on snowshoes. That was a funny thought. Have you ever thought about who stood where you are now, say, two hundred years ago? Who farmed where you built, who rested where you park, who listened to the wind where you hear more? My relatives might have wondered why anyone would bother going out on new snow. Who knows? Maybe they stayed by their stoves; or maybe they visited the walls, like me.

In any event, I took the white. I pulled on wool socks, waffle long-johns, faded blue jeans, sweatshirts and mittens. I pushed arms through a winter coat, head into a cap, covered both ears. Feet went in boot liners, then L.L. Bean boots. Old-timers probably did something similar.

Then, I headed out. Always I went through the woodshed. It jutted from our main house at an angle. It was a throughway, not a destination. The floor was all woodchips. These were not imported. Each sprang from wood hit by the axe, swung by me. To one side was a wood pile. To the other, a wall, things dangling on rusty nails. Against the wall rested a pair of wooden skis. Near the skis, a kerosene lamp and farm tools. Along window sills were cans and bottles of nuts and bolts, screws and nails.

Random coils of rope hung at levels, different lengths, colors and thicknesses. They clung to the shed like passengers from an Indian train, all ready to fall off. We never knew when we might need rope. It lashed things down, dragged things out, penned them in. Coils were not ovals, not like the store. They were neat, hung in a row, and bore signs of use. They were regularly recoiled, now gray, tan, stained green or dirt. All had started white. To make a coil, we looped rope around one elbow. The result was imperfect loops, no tangles.

Looking up, a peavey rested on spikes. That was an old logging tool. Also there, a hand auger, which required inordinate elbow grease. With them, leather crampons, used on slick ice. These were the sort that gave boots shark's teeth, and got that icehouse off the lake. The woodshed did have a distinctive odor, split pine, chipped maul, rusting nails, banged boot mud and old fertilizer, a little dust and spider webs, gasoline and hinge oil. In later years, to it we added dog.

Hard to forget, the woodshed scent never became a perfume. But I related to it. It smelled of "getting things done," perspiration, preparation, and task completion. The smell did not bother me. Still, I seldom lingered, except to work.

On the floor, you did find an old axe, wedge-shaped maul and sledge. They were compatriots, loitering together like ne'er-do-wells. They leaned against a scarred stump. They seemed content to do nothing, but appearances were deceiving. The old stump was a railyard, deep cuts. Each stripe and nick came from the axe, maul or sledge. Often they just stood about, but they could swing into action if needed. The stump was thigh-high, big as a tractor tire. Anyway, the axe, maul and sledge were also friends. We split wood together. Not quite snowshoeing, splitting was therapeutic, and useful.

Of course, the woodshed had other features – flecks of curled paint on window sills, dust between bottles and cans, row of cloudy windows. I am not sure what they were for, since we could not see out them. Condensed milk cans held roofing nails, all galvanized. These days, people would say we repurposed our cans. We did not know that word, or therapeutic. Baby food jars got washers, screws, odds and ends. Add a paint scraper, hammer, and a few flower pots. That was the woodshed.

One last quirk. In winter, we reverted to going in and out through the woodshed, giving snowy boots a place to dry. At one end lay the latched house door. At the other, a door that opened in, no latch. The outer door was an example of Yankee engineering. One kick jammed it snug. One pull popped it loose. Over the years, it was tailored to the frame. It never jammed too tight, or took more than one yank to open. Both doors sealed, the inner clicked, outer jammed trim.

Back to the aftermath! On my toes, I got down the bear paws, gave the outer door a yank, pulled it snug. I strapped them on, and paused to take things in. White chased the horizon in all directions, mounded on limbs. Silence abounded. All was muffled and still.

I could go anywhere. Breathing was prickly, like peppermint. The air was alive. Lungs loved it. Frozen air tingles. It was clean, rich with oxygen, stunning to inhale. It woke me, the way mud tickling your toes wakes you. It was stimulating. This was real winter, and at its best.

An observant listener did hear something. It was hard to peg, not really a sound, almost imperceptible. The heart heard it, not ears. It was a feeling, a call. Gossamer thin and steel strong, it quieted the soul, invited exploration. Paradoxically, it invited both stillness and movement. It was excitement in the hush.

Finally, I moved. Soon, I was lumbering along, swinging arms and legs with conviction, crossing the vast snow. These outings were work, but not really. They were like a child seeing with new glasses. They awakened gratitude. To be on bear paws, striding toward any horizon, was bliss. In the bliss, I caught only my breathing, and then not much. I floated. Snowshoeing in silence was distance running, no footfalls. Stride became automatic. Eyes were in control, effort barely noticed. By degrees, I let go, found pace, in pace peace. There were no trails, the world was open, vastness immense. One became immersed in the white, no destination.

Sometimes, I tipped forward and ran. Other times I slowed, hearing my heartbeat. On occasion, I caught a tip, ended up face down laughing. My gait widened, toes rose, heels dragged, knees came up, until I forgot again. Gradually, my knees and stride found rhythm. Up and down, whoosh, whoosh, a million crystals fluttering to earth. Dry snow was weightless.

At some point, temperatures would edge up. When that happened, fluff packed. But early, movement was fluid and nothing stuck. I rode the snow like a wheel, legs churning forward, tracks pouring behind me, steady rotation. Knots untied, problems dissolved, no boundaries. Newness begat newness, outer change inner. The vastness over which I wheeled made other things insignificant. And then, before I knew it, I was home.

I would breathlessly unstrap my friends, shake them, give the outer door a kick, and replace them on the woodshed wall. In that moment, I was happy. Maybe they were, too. We had done it again, answered the call, passed through the door, travelled the vastness, wheeled the aftermath, and come home. Blizzards came and went, part of the continuum. In the aftermath, magic moments presented themselves – and you had to take them. I did.

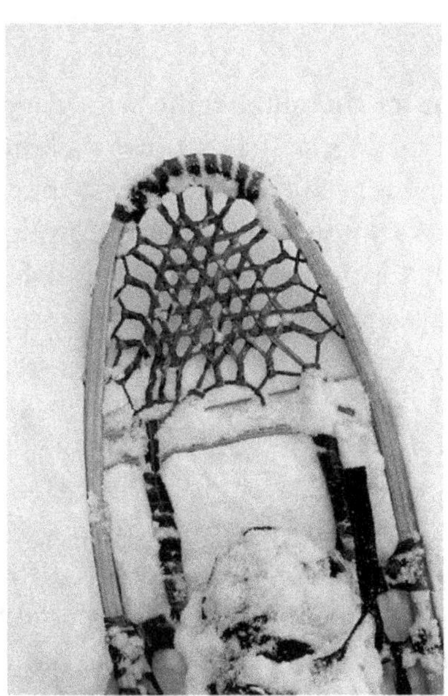

The enchantment of old snowshoes on fresh fluff

33. Diamonds and Daggers

Ice storms were rare. In their wake, snowshoes stayed on the wall. Branches fell, electricity was often lost. Anyone who stepped out went down, including adults. Harmless rain became silk, bright as diamonds, sharp as a knife. The world turned gorgeous and unnavigable, at least by cars. Tinkling on windows meant ice the next day, no school, treacherous going, awesome sledding.

Awakening, the forest was bejeweled, every single tree now royalty. For a time, Nature posed resplendent, just stood there, sparkling in the early sun. Branches wore bangles, notches and necks were bedecked, and shrubs shimmered. Birches, as mentioned before, seemed ladies in waiting, bent and servile, or perhaps just praying – for release from the ice. Pines swayed in satin gowns. Giggling duchesses gossiped in the wind, young maples. Beyond them, princesses stood everywhere, some tall and sleek, others short and stout, all stiff and unbending. Officers stood their ground, throwing light from limbs, row on row of reflecting medals. Squires loitered under the eaves with courtiers, attending to crusty kings and queens.

But ice storms, for all the glitz, came with daggers. Adults – at least some – found them irritating, restriction on walking and driving. A half-inch crust would not quite hold most adults, so they broke through, often broke something else. A trip out often meant unwelcome bruises. If adults managed to stand, if that ice crust was thick enough, if everything worked perfectly, there was the issue of propulsion. So, most stayed in.

The storm had daggers out for young trees, too. Ice abhorred svelte softwoods and slender birches. Full sun, rather ironically, was their white knight. It melted the ice. If temperatures rose, they stood tall again. If not, or if wind got into the act, all bets were off. Supple trees could snap. Snapped birches, shod of their tops, turned into giant paint brushes. The following spring, they were shaggy, wagging half-trees. Sometimes, they lived with the handicap; other times, they just could not. The forest was full of such stories, but suffice to say, ice was double edged. For all the grandeur, there was also some danger.

As kids, we cared nothing about this. Ice was fun. We had nowhere to go, no fear of falling, scant interest in tree shapes, and loved speed. What mattered was that an ice storm changed the value of a runner sled. If we dared to slide, we never stopped. Downhill runs on wooden toboggans, plastic tub sleds, metal saucers, rolls of plastic, and snow jackets were fine, even on packed snow. On snow, sled rides had a duration, distance, and predictable speed. Not so on ice.

Runner sleds, built with metal runners and wooden slats, sank into snow. On ice, they were incomparable. Suddenly, the issue was not gaining speed, but braking. We dragged feet on disinterested ice, stopping our only problem. What a problem to have! We became airborne platforms, some of us little rockets. We imagined the Olympic luge, skeleton and bobsledding. Since we were immortal, we had zero worries. We saw raw speed, and took it.

Holding a runner sled, we threw ourselves down the mountain, stomach muscles tightening as we hit the crust. And …over we went, grabbing the steering bar, hearts pounding loudly, nearly flying! Down we swept, in the grip of no friction, accelerating every yard and vertical foot dropped.

We were crazy with joy, and stupid as kids are. After the first steep descent, two successive meadows opened before us. Both tilted hard toward the woods. A stone wall ran across the lower meadow, dividing it from the woods. It had a gap, dead center. We aimed for the gap, shot for the opening.

Rod by rod, meadow by meadow, we built speed. As we gained, our eyes widened and watered. The slot became our sole focus. Growing speed compounded our fun, and confounded control. The swivel of steering bar, meant for snow, did less and less on ice – until it did nothing. Twisting runners cared less. Faster we went, the less the bar and runners mattered.

To the extent it could be done, steering was executed by feet and weight. Toes snagged bits of nothing, but that could be enough. A foot drag swung the sled and rider slowly one way or the other, never very fast. The rider had to do early calculations, line up on the slot, or face a nasty hit. The slot was the size of a wagon. The goal was to get the sled around, just keep it aligned. The only other option was rolling off and hoping for deceleration. The norm was holding, thrilling to acceleration, loving sled and ice, praying for that slot. We had to get through the wall.

Go, Go, Go! Whoa! Off center, watch it! Shift sideways, drag boot toe! Not too much! Other one! Lift both, swing body to 45 degrees, back on again. Hold tight! Twist stomach and core! Madly accelerating, we fishtailed and recovered.

Now to the other side! Get legs out, straighten up, and twist back! Straighten out! Little time now! Crazy fishtail, stop it! On target, lining up! Building speed, need that slot, need the opening. Go, no go, go! No way to stop now. A prayer.

Eyes watering, tears pouring left and right, hat over ears, wind roaring! Fingers cold, getting colder, holding tight. Focus, just focus! Need the opening. Who cares about anything, need the slot. Whoosh! And wall gone! History! Through! Wow, shot the moon again!

But that was only the start. Ice storms laid into woods, turning the path to a racetrack. The trail juked. We followed. It was lined with blurring trees and fuzzy granite, silent onlookers. Shifts of bodyweight became our steering. We just hung on. Legs and arms, head and shoulders, boot flaps and elbow ailerons took us on down the icy hill. No time for calculations, instinct called the shots. We ducked, swerved and swiveled in the nick, straight again, sled under us. If one missed turn bought a tree or worse, we owned the world. This day was ours, ice and all.

Actually, most turns allowed for reasonable navigation, within parameters. We knew these woods well, intimately. Turns and jukes did not change. A thousand times we had walked them, worked them, snowmobiled on them. The new variable was speed, the glorious ice.

So, we plunged the slope, aimed for the lake – and generally made it! Uninterrupted by an unforeseen banking error, we usually crushed the trail, human slurry to the last. Eventually, we got poured out on the frozen lake. There, we lay gasping, replaying the frenzy until we recovered energy to get up and walk back.

On reflection, while ice storms were a mixed bag – beauty and beast, marvel and menace, diamonds and daggers – they were a ton of fun. Robert Frost knew them, and their fun. In his famous tale, "Brown's Descent," an ill-fated farmer discovers our sport – one imagines with less enthusiasm. Wrote the bard:

Brown lived at such a lofty farm
That everyone for miles could see
His lantern when he did his chores
In winter after half-past three.

And many must have seen him make
His wild descent from there one night,
'Cross lots, 'cross walls, 'cross everything,
Describing rings of lantern light.

Between the house and barn, the gale
Got him by something he had on
And blew him out on the icy crust
That cased the world, and he was gone!

What beauty, fun, and treachery lies in an ice storm! Hmmm. We never tried sliding by lantern. Maybe one day …

34. Downhill Debacle

Glide, pole, pivot. Glide, pole, pivot. Glide, pivot, pivot. Glide, swoosh, stop and rest. Most days, downhill skiing was methodical and relaxing. Skiers took risks with care, choosing their pace, pitch and slope. Racers might zoom, old folks dawdle. Skiing was faster than crossing the snow on gut webs, more controlled than careening on runners. But not always …

At about ten, I stood atop my first ski slope, refreshed by a dismount into a face plant. No matter, I was back up and wiser, if not much. I was here – off the lift, ready to ski. I had zero training. Looking down, it seemed manageable. Truth was, I had no idea how to ski.

Others around me made skiing look easy. They knew what they were doing. People passed me laughing and swishing. Everyone seemed to move with an easy cadence. The sport seemed inviting. Awkwardly, I edged over the drop-off. This is when things went haywire.

Suddenly, I was falling toward the lodge, a tiny dot below. Where the groomed snow ended, air and terror began. My high boots kept me vertical. I realized, in a heartbeat, I knew nothing about skiing. No one in my immediate family skied. I had rented skis, boots and poles – taken the lift up. That was about it. Now in gravity's grip, I made a discovery: The faster I went, the harder it was to turn, tip or control anything. That may sound odd, but it is true. More physics.

Someone told me at the rental shop to put my tips together, form a wedge and "do a snowplow." In this way, I was advised to keep control, slow my descent. It sounded like wise advice. However, a cheerful parent at the top countermanded my rental clerk, scoffed at the idea of a "snowplow." She gave me firm advice. She could ski. I listened. "You do not need a snowplow, just put your feet together … and let the hill do the rest!"

That sounded very easy. Now, I was suddenly moving at great speed, unable to turn or fall, frozen from the inside out. I was like a young bird pushed from the nest, no instructions about how wings worked. I kept feet together, tried to figure it out … en route.

At first, there was lots of wind in my face, and exhilaration in fast movement. But before long, those joys passed. Acceleration took over. I just kept falling forward, gaining speed every second. Hurtling is a good word for it. Like a first-time parachutist, I fumbled about for the ripcord. Reality swept me – I had no ripcord. From behind somewhere, through mounting wind, came the parent's counsel. "If you can't stop, just fall over!"

Now, there was an idea. That easy, just fall over. *Why had I not thought of that?* I leaned, lunged, rocked, and tried to tumble over. My efforts came to nothing. High boots, designed to keep me standing, were doing so. Locked into bindings on runaway skies, they did not want me to tip. They were made to help me. They were not persuaded that I really wanted to go down.

Soon my eyes were watering, cheeks stinging, mind in a dither. I leaned back, more and more, but no luck. I stayed ramrod straight, accelerating. I tried to lean left, no go. Right, no go. The downward draw just got stronger, chance of pitching weaker. Incredible, but I could not tip over. Speed grew and grew.

For a split second, I recall wondering what this looked like from outside me, from above or below me. I was staying up on my first run, but that was not so good. I was out of control. I could not fall, hard as I tried. And I was trying. *This must look bizarre,* I thought, *a wretched first-time skier, desperately trying to stop, no ability to influence the course of his movement.*

Then, my mind returned to the issue at hand. I *needed* to fall. Barreling through controlled skiers large and small, young and old, I left apologies in my slipstream. That was no good. Between apologies, I was cursing the parent who said this was easy. I was also becoming deaf. Faces turned toward me and shouted, I heard nothing. Then I saw it. Directly ahead, coming at me like a locomotive, was a picture window. In front of me stood the glass face of the Ski Lodge. It filled my fogging goggles. I was about to go through it! Panic set in.

The more I strained to fall, the more up I stayed. *Why did they make boots like this? Why did they put plate glass windows at the bottom of ski slopes?* The faster I went, the bigger the window got. I recall seeing heads inside turn, eyes widen as I neared. The white between us was disappearing. Nobody ran, but I could see horror in their eyes. I must have had some in mine, too.

All of a sudden, my failure to fall, inability to demonstrate that simple skill – seemed ludicrous. I threw myself completely to one side, overriding the boots' stability and power to paralyze. Gratefully, I toppled like a three-legged fire tower, and slid. All arms and legs, flying cotton and wool, poles flailed, boots released, and skis went somewhere. I hit the snow hard, passing ski racks on my back, spinning like a top. Involuntarily, I collected skis and poles, mowing down well-placed sticks. The avalanche kept coming. Time slowed as I saw more clearly the inevitable mess that was – me. Somehow, mid-wreck, I wondered how it would end. Then it did.

Going down, I cursed this blasted sport. I watched the lodge window approach. I was nearly upon it, the world gawking. Gaping eyes, open mouths, slack jaws and pointing fingers popped through the glass. Chairs were pushed back. Folks inside could not believe what they were seeing, nor could I. I could not believe what they could not believe – that I was about to join them inside the lodge. My every thought strained to be stationary. And then, I was. I slid up against the glass, be-goggled face full of snow. Skis and poles clattered against each other and I stopped – below incredulous eyes. Embarrassing? A bit, but I was thrilled to be on my side of the glass. My first ski run … was hardly auspicious. It was memorable. From that point forward, things improved. They had to.

Half a dozen years later, I was a downhiller. Never competitive, I did grow more confident. Most days, I went top to bottom without calamity. Control made me a cheerful, recreational skier. Turns out, skiing involved method. Prayers worked, but learning how to traverse was better. Focus switched to keeping skis aligned, poles forward, feeling the grade under me. The more outings, the better skiing felt. By my late teens, skiing had become a weekend activity. Lift tickets were affordable, and friends split the driving and gas costs.

Then came the debacle. It was subzero, and wind. Sugarloaf was the venue. Host to the 1971 World Cup, the slope was a local favorite. Maybe the day was just a bad choice. We imagined we could manage anything. Cold days meant fast slopes, fewer skiers, more clothes and face wear. We might need layers, but so what?

As usual, we skied all day, taking only short breaks to warm fingers, faces and toes. Then we dashed back up the slopes. By 3:45, the sun was nearing the horizon, almost touching it. Light was fading, perspective hard to keep. Only my friend Mark and I remained on the slopes. Everyone else seemed to be sipping schnapps in the lodge, or peeling layers and enjoying dry shoes, wiggling toes, hot food and hot chocolate.

We were the stalwarts, proud to be crazy, like fans last to leave a rain-out. At this time, the big slopes got dim and barren. Somewhere, grooming snowcats started to growl. They were preparing to retake the woods, remake the trails. Through trees, little lights twinkled. The cats were awakening, but not out yet. Ski patrol was still above.

By day's end, our quads were burning, arms tight at the elbows, knees wobbly. But we wanted to wring full value from our tickets, squeeze in a last mogul-carving run. Final runs were tough, but satisfying. Sometimes, they spelled trouble. Common sense told us to go slow. Plunging a dim slope, with tired legs and frozen toes, was not smart. But we were young and stubborn. We felt the need to use last light.

So here we were, standing atop a black diamond. We might have been looking down Haul Back, Ripsaw or Flume. As it was, we stood over Widow Maker, not a soul in sight. These trails were favorites of the US Ski Team. The trail's name stuck in one's frontal lobe, quickened the pulse. Or did mine. Covered in moguls, walled by trees, this was a challenge by day – more at dusk.

Widow Maker began near the gondola. It dropped between Misery Whip and Haul Back. Widow Maker was a descent, but not as steep as Ripsaw. It seemed perfect for our close-out run. A harsh wind swept up from below, blinding us for a moment. We stood looking. Below, fire and drinks waited. Up here, just cold. This was definitely the last run – had to be done. And "if it were done when 'tis done, then 'twere well, it were done quickly" – or something like that. The other Bard. Macbeth was probably not the right inspiration.

Personally, I was pumped, but cold. I was on slightly used skis – brand new to me. Blue, they were of an unknown make, model and age, purchased at a yard sale. They kept me from renting, which made them special. So far, they worked well. Some people sold things cheap. My skis came with poles and boots, all new to me. And blue was a great color. Sugarloaf was a great mountain. Widow Maker was a great trail. This had been a great day, now just one run left.

I tucked my chin against the gusts. Dusk was gaining. Mark was cold too, I could see. The lifts and gondola had stopped. No more skiers. Ski patrol would be down soon. A skier's enthusiasm can be blind. Ours was. Everyone else had peeled off. The mountain was ours.

"Slope sure is empty…" I noted.

"Sure is, and icy," Mark chuckled.

"Below zero now …"

"Guess we should take it easy … eh?"

"Lot of moguls on this one …"

"Hard to see in the light …"

"Guess we ought to get at it."

"Yeah, guess so."

Somehow, in fading light, the slope looked steeper. We lingered. Light kept fading. Suddenly, our dialogue took a radical turn – for the crazy.

Inspired by my "new" skis, I suggested a race. I did not think about the age of these skis, novelty of their construction, wood inside fiberglass. I thought about taking advantage of an empty mountain. We might test our mettle, race down Widow Maker. Mark was slow to respond. He was not so sure about this idea.

He was right to hesitate. In this light, racing was nuts. There was no reason for it either. We could take our time, enjoy the final run. What was more, we could barely ski this mogul monster in good conditions. With wind, ice, limited light and sub-zero temperatures, everything would be harder. Gone were the give-away shadows, making moguls navigable. Gone was the morning fluff that allowed lift and carving, blown and scraped away. The slope was depthless, a vertical field filled with shapeless dips and shapeless piles. Between the piles, unforgiving ice.

Mark laughed. He did not laugh dismissively or derisively, just at the absurdity of a race. He was a good friend. He skied with care, focus and intention. To speed this course at day's end was asking for trouble. He had the good sense to understand my suggestion was not good sense. It was over the top, especially under these circumstances.

"You really want to … race?"

"It's a thought … we have the slope."

"Yeah, but … now, here?"

"Sure, why not?"

"Pretty icy…" Mark was pondering the thing, and applying some judgment.

I offered that there was probably no better time than this to ski without interfering with anyone. Having foolishly suggested a race, I hesitated to drop it. After all, we both liked speed on skis. We were competent, although not exactly good. Why not pick up the pace, turn this roller coaster into a memorable last run? Mark was highly capable, better than I was. But I had something he did not – "new" blue skis. The way I saw it, we were about even.

"Well?" I asked.

"Ok," said Mark. He laughed again, a quizzical "why not?" laugh, the sort that gets kids in trouble. He was thinking about this whole thing rationally; I was imagining an open slope where the 1971 World Cup had been held. "Ok," he offered, without conviction. "Ready?" he asked. "Yep," I said, "let's go on three." We examined the slope one more time. Chill was catching, wind unrelenting. We had been standing too long. Time to go. "One, two … three," I said. And … we were off!

Moguls – giant rounded mounds of fluff – were funny things to look at from any direction. They were funnier to ski around – or over, as the case may be. We found them on steep slopes, made for experienced skiers. Carved well, they looked like a dozen fresh eggs. They passed in gentle, artistic arcs. That was the theory. Coming off them was fine, as long as a skier maintained control. A good skier used weight and edges, leaving a symmetrical, repeating "S" down the mountain. Neat as icing on a birthday cake, mogul trails painted the slope.

Now, that was not me. I was hardly consistent. If a skier is iffy on big moguls to start, expect less late day. As skiers can be in perfect sync, they can be perfectly out of sync. If a skier hits a big mogul wrong, watch out. He is likely to go airborne for several seconds, then bounce over successive peaks until control returns – if it does. He might discover a way to muscle through, but the longer it takes, the likelier a spill. I remembered too late. Like skidding around a corner on pebbles, once the moguls were lost, they were hard to re-find. Fate took over. The skier might hold on, or lose the chance. This was my discovery halfway down Widow Maker. Enthusiastic on new blue skis, I lost the S, never got it back. Try as I might to regain control, a mogul rose up and ate me.

Mark leaped ahead, sweeping back and forth, carving up the mountain. Moving nimbly among mini-mountains, he swept to the bottom. As he did, I tumbled head over tea kettle for some incalculable distance – down, down, down, until I stopped. Uninjured, I shook myself and looked around. Half the trail lay below. In a fit of resolve, I refused to admit defeat. Neither binding had popped, so I was good. I stood up, threw myself back at the base, down the slope.

Half a dozen feet, and I was upside down again, covered in snow. I stopped so fast there was no momentum to carry me. My goggles were clouds. I felt for the bindings. Both solidly on, neither had popped. Lucky me! Again, I threw at the bottom. In seconds, I was tumbling H. over T., T. over H. – sliding down, down, down. The slope was steep. This was getting old. That tumble, I rose to see Mark waving madly. He was standing at the bottom already, shouting something inaudible. Couldn't make it out. Maybe I was second, but no quitting. I pushed once more. This time, I noticed something odd. My left ski shot out, right stayed stuck in snow. Then everything went white, and I was sliding again. This time, I got up slowly.

Goggles off, I looked down at Mark. He was still waving and shouting – at something. He was pointing up the slope, above me. I turned around and looked up. A hundred feet over me – lay half of my right ski. The beautiful blue stood out, even at dusk. How could that be? Both bindings were locked, boots attached to my skis. Neither binding had popped. I looked down in disbelief. My right binding held tight, to half a ski. Somewhere, the binding had not popped. It was my leg or the ski – and the ski had gone. I was darned lucky.

Unthinkable really. I had never heard of such a thing, a ski snapping in half, jaggedly too. *So,* I thought, *that is what wood and fiberglass gets you!* My right ski hit the mogul, binding refused to pop, and ski sheared off! I knew that could – by all rights *should* – have been my ankle, or leg. I was a lucky guy, two legs intact. That explained all my tumbling, or most of it. I had only one good ski. The other was a trumpet of frayed wood, flipping me over every time.

Otherwise uneventful, the day was suddenly memorable. Who ever heard of snapping a ski – on any slope? The experience was novel, worth the lift price. Where better than Widow Maker? Gone were my new skis, in exchange for a story. Mark got a good laugh. We both did. Here we are, again! My next pair was *not* from a garage sale. Having missed the plate glass window and broken leg, I was careful – even selecting skis. Back on the slope, I stayed with an easy cadence. Glide, pole, pivot. Glide, pole, pivot. Glide, pivot, pivot. Glide, swoosh, stop and rest!

35. Super Fish

You think you have seen it all, then "behold, something new!" Happened throughout the 17th, 18th, 19th and 20th centuries. Things popped right and left between plagues, wars and fish stories! People were in the right place, right time, made history. Could happen to anyone. Gravity, electricity, penicillin – all flukes. Sir Isaac Newton gets an apple on the head – bang, three laws. Ben Franklin flies a kite – shazam, spark, light, power grid. Penicillin, the same. Alexander Fleming scrapes mold off bread – wham, a Nobel Prize. Chance made destiny. That's the way we saw it. No mistaking it, anything was possible. And say, we got signs!

Before I share our glancing blow with destiny, take this to heart: Lots of discoveries are accidents. Even with foods. In the 20th century, a baker poured bits of chocolate in a cookie – viola, chocolate chip cookies! Ruth Wakefield, Toll House Restaurant, thus Tollhouse cookies. Take a Popsicle, summer mainstay. The discovery was by 11-year-old Frank Epperson, in 1905. Just had an idea, left sweet liquid on his back porch – with a stick. Next morning, Popsicle. Eighteen years later, patented it, made a bundle and history. No kidding.

Doubts? Banish them. Accidents happen. Some are good ones. Anyone can make a discovery. Consider the lucky researcher at that New England military installation, few years back. Every time he walked past the radar tube, his chocolate bar melted. Curious thing, and messy. He put un-popped corn in his pocket. It popped! From this "Eureka moment" came – maybe you guessed it? – microwave ovens! Point? Keep your eyes open, anything is possible.

As kids, we were always wondering, a good state of mind. We believed more was yet to be found. Why not? Growing up, we assumed countless things awaited finding. If it worked for Newton, Franklin, Fleming, Wakefield, Epperson and the microwave guy, why not for us? You just never knew .... Maybe "wrinkles in time" did exist, and Madeline L'Engle was right. Or Isaac Asimov, tumbling through time to his "pebble in the sky." Newness was always possible. We remained alert. Mysteries existed, like the aurora borealis, albino deer, hypnotizing lobsters, what we pulled from the lake. You know?

Hiram Maxim once lived in our town. No joke, he did. Reputedly invented the light bulb, but lost his race to the patent office. Who knows, maybe Edison had faster feet. Maybe Maxim overslept. He got rich anyway, patented the machine gun and other improvements, including a "better mousetrap" and steam pump. He invented the "steam inhaler using pine vapor" for what "ailed you," amusement rides, un-flyable airplanes. Maybe the light bulb was his high point.

As a whole, Mainers have made many discoveries. In the 1830s, industrious Jacob Davis was an enterprising tailor, just immigrated to the United States. He set up in Augusta – not far from where we grew up. Later, he went west, but first he got a joint patent with Levi Strauss – for *blue jeans!* Entirely true. By trial and error, Davis discovered denim-and-rivet blue jeans. That's right. Levi Strauss just provided the material. Unfortunately, like Maxim, Davis overslept. Strauss got naming rights, or we would be wearing Jacob Davis blue jeans. Anyway, jeans owe something to Maine. Where do I stop? Green tourmaline – well, you know about that. Earmuffs – well, credit a Farmington native. As kids, we kept our eyes open.

Then one day, it happened! We had our rendezvous with destiny! Nature gave a discovery, that's how we saw it. No practical application, but riveting still. We imagined ourselves in the company of Newton and Franklin, if not Epperson and Davis. Here it was: If cats had nine lives, fish – we discovered – got two! That's right. What's more, it all happened in our kitchen. Here was a leap for cryogenics or metaphysics, possibly both. *Fish had two lives!*

The discovery occurred on an unexpectedly cold January day, the sort that probably slowed Maxim and Davis to the patent office. Our family had been ice fishing. Winter weekends, we often headed out to fish. We fished all day, retreating to the ice shack as needed. Fish, we left on the ice. On this particular day, we zoomed down, caught a "mess" of perch and pickerel. Late day, we headed home. Snowmobiles hauled toboggans with fishing gear – and fish. After a good day, we chipped the rock-hard fish off ice, and zipped home. That day, temperatures were frosty, turning fish to bricks, making each an ice block. Temps fell into the single digits. The lake boomed and groaned, as ice thickened.

By the woodstove, we kept eyes out for popping flags. When an ice trap's flag went up, we shuffled to the hole, broke the film of ice, hooked the fish, pulled hand-over-hand, and tossed our catch onto the ice – far enough from the hole to keep it from wriggling back down. We rebaited the hook, dropped the sinker, reset the flag, and ran back to the shack, palms to the stove.

Jigging a line gave life to bait, but some days we just let the line, trap and baitfish do the work. Without jigging, we landed fish all day, maybe ten. By sunset they were granite rocks – concrete blocks. They got chipped, chopped and kicked loose, tossed in milk crates, roped to the toboggan. All the way home, these bricks got sprayed with flying ice and snow. Snowmobile treads throw chips like mill saws throw dust, especially climbing hills. Bouncing zigzag, the toboggan was covered. A live animal might have bruised, but frozen fish were chunks of steel.

Home at last, we downloaded. In came our tools, traps, bait bucket – and frozen fish. Everyone did their part. Along the way, someone dumped the white bricks into our kitchen sink. Bang, bump, clunk! The sink was full of rocks. Most days, our fishy bricks thawed, got tacky and malleable, and were finally filleted for dinner. No big deal, no big fuss, just a process.

Today was different. I was really hungry. I imagined warm water might accelerate thawing … and dinner. So I ran a sink of water, turned it off, and walked away. Then, I forgot about the frozen fish. What with putting things away, peeling off layers, bringing in wood, time sneaked by. One thing led to another. We forgot about the fish. Until I heard something in the kitchen. Then I remembered. I moseyed into the kitchen, and looked into the sink. My eyes narrowed. Splashing was happening. It defied logic. Before long, I was hollering. "Come look at this!"

No one quite believed it. Newton must have felt this way. And Franklin and Maxim, maybe even the fellow from Farmington. Our discovery was one for the record books. Imagine … frozen fish coming back to life! Cold-blooded perch, one hour ago frozen as granite, now flopping freely. More than that, they were swimming in circles. We had an aquarium. This was not normal. These were wagging, flapping, lively fish! *But how?*

How could fish revive from deep freeze, flex their once frozen gills? How could they breathe oxygen, swim drunken circles in the sink? These fish were alive, touring the afterlife, a very small lake. How could this be? We alternated between silence and exclamation. Mostly we gawked and laughed. Impressed by our discovery, we marveled aloud: Fish, once frozen hard as bricks, could return to life. We watched as they paraded in a clumsy line, exploring the sink's corners, time travelers of a fishy sort. Maybe there was something to that "wrinkle in time," Asimov's "pebble in the sky," Robert Heinlein's "door into summer." There were certainly surprises afoot, and we had found one. We had fallen down a slide into science, underscoring the value in being curious. That evening, we felt part of history. Not Popsicle or earmuffs, perhaps. Not lightbulb or mousetrap. But it was a discovery. And then, we had dinner.

36. Lake Salmon

Every winter morning, as part of the celestial order, direct and flecked sun hit treetops on our side of the mountain. Already, these shafts had lit the other side, making it popcorn bright. By the time we got it, the sun was turning more of a crackerjack gold, but it was welcome.

Many winter weekends, we fished on ice. This particular one, we did the usual, lashed bait buckets, traps, food and wood on toboggans, hitched them to snowmobiles, and headed down to the lake. We had our shack in position, and knew the heading by heart. Ice fishing was a bit like opening a crackerjack box. You never knew what you would find – or catch. There was an element of surprise. Hidden under the ice might be anything, white or yellow perch, pickerel, maybe even an odd cusk.

Down our hill we went, zipping around well-packed turns, watching out not to topple the toboggans. Terrain undulated, and then we arrived on ice. The lake was inevitably snowy, brisk and refreshing. At our icehouse, we downloaded gear, chiseled holes, put wriggling shiners and tommy cod on hooks, and lowered lines to depth – three feet from lake's bottom for perch, just under ice for pickerel. Pickerel were boney but tasty, once you deboned them. Then we went inside, set a fire in the stove, and waited for a flag to pop. This was the moment when we sniffed around the crackerjack box, wondering what we might get, dreaming of a big surprise.

On rare occasions, we dreamed of the ultimate, an elusive fish that had never managed to find my hook. Rumor had it they swam in our lake, had been sighted. State records suggested the same. But no local I knew had caught one. Someone upstate claimed to have pulled one out, but rumors were just rumors. No local vouched for their presence, which could cut either way. Still, we maintained hope, and the sort of dreams that attach to lottery tickets, and a crackerjack box.

This phantom fish was considered, in some circles, more a tall tale than square tail. The fish was a lake or landlocked salmon. Reputedly, landlocked salmon – in uncertain numbers – cruised our lake, too smart to be hooked, leftovers from a distant stocking. That was the big rumor – just a crazy story, never substantiated, like finding a Loch Ness Monster on your line.

This particular day went more or less as predicted. A few white perch came up, one or two pickerel. We knew which lines were at what depths, so when a flag popped, we knew what to expect. Occasionally, we got something – what we expected. One year my mother did snag a cusk, off the bottom. That made good eating. Still, we thought we knew what lay below the ice.

Suddenly, a flag popped. It was my trap! I grabbed gloves and hat, went to the hole. This was a line set just under the ice, for pickerel. I reached down, gave it a good yank. The line ripped out of my hands, and then went slack.

That was odd, I thought. Suddenly, the line flew off the spool. This fish was running, going somewhere fast, taking everything but the trap with him. Out went the monofilament line, and down I went on a knee. I grabbed barehanded for the spitting, screaming line.

This was different! This was not a usual fish in winter. As I heaved the light line, it yanked right back, like an angry kite in a gale. I might as well have been pulling up an anchor. The fish did not want to come; it wanted me to come to it. This fish was giving me a lesson in who controlled the lake. The underside did, of course, not those of us in gloves and hats, above the frozen plane.

Now, this was exciting! This was a huge fish on two-pound test. It was showing me that it could pull twice as hard as me, maybe three times. I pulled, it pulled. I let out, it pulled. It gave back, and I took. I pulled, it took back. It pulled, I gave. I pulled, it came. This was something.

Gradually, line piled up on the ice, inches at first, then a coil. Gradually, with patience and cold hands, I got the edge on the fish. Whether it was tiring or I was learning the game, I am not sure, but it got closer to me. This was a fight. I was a fighter, too – an ardent fisherman at age twelve.

Back in the icehouse, curious eyes gazed out frosty windows, wondering what was giving me such a fuss, taking so much time and line. Why was I on my knees, wet to my elbows, halfway down the hole, consumed by a fish? Inside, warm hands cupped hot tea, touched up with condensed milk. Some were reading, others chewed on hot dogs. The woodstove rattled. But people were curious. What was up with me?

Out on the ice, I was curious too – what was up with this odd fish? What in the world was this crazy thing under the ice? This was the darnedest, most contrary, irreverent and insubordinate pickerel I had ever hooked, seen run a spool, or tried to reel in. What an attitude this bruiser had!

Now I could feel the fish losing ground, off balance. I pressed my advantage. The battle raged, fish against me, but I was winning. What a battle! I did not have it yet. There was no net, no magic for landing a big fish on ice. The hole was just so big. I did not want to lose it.

At last, I saw a shape flashing back and forth in the blackness, beneath the hole. It was pink. Pickerel are not pink. Suddenly the bruiser saw sunlight, and determined to have none of it. In quick passes, it gave nasty yanks. Maybe it wanted to leap the ice in a big arc, break my line, fall back and disappear. It had a pearly underside, top of silver and plentiful flecks, like a magnificent opal. This was not a pickerel! This was a gem.

The fish was brighter than a perch, no scales. It was bigger than the biggest pickerel, no qualms about throwing its weight around. The battle continued. Many times I thought I had lost the big fish. Getting it through the hole was a labor of patience. For a kid used to jigging a line, gently pulling up perch, maybe wrangling up an odd, fat-bellied pickerel, this was a thrill.

Water rises in a chiseled hole, but fish are heavier in air than water. Somehow, they know it. If they can break a line, they will. If they can escape down the way they came up, they will. Fish splash, wiggle and twist, too often leaving fishermen frustrated, and empty handed. That is why so many fishermen tout stories of "the big one that got away." I could not let this one get away.

Eventually – and that word has special meaning in winter – it got into the hole. With a swift pull and one firm hand, I landed the fish. And what did I land? The only landlocked salmon ever to grace my hook. He weighed nearly four pounds. That put an end to our guessing; the lake had salmon. And he gave me something else, a fish story to tell for forty years.

No one really knows how landlocked salmon (*Salmo salar Sebago*) got locked in Maine lakes. Or how they turned into inland fish. Their cousins are ocean-going Atlantic salmon (*Salmo salar*). Originally, scientists thought these were the unlucky few, migrating ocean salmon just caught by receding glaciers. That theory is fading. Prevailing thought is they chose to stay.

Today, landlocked salmon are found in more than 170 Maine lakes and more than 40 rivers. They all started in four Maine lakes, Sebago, Green, Sebec and Grand Lake. Other populations appear in Michigan, Canada, and parts of Scandinavia and Russia. These days, they are homebodies. Turns out, their ancestors probably had a way back to the sea, but preferred the safety and smelts of Maine's lakes and rivers. They freely renounced shark-filled waters.

In any event, speaking of easy eating, that beefy salmon certainly was. After the collective shock and laughter passed, we weighed the big fish and headed home. Up the mountain we went, sun on a far horizon, ashy shadows and dusty rose patches around us. Seated for supper, sun no longer crackerjack yellow, we had our surprise. To the west, tangerine streaks evolved to an improbable fuchsia. The sky mellowed to burnt umber and pink – exactly like the improbable salmon meat on our plates. That was the day – and the only day – we enjoyed lake salmon for dinner.

37. Campfires

What is it with campfires? Something. A couple of dry logs, loose sticks, a handful of birch bark, and a match. But a campfire is far more than the sum of these parts. Suddenly, souls are being soothed, peace sets in, light chases out shadows. Contentment flows like warm water. Minds uncoil, eyes transfix. Like a chamois or shaft of sun, campfires warm everyone. In every era, campfires have breathed life into what was cold and still.

Primordial and uplifting, the campfire's spell is timeless and reliable, like stars themselves. The campfire is starlight captured and placed at our feet, tamed and sized to our needs, modest, mollifying and mesmerizing. The star at our feet warms shoe soles and hand palms, brightens faces, bemuses and befuddles, becalms and radiates joy. That is one reason I loved camping.

Packs and sticks were set down, tents and lines put up, and we sat in our circle, a little bubble of light. All eyes went to the flame, and became blind beyond it. But we were happy. Minds stopped worrying about foot placement, roots and stepping stones. They came to a rest. Tired bones settled, reformed into one unit. Around the fire, we sat on stumps and webbed chairs, caressed by invisible waves, each a sand beach.

Imaginations came to life. We saw anything and everything in those flames, rethought the distant past, replayed the recent day, dreamed of what might be, sometimes what might have been. Sabers twisted and jabbed the night, tapered in high, fleeting spikes, flashed and were gone, leaving spots and splotches where they struck. All eyes appreciated the antediluvian dance, interplay of light and dark, hope and heat. The campfire took us away to somewhere, stirring shapeless thoughts, some clear, some intangible, some just visceral and evanescent. Sometimes a new idea appeared in the flames, here and gone. Or the idea lingered like wood smoke, filled one's eyes and mind, until you moved. Sometimes the idea moved you.

Something else inhabited a campfire. Undoubtedly, it came from deep in our species' unrecorded history, eluded identification. It was felt by those in the circle, had no name. It was inviting, evocative, almost irresistible. It was silent. No one talked about the feeling, or taught about it. It just was.

Maybe it was Yarmouth Man, hunter of the mid-Pleistocene epoch, cooking a beast on which his family's life depended, sending through time his adoration for fire. Maybe in the flame was a message, a feeling he had passed down through this medium to our generation. Maybe it was a thousand pleas for survival, sent by Sangamon Man from a hundred thousand years ago, as he felt the Wisconsin glaciers drifting in his direction. Maybe fire was his way of subverting time, each lick and flicker an outstretched hand. Maybe it was just the aggregation of a million years of terrified animals, a billion human sighs, and protection in the flame. It was something, more than peace and distraction, more than a mere breeze. Maybe it was one end of a tunnel, history leaning forward to tell us something, holding us rapt. For a moment, suspended between real and not, we felt it. Then suddenly, we were back on a log, waving away smoke, just here.

Whatever else a campfire did, it took the chill off. It lifted surrounding hearts, those at ease and those heavy. It was balm for all comers, coal pokers and quiet trekkers, old explorers and youthful scouts. We never got tired of it. In some faces, the fire inspired reflection and introspection; in others, relief from any thought. To some, it opened a door; to others it bolted one tight, kept worldly concerns at bay. One campfire, many effects, a mystery. The campfire was absorbing and disgorging, retiring and inspiring, winking and whispering, but always delivered what every log sitter needed.

From where did a campfire draw power? Chairs, tables, and logs did not have it. A window might, depending on what it looked out on, but only a little. The campfire could brighten and charm, still and disarm, heal what ailed those looking into it, put us to sleep. Like a trusted friend, it kept wild animals away. Dampness, too. It sparred valiantly with the encircling darkness, won until we agreed to let darkness back. Little was asked of us, just keep it going.

On cold nights, a campfire curled at one's feet like a faithful dog, begging another pat, snack or bone, another twig, stick or branch. Like the old dog, she stirred and murmured, animated by an inscrutable, wordless dream. Do campfires have dreams? Are they composed of them, one on the other, like burning logs? All the while, it pulls you close. Within its radius, all is safe.

On a good night, congeniality splashed from a campfire. Boats shifted at anchor in the harbor, bobbing on the fire's ripples, here and there clinking of a mainmast. All felt protected. Time slipped, fingers and faces unclenched. What was vital and urgent was less and less so, until not so. Worries dissolved in the harbor's lulling waves. Whoever the harbormaster was, He knew his job. Ships in need got a break. The campfire induced forgetting, and remembering.

When we went camping on overnight expeditions as a scout troop, part of the excitement was building a campfire. On dry evenings, a fire ate voraciously, chewing on everything within reach. On wet ones, it showed temperance, nibbling and chewing with deliberation. On both, it ate what we fed it, which depended on what lay about. Scouting nights were filled with fireside pops and bellows, laughter and jokes, whispers, chortles and sighs. After we had drained ourselves of noise, we listened to the fire ruminate, until we fell asleep to the murmuring.

Half my love of a campfire was color, the irregular flashes of yellow, green, orange and blue. They cast a spell. Tints ebbed and flowed, appeared in shafts, little aurora borealis bits. Pulsing, rising and falling, fires had a candescence, just like the northern lights. Color chased out disharmony, synchronized thinking, created a dynamic and impressionistic painting, a thousand in a night. Colors waxed and waned with wood and temperature, jumpy yellows to rosy glows, darker still to ruby coals; high to low, low to lower, until the curtain shut.

So much mystery in such a little pool of light, the campfire. A couple of dry logs, some loose sticks, a handful of bark, and a match. Nothing much, and so very much. In that little place, shadows were chased and chastened, souls soothed and settled, peace protected and perfected. Not much, in the grand scheme, but enough – enough to keep us coming back. There was something timeless about a campfire, puff of stardust, cup of moonlight, aurora borealis in the night.

38. Through the Ice

It was deepest winter – cold. But we were camping. Maine scouts did that. Shivering, bantering, preparing for the coming night, we felt intrepid. We were out for fun, temperatures notwithstanding. We thought we knew everything – knots and whittling, orienteering and campfire building. All we lacked was common sense, something we had yet to appreciate. Otherwise, we were ready, canvas tents pegged down, brimming with food and enthusiasm, sleeping bags rolled out.

Tents back then had no bottoms, just a ground cloth, which was okay. No one knew tents should have bottoms, so we did not miss them. For warmth, we dug squares in the snow, laid down hay, then a ground cloth. My buddy Will and I pegged down our two-man tent, then went to find firewood.

Each two-man tent was allowed to build a campfire, and we wanted ours to roar. So we launched ourselves into the dimming forest, in different directions. My goal was – as always – to find birch bark, God's gift to scouts. That bark's oil makes fire starting easy. Turned out, I left everything in the tent, including what common sense I had. The omission would prove telling.

Nevertheless, on I pressed into the woods, eyes peeled for birches. I saw little ones, so knew there were bigger ones, with more bark. A big birch could shed swatches the size of a newspaper, and no harm to the tree. I pressed deeper. Dry branches were easy to gather, but I wanted birch bark. Looking around, the woods were hard and soft. Maine being Maine, a big birch had to be here, somewhere. Even in deep snow and fading light, I was undaunted.

Suddenly, I saw one! Oh yeah! There it was! Across that shallow valley, biggest birch I had ever seen. And it was shedding, almost throwing bark at me. My faith was rewarded, quest nearly complete. This was a granddaddy, too. This was a white clock tower, bequeathing bark in layers, Big Ben reaching up into the upper forest. The trunk invited inspection. It was just a short hike. I needed to climb the snowy slope, once past the gully. Common sense would have cautioned me: *Beware of unassuming gullies, in dim woods. They look like snow, may not be empty.* This one was not empty.

Around me, snow mounded unevenly, about waist deep. I could see my goal. I could see the bark falling like wallpaper. I stepped into the gully. Only at the last minute did I realize it was not an empty gully. I was crossing a small river, iced over, enshrouded in snow. Under the snow, a low gurgling. I could hear it now, muted but there. Suddenly, my predicament was obvious. I was standing on ice, over rushing water. For now, the ice was holding me.

I was already half across. *Best to keep going.* Six feet in, I felt something give way. I launched for the far bank – and made it. The embankment caught me. I slipped to a halt – dry! Behind me, the crack's clap echoed. *That was close!* A visible crack split the snow, ice below. *Whew, now for that bark!*

I shrugged off the close call, and made for Big Ben. A few sheets would start the fire nicely, few more would start everyone's! From the monstrous tree, dangling bark fell into my hands. I did not have to use a knife. Ben was giving it away. Bundles in both hands, I headed back to camp.

While it was getting dark, that was not a concern. The only issue was that gully, no longer so unassuming. I had to cross it somewhere, then plod back. Light was receding. I needed to be efficient. I looked upstream and down, obviously could not cross where I had before.

Finally, surmising ice was equally thick both directions, I headed upstream along the embankment. Far from the crack, I kicked the snow and tested the ice. Here was a solid patch, thick enough to get me over. I would "think light," move quick, be over. My strategy was simple: Be a dart, touch-and-go, never stop. I tested the ice again, comfortably thick. Here is another piece of wisdom: *Edges are often thicker than middles.*

Buoyed by unfounded confidence in thick ice, I changed strategies. Rather than lunge or leap, I would proceed slowly, be more patient. I would slide one foot, then the other, no hurry. I would not jar things. I would use care, not speed. *Why dash when I could walk?* Stuck in a ditch, cars crept out. Taking my time, I would creep across this mid-forest obstacle. Point missed: *Cars in ditches are different from scouts on thin ice.*

Stepping onto the stream's frozen ripples, I heard no unsettling sounds. The layered ice was dusted in white flakes. I gauged the distance bank to bank – only a dozen feet, not more. With purpose, holding my bark, I slid another foot forward, then another. Repeating this process, I heard no signs of cracking. All was good. The return was going just fine.

My confidence soared. Moving like an inchworm, I could leap either way, if needed. To my delight, the ice held. Like New Hampshire's famous granite outcropping, "Old Man in the Mountain," this ice was good for the ages. I breathed much easier. Shuffling, the mind wandered. I imagined the roaring campfire, nearly built. Others would marvel at my find. I had found real treasure, enough bark for all fires. Theodore Roosevelt could not have been happier. With each step, doubts receded. I was crossing a frozen stream – in a grand place, on a great mission, doing okay at center stage. Only thing was, the trap door …

Mid-point, I realized current ran fast here, right under me. A long leap either way would fall short – but I was almost there! I drew in a long breath, focused on the other bank. That was the last of my cogent thinking. Theodore Roosevelt suddenly vanished. And I did through the ice.

Vertical movement replaced horizontal. I entered a different world. No warning, and the ice gave. Down I went. In less than "Whoa!" I was standing waist-deep in icy knives. The water was sharp, shocking, and for a moment immobilizing. Suddenly, I was here and absolutely not here. I was standing in the rip, an arctic current. Meantime I disowned everything below my belt. That half must belong to someone else; it could not belong to me. It was so cold that I consciously tried to think myself elsewhere, maybe on a different planet, anywhere but here. Only I could not escape here, or my frozen nether regions. The stinging was persistent.

No prose can do justice to this event. I was breathless, lost in darkness, meanest space. I was caught in a pocket of the Siberian Sea. I was a polar bear, with no fur. I was a featherless ptarmigan, a shivering Inuit, a feckless, fumbling, frozen Boy Scout. And I wanted out – now! For a fleeting moment in this absurd, out-of-body-but-regrettably-also-in-body situation, my mind gnawed at the novelty, paused to watch. It tried to piece together the fractured world. It struggled to understand the unfamiliar, like processing an injury or bad news. Not injured, this was bad news. My mind wanted to "rewind" and start over, make things different. Then it realized, no, not possible. Time was passing, knives out. The luxury of thinking had to be postponed. If time refused to go backwards, I had to go forwards – and get out.

I was not standing in water over my head, thank goodness. That was a consolation. I knew this was just a big inconvenience. Nevertheless, the stream was breathtakingly cold. Taking action was necessary. Odd, how the mind works under pressure. With no memory of how the feat was accomplished, I scrambled up the far embankment, stood breathing hard and – I noticed – was running. I was also shivering uncontrollably. I watched myself, in this hilarious sketch, attempting not to feel.

Finding "dry" required the tent. I therefore dreamed of the tent, imagined being in the tent as I ran. I took consolation in the power of my imagination. Pant legs started to harden. At the same time, I was relieved to think of nothing but the tent. Mentally I was there, beside the roaring fire. Physically, I was still a long way off. The two worlds were kept separate. I stayed in the first one, as much as possible. In the second, bending knees got progressively harder.

I made a beeline through the woods in a stiff-legged, high-speed strut. Focusing on unbroken strides, retracing my deep tracks, forgetting as much as possible my lower half, time passed. I stumbled, walked, stumbled more, and left a trail of water. My inseams were scuffing. Before long, I was clattering. Suddenly, I knew how the tin man of Oz felt. I kept telling myself to look ahead. At the tent, I would de-ice, rediscover the meaning of dry.

Like the last minutes of a marathon, when a runner dissociates from legs, I feigned no interest in them. Minutes passed, seemed hours. I was indifferent to snow, lighting, or land contour. None of it mattered. I just needed the tent. Half way back, I realized that I had not dropped the bark. That lifted my spirits. The bark was still crushed in my fists, which refused to unclench. I did not bother thinking how this happened. Somehow, my body had decided not to surrender the bark. As far as I could tell, my mind had nothing to do with it. Frozen as I was, I took heart in the bark. It would start a fire.

After an interminable period of bull moose-ing through dark forest, ignoring my legs, I arrived stiff-legged in camp. I paused for no one and nothing – no words, just dropped the bark, untied the flaps, stepped inside, and stripped to the skin. Shivering uncontrollably, I grabbed a towel, redressed. Dry never felt so good. *Relief!*

Once dry, I began to feel again. I moved from quarter to full breaths. I appreciated dryness as never before. I luxuriated in fabric. Dry, dry, dry! And warmth. I reemerged from the tent, appreciating life tenfold. Enveloped in thermal underwear, double socks, thick pants and multiple shirts, I regained my bearings. A fire was still needed. Life had slowed. I could think. Soaked and frozen, my boots would soon be rocks. Luckily, I had sneakers. Scouts assembled to hear the tale. By the time I was done, my trousers were marble, frozen hard.

I wasted no time converting bark, twigs, sticks and logs into flames. The magic bark worked. In minutes, spikes pogoed into the darkness, spitting fireflies. At last, I was sitting down. My mind replayed the adventure, to the point where I fell in. At that moment, the screen blanked. Recollection resumed speed walking, hi-tailing it back to camp. In the God-given warmth of a campfire, I blinked and stared, blinked and stared, poured gratitude, warmed aching toes and knees. I could not get enough of the fire. I welcomed every wisp and curl of indecisive smoke. From the fire's light, I drew contentment. Here was a friend.

Replaying my stupidity, I felt lucky. Common sense returned, to a degree. One last lesson came from that campout. My marbleized pants, brown corduroys, needed thawing. I only had three pair. Frugal, Mom patched and cared for our clothes. I had to rescue these pants, dry them out. I pried them up, bent them into shape for hanging, and looped them over an unbreakable stick. The stick was thrust deep in the snow, back from the fire. They would be dry by morning. Supper eaten, dishes cleaned with snow, I turned in – and slept like a rock.

Next morning, we rose early. The prior night's fire had burned late. We needed a new one. I threw on a tee, sweatshirt, dry pants, cold socks, thrust my fat feet into sneakers, and flipped up the flap. I expected to see dry corduroys. Stepping out, I rubbed sleep away, took in the scene. Fire out, something was wrong. My pants were nowhere. Two days, two shocks. My brain was slow. *What had happened?* In the fire pit lay a work of art, ashes in ripples. The pit was filled with delicate waves, stripes, and folds. The ash mimicked a rolling, tree-lined landscape, row upon row of ridges, undisturbed by wind. They climbed the side, ending in a half-burned branch.

I did not know whether to laugh or cry. The ashes were remarkable, poetic. They were tragic, epic. I just stared. Beautiful ashes stared back, my pants – burned up. I was mute for a long time, imagining what my mother was going to say. These were my good pants, not cheap. She would not be happy. She would ask about my common sense.

Suddenly, Will appeared from behind the tent flap. He stood up, looked around, looked at the fire pit, looked at me, and looked back at the fire pit. He took in the contoured ashes, missing corduroys, and burned stick. Suddenly, he exploded in laughter. He looked away, looked back, looked at me, and could not contain himself. All at once, I was laughing, too. The situation was preposterous, if predictable. The tragedy became high comedy, my second drama in two days. That was how we learned common sense, the stuff between merit badges. Will and I laughed until we cried, then had breakfast on a fire, built on fine art. Somehow, my mother understood. Boys will be boys. May it ever be so!

39. All Boys, Once

Boys will be boys, and once – not so long ago – town elders were boys. Our boyhoods differed, even if they share similarities. This is a follow-up, another visit with Richie, who you may recall found himself in the thick of World War II's Italian Campaign at age eighteen.

I had not seen Richie in a while, so found him at a Maine Veteran's home. He insisted he was comfortable, seemed content. Asked if he had "good days and bad," he responded, "Nope, just good days." This one was sunny, in early June. He had a room to himself.

We talked deeply, as never before. After this visit, I swung by many times, but conversation never took this tack again. Richie's eyes were bright, impish. On this day, he was crisp, ready for conversation. The prism of life flashed about him, in the colors of war. Maybe it was the place, filled with World War II veterans. Maybe it was someone's willingness to listen. Maybe I was close enough yet not too close. Maybe it was a stage of life, maybe another season to which *Ecclesiastes* refers.

That day, I entered the room to hear him saying he was cold. A hot summer day was ending. I turned his fan low. He said that was better. He seemed glad to see me – and surprised. Did he have many visitors? Oh yes, quite a few. How was food? Pretty good. How was he? Not bad.

Conversation flickered from the new digs to his family, eventually to town history. His 92nd birthday, he told me, was just that month. He seemed surprised at that, too. "Things pass so fast …" he mused. We talked of his boyhood, attending school by sleigh in winters, swimming in the Mill Pond summers. He said he preferred summers, that he and his three brothers – Bunt, Gib, and Tink – had been "hell raisers." I chuckled at that. He reminded me his father was postmaster, later also his brother. I imagined not much got by the Wayne Postmaster.

Perhaps because it was a topic of prior conversation, or given where we were, when I mentioned his military service, he picked up the topic – with some urgency. Obviously, he had been thinking about it. Now, he seemed to want to say certain things, things not said before. He now wanted to talk about it. I wanted to listen, and it was my turn to be surprised.

"Anzio was hell … war is hell … trigger, trigger, trigger," he looked away, "it just never stopped." He made finger pulls in the air, as if reliving something, "hell, hell, hell … the Germans fell, kept falling." He stopped, looked away again, and lowered his voice, "it was hell."

I was not sure what to say. "It must have been," I mustered. "Did you think of home?" "Yes, every day we thought of home, every day, and every day I thanked the Lord I was still alive, I thanked the Lord every day." Again, he seemed to switch to another place in his mind. "It was hell … you see things you never thought you would see, did things you never thought you would do, just kept going, hiding, and then shooting, it never stopped…" Back to me, he said "I was a First Scout, we had to find the Germans, where they were, and bullets were everywhere, hitting around me everywhere in the dirt … I hid behind rocks, anything that could save you, a pebble, bullets on all sides …"

"But you made it home," I tried to console. "Yes," he said, "even now I sometimes ask how I made it home, it was hell … just hell. Maybe I survived because I was small, could hide, but the Lord saved me, I just wanted to go home." I had never heard him speak this way, nor with this passion. I let him talk. "When we got to Rome, it was hard getting there, the hills were hard, but every hill was a place to hide, and the Germans were hard fighters …" He was quiet for a time, as if transiting the hills under fire again.

"But when we got to Rome, they knew they were defeated, you could tell. We all just wanted to go home, we thought the war was over, we finally got a chance to sleep … From Anzio we never slept, in Rome we finally slept … we all wanted to be home." He was quiet again, eyes open – momentarily in a place only they knew, and to which he did not wish to give words.

Finally, he said again, "war is hell …" Asked, he retold the story of successfully hiding in culverts, adding important, formerly untold details. In one instance, he had stayed hidden in a culvert for two days, perhaps longer. There was constant strafing, and Germans everywhere. A passing truck spilled food, fruit – it never tasted so good. He had eluded the Germans. Then, the farmhouse. More details. Yes, his unit was stuck there, but the farmer was no friend – they were being held and told not to leave. He had sought reinforcements down the ravine, yes, but only when the farmer stepped away. Of the others, some were captured, others got away. His tone was momentarily intense and defiant, for a fleeting second victorious, then the pall fell. Hard this time.

"Home, we all just wanted to go home …" he said. I tried to console him, put my hand on his arm, looked him in the eye and reminded him "but you got home, you survived, you did get home, you were a wonderful influence on us, you and the others, on my age of kids." He seemed to take that in, acknowledge it, then let something else out. "Tink could not believe it when I told him what happened to me, the hell of it … Bunt was like a grandfather … he told me, 'look it is over, it was hell, it has to be forgotten, you have to forget it, it is not real now, not something you can keep thinking about, have to forget it.'"

Richie, so historically strong and cheerful, laconic and humorous, now seemed to skip a gear. Only after a minute or two, did I realize this was tied together. He did not skip a gear at all – what he said was a follow-on. "Bunt told us to forget it … I came back and got a good job, I sold cigars around Maine, Kittery to Fort Kent … never smoked a cigar, but sold them everywhere, travelled sometimes a thousand miles in a week, this side of the state to that, all over … it was a great job … it kept me active." He stopped, and looked me in the eye. "You have to stay active, that is the only way, only way … to forget." Now I understood, and how much the war had affected him.

I made another attempt to express appreciation, that deep appreciation so many feel, which is sometimes so hard to get out. "You know, you really protected us twice, once when you went over there and once when you came home, not telling us things, when we were kids." Richie got focused again. "Yes, there are some things you cannot say, you cannot imagine, cannot realize you saw, that you did, but you had to … war is hell, and we just wanted to do what we had to and come home."

Suddenly, his eyes filled. He repeated, "War is hell, and we just all wanted to come home." I put my hand on his arm, tried mightily to change the topic, offering consolations. One last time, he said, "Bobby, war is hell, hell, it is hell." Other stories were told, some graphic and others descriptive, but this was the abbreviation, conveying truth and capping the awful truth in a word. Only that gushing well, as I now knew, could never be fully capped.

Happier topics followed, but only at my prodding. The importance of that one topic – he did not want me to miss. He agreed that history is only what we write down, or pass along to the next generation, the rest is lost. He agreed that the "sacrifice" – his word, not mine – was for a higher purpose. It gnawed at him. I reminded him, you had to go, if you had not gone, did what you did, we would not be here, not have our freedom. I thought, and verbalized, that God puts us where we are meant to be at any given moment – and he had to be there. Richie looked up, "I agree with that." He became pensive. "I cannot imagine if the Germans had won …"

For some reason, that statement, earnest and sudden, jarred me. I realized, because it was the awful truth of his youth, they could have. The Nazis could have won. In his time, that was a real possibility. That was scary. Except for people like Richie, who put it all on the line, the Nazis would have won. Somehow as a teenager, Richie had managed to confront evil and survive. With hindsight, reading battles in books, outcomes look so simple, almost inevitable, sterile, just numbers. But they were none of those things, simple, inevitable, sterile or just numbers. They are lives, millions of them, lived with courage, humility, faith and determination, like Richie's.

He noted that, when he and his three brothers signed up, it was not with enthusiasm – "we just thought the world was ending." In other words, America was facing an existential threat; they had no choice but to defend all they loved. Even when he and others arrived in Italy, they were afraid, wanted to get the job done and get home.

Quietly sitting with Richie for two hours that day, hearing his stories retold – actually relived – forced me back to the stacks. What I found with further research on him, the 88th Infantry Division, and the Italian Campaign was arresting. The complete story was as riveting as his geographically separate pieces.

The final, nutshell version of Richie's tale is this. He went to war in October 1943, three-quarters of a century ago, along with his three brothers. He soon found himself in the US Army's 88th Infantry Division, training in the United States and North Africa, then joining the 5th Army at Naples, February 1944. Wearing a blue four-leafed clover on one shoulder, the division was said by captured Germans to "fight like devils," according to a 1947 encyclopedic, battle-by-battle account by General John Sloan, duly entitled *Blue Devils in Italy.* They took the name with pride, and were constantly on the front lines.

By mid-April, the Germans and Allies each had more than 20 divisions in Italy. From 11 May forward, the Blue Devils led the advance at Minturno, Formia, and in battles to recapture dozens of Italian villages, constantly navigating mountains, scaling cliffs, encountering German machine gun nests, and pressing hard-bitten Nazis north. Along the way, names stand out – Santa Maria, Castleforte, Monte Grande, Mount Diamono, Mount Ceracoli, Mount Rotondo, and Cassino. The 88th led an assault on the Gustav line, eventually broken left and right. As Sloan notes: "Once through the Gustav Line, there were mountains and more mountains." Some call these engagements, including Monte Cassino and surrounds, the hardest of the War. Monte Cassino required four assaults, massive aerial bombardment. Everywhere, the Fifth Army encountered intense German resistance. There are movies made about these battles.

The Blue Devils pushed on into Spigno, Mount Civita, Itri, Fondi, and Roccogorga. From there, the Fifth Army's reinforcement coincided with the long-awaited Anzio break out, which occurred between the 25th and 29th of May. From there, the Blue Devils pursued the Germans relentlessly to Rome.

Richie was a first scout. By day, first scouts, a term still used for reconnaissance specialists in the United States Army, including Army Rangers, led advancing troops by 25 to 50 yards. At night, they crept to the German lines, intentionally illuminating troop positions and artillery, conducting close-quarters reconnaissance, scrambling to get back alive. As he told me "bullets were everywhere, hitting around me everywhere in the dirt … I hid behind rocks, anything that could save you, a pebble, bullets on all sides …" That would, as books affirm, aptly describe it.

Not surprisingly, Blue Devil casualties were inordinately high, and higher among first scouts. A reported 14,000 Blue Devils were inserted at Naples. Of that number, more than 9,000 were removed from the battlefield as casualties, another 2,298 – according to the current Secretary of Defense – were killed. And so, any individual member of the 88th had less than one in five chance of returning home unscathed. First scouts were the least lucky of the bunch, with a turnover rate of nearly 100 percent. So yes, a miracle that Richie got home, to Wayne, at all.

The Blue Devils were the first unit to arrive in Rome. As Richie said to me, "then we slept." Yes, there he celebrated his 19th birthday. Notably, he wrote letters home to his father, the postmaster. As operational security was high, there was no way to tell the family where he was. So Richie developed a code he hoped his father might decipher. He changed his middle initial, on each successive letter home. His father got it. He knew he was in Rome.

The taking of Rome was of enormous significance. Think about it. At that exact time, the Supreme Allied Commander, Dwight Eisenhower, sat rolling on the Atlantic. He and 156,000 Allied troops lay over the horizon, preparing for D-Day, an all-or-nothing assault on Normandy, France. He had a limited window for that launch, accounting for tides, weather and need for a full moon. The weather on June 4, 1944, in Britain and France, was miserable, clouds heavy, low light, high winds. If Ike waited, he would lose any chance of a June landing. In hold posture, he learned of the Allied victory over the Germans at Rome. The news must have heartened Allied troops, especially the officer corps – for their pending beach assault.

On June 6, 1944 – two days after Richie arrived in Rome, Allied boys hit the beaches of Normandy, 1,000 miles north. But the Blue Devils were not done. Neither was Richie. On July 8th, 1944, they attacked the "fortress town" of Volterra, another legendary assault, movies about that too. They liberated the town in a day. Four days later, they took Laiatico. Five days later, they took Villamagna.

Within a week of Villamagna, they retook San Miniato, where Nazis killed civilians and mined the city. The 88th then crossed the Arno River – bringing tanks, artillery and trucks, and facing "bitter Nazi resistance" from Pisa to Florence. Between Volterra and the Arno, the 88th suffered 142 officers and 2,257 enlisted men killed, wounded or missing.

As the Nazis retreated, they blew up bridges. Americans built pontoon bridges. These got swept away on high water; Americans rebuilt them. There was no stopping the Blue Devils. Having smashed the Gustav line and taken Rome, they helped liberate Florence, then beat the Germans in battles at Mounts Battaglia, Capello, and Grande, then Verona and the Brenner Pass.

Richie was recognized for his courage in places like Minturno and Formia, Anzio and Rome, the Arno River, Apennienes and Po Valley, Bologna to Verona. He received the European/African/Middle East Theater Campaign Ribbon, three battle stars and other medals, eventually a Bronze Star for heroic actions. The gist is this – he did what he had to do. On return, his brother Bunt told him he had to forget it. Richie did what his brother told him. He forgot much of it – the best as he could – until recently. Then he remembered, in detail. Bits and pieces of these battles got retold on that summer day, not long ago.

Reflecting on what Richie shared, and on research affirming the miraculous history of the 88th Infantry Division in Italy, I thought perhaps a short note of recognition from a notable figure might be in order. Knowing a colleague who had worked with retired Defense Secretary and Senator William Cohen, I wondered if the retired Secretary might draft a note for Richie. The response was overwhelming – and positive.

The former Secretary and Senator promptly penned a letter to the aging Blue Devil, and first scout from Wayne, Maine. Then, he purchased a recent book on Anzio, inscribed it to him, and had the former Vice Chairman of the Joint Chiefs, General Ralston, and former head of Materials Command, General Kern, also inscribe it. Somehow, Secretary

Cohen then managed to have the current Secretary of Defense, James Mattis, inscribe the book to Richie.

Several days before I was to present the letter and book to Richie, I was told that Secretary Mattis, probably the most decorated living Marine and a leader with much on his mind, had also penned a hand-written letter to Richie. On reflection, I think Mattis was amazed a first scout from the 88th was still alive. These letters were duly presented before a group of local Maine veterans.

From Defense Secretary James Mattis, in his unhurried hand and all caps:

"DEAR MR LINCOLN,

I WRITE TO PAY YOU AND YOUR BROTHERS-IN-ARMS THE RESPECT OF TODAY'S U.S. MILITARY. THERE ARE NOT WORDS SUFFICIENT TO DESCRIBE YOUR GENERATION'S DEVOTION TO DUTY IN THE FACE OF THE GRIMMEST CIRCUMSTANCES. NOWHERE WAS THIS MORE TRUE THAN FOR THOSE WHO LED FROM THE FRONT IN CLOSE COMBAT.

YOU AND YOUR COMRADES SET THE STANDARD FOR PATRIOTIC COMMITMENT. TODAY'S SOLDIERS BUILD CONFIDENCE FROM YOUR STOIC EXAMPLE, KNOWING THAT WE WILL NEVER FACE ANYTHING WORSE THAN YOU OVERCAME.

PLEASE ACCEPT THE RESPECTS OF US ALL IN THE DEPARTMENT OF DEFENSE.

JAMES MATTIS, SEC DEF."

The second letter was from retired Secretary and Senator William Cohen. Slightly longer, the letter's essence included personal gratitude to Richie for his "military service to the United States of America as a First Scout in the 88th Infantry Division," and for his heroism "in the Italian Campaign of World War II," for which Richie received the Bronze Star. Cohen further noted the difficulty of transitioning from North Africa to combat in "the cold and wet marshlands, surrounded by mountains in Italy," observing that, "despite heavy casualties and epidemic conditions, resulting from Malaria-carrying mosquitos, you repeatedly risked your life on the front lines" and "demonstrated extraordinary bravery, enduring dangerous enemy fire to launch flares to illuminate enemy weapon batteries."

In addition, the former Secretary of Defense affirmed, "the 88th Division was part of the Fifth Army and it was the first Division to enter a combat zone in WWII," being "made up of mostly draftees." Cohen added, "You fought so fiercely on your way to capture Rome that German prisoners historically remarked that the troops of the 88th fought 'like devils,' earning the Division's nickname the 'Blue Devils,'" and "even under the worst circumstances, the men of the 88th played an integral part in the defeat of the German Army in Italy."

Becoming more personal, Cohen wrote: "Your many acts of courage, and the troops who served alongside you, contributed significantly to the Allies' successful capture of Rome, the ultimate wartime victory, and the assurance of the freedom of future generations." As a result, "it is indeed a privilege and an honor for me to recognize you as one of Maine's true heroes, Richard, and I would like to extend my personal gratitude to you for your unwavering commitment and dedication to our great nation." He closed: "Sincerely, William S. Cohen, United States Secretary of Defense, 1997-2001."

Four inscriptions lay within the book. In order, they read:

"TO MR. RICHARD LINCOLN – YOU HAVE THE RESPECT AND AFFECTION OF TODAY'S MILITARY. YOU AND YOUR BROTHERS-IN-ARMS ARE THE PRIDE OF OUR COUNTRY. LET ME TAKE THIS OPPORTUNITY TO THANK YOU FOR YOUR COURAGE AND SACRIFICE. WITH GREATEST RESPECT, JIM MATTIS, U.S. SECRETARY OF DEFENSE."

Then:

"To Mr. Richard Lincoln, Your courage, service and willingness to sacrifice life and limb for our nation makes you a hero to me and the many millions who enjoy freedom in America and abroad today. Thank you for all that you have done for us. William S. Cohen, former Secretary of Defense."

Then:

"Mr. Lincoln – You are a remarkable man who was part of the toughest fighting in WWII. The 'Blue Devils' set a standard for all to be measured against. I am grateful for the sacrifice you made as a young man and thankful you are still with us to receive my thanks. Paul Kern, GEN. US Army (Retired)."

Finally:

"To Mr. Richard Lincoln, I am deeply grateful for your service to our Nation. I have visited Anzio and was truly moved by the sacrifices you and your brave colleagues made during that battle in 1944. With deepest respect, Joe Ralston, General, USAF (Ret), Supreme Allied Commander Europe, 2000-2003."

On that bright fall day, as we read commendations to our quiet Wayne warrior, once part of the indomitable "Blue Devils," everyone got a chance to thank Richie. By unexpected good fortune, we also had the chance to replay to him a speech made by Secretary Mattis before the Association of the Army, in Washington D.C.

In that nationally televised speech, America's Secretary of Defense singled out Richie for recognition, an example of what is best about America and those who defend her from small towns coast to coast. If you are curious and possess Internet access, you may search: https://www.c-span.org/video/?c4686104/richard-lincoln. You will see what many in his town, including me, watched with pride and surprise – a real tribute.

So, going back in time to that long and emotional, early summer day when we first talked of these difficult things in depth, I finally turned our conversation to other topics. Richie's trip back in time had been tiring.

I offered an update on town news, arriving summer folks, a pending supper at the yacht club, an auction at the church. I told him we missed seeing him in the Wayne General Store. He chuckled, reminding me that tourists used to be called "summer complaints." I told him Tubby's ice cream shop was doing a smart business. He told me his favorite flavors. I put the thought away, for a future visit.

"Is there anything I can bring you? Anything you do not have that you want? Radio, books?" I asked. "No, not really, I don't think I need anything." "Do you watch television?" I asked, seeing one in his room. "No, I think the world just turns and turns… no need to watch." "Do you have a favorite candy bar?" I tried. "Well yes," he smiled, "I like *Oh Henry!*" "Great," I said, "Let me see what I can do about that …" I had not seen an *Oh Henry!* bar in years. "That and *Hershey,* none of the others." "Ok," I said, "next time you see me, which I expect will be later this week, I will have an *Oh Henry!* for you!" "That would be nice," he said.

"Can you use anything else, anything at all?" I asked, a final time. "Just conversation … I like having a good conversation … thank you for coming." "Well, I enjoy our talks, I always have, and I will be back again, end of the week – with an *Oh Henry!*" And I was. He was happy when I returned. We had another conversation, lighter this time. We had many after that, including the day those letters were read among friends.

Only now do I realize how much Richie carried and for how long. He did it quietly, for all of us. How much he held back I never appreciated – until that June day. When I visit him these days, it is with deeper appreciation. He has an American flag on his wall, full size. He has a couple of plants. He still insists there are no bad days. Somehow, I wonder if he is still protecting. But with his impish smile, he insists. We owe debts we can never repay. We can only acknowledge, remember, and hope to do our part when called. Richie's boyhood was different. Because it was, mine was.

Richie in his early 20s, back from WWII, sporting his new tobacco wagon. Having seen war's worst as a First Scout in the 88th Infantry Division (famous "Blue Devils") during the Italian Campaign, he took his brother's advice – and stayed active. Over the next 25 years, Richie drove – as he liked saying – "from Kittery to Fort Kent" selling cigars. He and wife Nan raised two daughters, Elaine and Lisa. Richie was one of the four Lincoln brothers who saw combat in WWII.

Richie, age 87, at The Old Post Office, once run by his brother, before that by his father. American flag to left, POW-MIA flag to right. Richie marched in 58 consecutive Memorial Day Parades. (Photo credit to Dean Gyorgy, who also located boyhood photo of Richie and Paul)

Richard Lincoln, in hallmark bow tie, at his 2017 recognition ceremony, age 92

40. Depth Perception

Linc is a gentle sort, upbeat, down to earth, a gentleman – and cheerful, like Richie. He was my English teacher. With patience, he taught me to write. He insisted I learn how to write, never lowering standards for those he knew could, with some effort, meet them. He is now in his 90s. His story, like the others, will remain forever untold – unless told. So, here it is.

Calling him, I asked if we could visit. He was quick to accommodate, although still heavily scheduled. Somehow, he never slows down. Maybe there is something to Richie's and Priscilla's maxim that we are kept young by staying active. At the appointed time, I padded up his driveway. Through a bay window, I saw Linc studiously reading his newspaper – no moment wasted.

Inside, he first had to know – like Priscilla, Richie and others – what I was up to. How were my siblings, kids, mother, work, life generally, in that order? Per my obligation, I caught him up, and then – finally – turned to his wartime record. Odd, I thought, that in the four decades I had known him, we never spoke on this topic. No matter, we would now.

"Well," he began, "I put my junior and senior high school grades together, graduating at sixteen, and enrolled at Brown University." This I had never heard. It seemed an auspicious beginning for a World War II veteran. Linc soon disabused me of my admiration. "I flunked out in one semester, failing every course except English, where I got a C plus." My eyes got wide. "At seventeen, early 1944, I enlisted and became an apprentice seaman."

Here began the real story. "My boot company consisted of 120. In the group, two of us had unusual eyesight, perfect depth perception. Back then, there was no radar for the big guns. Gunfire was controlled optically. So, we were trained to use optical range finders to determine distance, speed, direction." Linc paused. "I sometimes say my eyesight saved my life … The rest of the boot company got assigned to a light cruiser, which was sunk and two-thirds of the crew died." He pauses. "I would have been on that ship, if it hadn't been for my eyes."

I ask my old teacher how the event affected his thinking. "I thought 'Thank God, my eyes have saved my life' and … how lucky I was." For a moment, Linc draws a line to his father, and his father's luck. "My father was a friend, and in this I was lucky too. He was serving as paymaster for the 5th Marine Corp, which fought at Okinawa, but as paymaster, he was required to stay back in New Zealand." He pauses again. "My older brother George went into submarines, saw a lot of action. I wanted to get into the Navy, and get to the Pacific." Later he adds: "Interestingly, my father, brother and I all served in the Pacific at that same time."

Linc then explains his eyesight has always allowed him, even now, to "see depth to a measurably more accurate degree" than most people. As if to illustrate the point, he notes that a pen I gave him–sitting five feet away on the table–was "made in China." I am aghast, as I have given these pens away for years, never seen any sign of foreign manufacture. He points out the miniscule lettering, on slivers of the clip – one side "made in," the other "China." Even showing me, I can barely see these indentations. His sight is remarkable.

"After learning gunnery on the Battleship Wyoming, I took a ship through the Canal to Pearl Harbor and on to the mid-Pacific, where I transferred to a destroyer escort." He chuckles. "I and one other became the 'gunnery department,' managing the Quad 40-millimeter gun positioned in the bow … that was my battle position." He explains that, after several months, he was transferred to another destroyer escort, 100 miles off Japanese islands, from there to Landing Ship Medium at Okinawa, called simply LSM 201.

From here, things got more exciting. LSM 201 was destined for Iwo Jima, the invasion. He trained for the invasion, and his ship was assigned to "one of the invasion flotillas." On one hand, he was eager to be in the mix; on the other he notes that – somehow – fate again intervened and "saved my life." As his LSM prepared to invade and disembark Iwo Jima, the engine broke down. As a result, his team had to wait three days, before arriving on Iwo Jima. "By that time, we were not needed, so we were sent to Okinawa …to train for the invasion of Japan."

Here, an unlikely line falls from my old teacher, a man who spent his professional life in The Academy, as far removed from modern politics as life will allow. "An invasion would have been very bloody … because the Japanese did not give up an inch without exacting a human toll." He continues. "We were on our way to Japan … when America dropped two atomic bombs." So, it was close again; they were underway for the invasion of Japan. "By the time we got there, no war … we stayed several months, then to the Philippines, then back the United States." Somehow, he again seems acutely aware of his good fortune. More grateful than wistful, he adds, "I was where the action was taking place, but always just missed it."

Two last surprises lay in wait. "On the way home, mid-Pacific, we lost our generators. Navy ships all took on water; we needed those generators to pump water from the hull, otherwise the ship sank. We were nervous. It took two days for another ship to come, generators to be fixed."

At Pearl Harbor, he rendezvoused with his brother George, who had stories to tell of submarine warfare. Linc recalls George's sub – like all of them – was "named for a fish." Linc then gets serious. "The last leg, from Pearl through the Canal to Norfolk, nearly cost me my life …" War over, many officers were decommissioned there in Hawaii, including his ship commander. "He was replaced with a music major from Yale, who did not know the ship, but insisted on navigating. Off the coast of Mexico, the Fox radio barked … We were told, 'Turn everything off, all, everything!' He had gotten us into the middle of a U.S. minefield, fifty miles from the Canal. We turned everything off, and waited. He was taken off the ship, replaced by a high ranking enlisted, who took over, got us through the Canal, stopped in Cuba, then to Norfolk."

Linc pauses, as if to let the totality of it sweep me, and perhaps himself again. "Three weeks later, I was back at Brown. They took me back as a member of the 'Veterans College,' but I did well enough to get transferred to the regular college and graduated in three years. My brother George also graduated from Brown; we went together." From there, Linc got married, proceeded to PhD studies at Virginia and Duke, had kids and moved to Maine, where he then taught high school for decades to eager kids, including me. Over the years, he has served on many local boards, among them boards for Maine Public Broadcasting, Bates College, and Senior College for the University of Maine. He is always giving back.

Having finally heard his Navy record and the series of fateful near misses, I asked if any special feelings attached. He was quick with an answer, one I did not expect. "I learned how to take responsibility … I learned how to fire those guns. I learned how to learn what I had to learn. And I learned how to make friends with those whose backgrounds were very different. I learned how to do what I set my mind to learning. It was not easy. I was very immature. Once I learned, I really felt proud. At first, I was scared that I was in something over my head, but I learned no – that if you find out what you have to do, learn it, you can do it. It gave me confidence. That was the most important gift from those years." That is the gift that he gave to many of us.

And there it was, in a nutshell. Linc had more than one kind of depth perception. The English teacher who gave me confidence, learned his confidence as an apprentice seaman, training on guns of the Battleship Wyoming, preparing for the Iwo Jima invasion, then the invasion of Japan that never happened. He used his newfound confidence to excel at Brown, Virginia and Duke, then to teach kids in rural Maine to write. And one of them, among the hundreds he taught, finally got on paper a bit of what motivated him, to motivate us, to do a thing like this. Linc is a gentle sort, an English teacher with unusual depth perception.

Lincoln Ladd (Linc) in uniform, WWII-era photo, destined for the Pacific

Linc today, thriving in his 90s, my former English teacher, elder of a grateful town

41. Ebony and Ermine

Count them, exactly 36 ebony and 52 cream. That was the number of keys our lacquered upright piano had. Used to be, everyone had an old upright. We were among the "everyone" who did. Ours dated, like most uprights, to a time when music was more often played than bought. Not long ago, that was much of America. And people hung onto their uprights. Mom liked to play.

The upright stood just inside the woodshed door. We passed it every day, mostly ignored it. We came and went, went and came. It never changed, never moved, never spoke on its own. It had horizontal surfaces, which was dangerous in our house. Books got piled on the top board, papers on corners, art projects and mail on fall board. The upright was what you might call a utility infielder, catcher of every pitch, whether being played or not played.

Of course, the upright got musical use, too. More than one family member tickled the ivories, filling the house with warm notes, especially at holidays. Then, we were back to ignoring it, piling it high with books and papers. That was the routine, until one bizarre day. On that day, everything changed. I never took the upright for granted again. I always passed the dark lacquer, half hoping for another shooting star.

If not quite midnight, our upright was dark and dignified. The keyboard was an enchanting mix of dense forest and bright tusk. My sisters dabbled at the keys. Mom played Christmas and Broadway favorites. When Mom played, we all sang. Central to our living room, the piano stood among woodstoves, a nondescript couch, cluttered table, unreachable mantle, phone stand, floor-to-ceiling bookcases, old organ and gun rack. Stage center, it was a star, if overlooked. Over the years, we just took it for granted.

That changed one afternoon. The family was ice fishing. I was stuck at home, doing homework. Mom was a teacher, so fishing waited on homework, not the other way around. The day's duties lay before me, chiefly math and physics. I was stuck at the wobbly kitchen table, around the corner from the living room – out of sight of the upright.

Outside, things were cold, inordinately so. Between pondering equations, I got up and made the rounds, re-stoking fires. We had two stoves in the living room, one in the kitchen, all wood-fed. Now and again, I absentmindedly picked up wood, flipped up a stove cover, fed the coals, and returned to my seat. Eyes get tired. I just wanted to finish. I worked at it. In the kitchen, I spread out papers. When bored or hungry, I walked around. Sometimes I warmed my hands at a stove. Sometimes I opened the fridge, just looked. Then, I came back and sat down to work.

Late day, the sun laid beams across the table. Temperatures were falling. All three fires were hungry, needed tending. I could feel the chill through the window. Outside, light was slipping away. I turned on the overhead, and kept steady at my work. The family remained away, but they would be back soon. I kept turning pages. "Unless acted upon by an external force, a body at rest will remain at rest … in motion will remain in motion." So forth and so on.

I chewed pinwheel cookies, read, wrote, paused to think, and paused to pause. My homework kept me focused. Now and then, eyes needed adjusting. The last thing on my mind was the upright. I just needed to un-fuzz my brain. I decided to make a slow circuit around the living room, warming hands at each fire, gazing on the lake. I made the circuit once, uneventfully – kitchen, living room, phone table, small stove and upright, potbelly, window and back. I was looking forward to "calling it a day." The fog of over-focus had me.

Before long, I was on another circuit – through the doorframe, past phone table, stove, upright, potbelly, window, and back. Nothing unusual. More studying. Finally, I rose for a third blasé perambulation through the living room. Despite the cold, our house was tight, more or less.

Rounding the corner from kitchen to living room, I suddenly stopped. Something was not right. Something was off. *What was off?* I hunted for an anomaly. Maybe it was just my imagination. *Why did something seem not right? Why were my senses telling me engage?* All of a sudden, I was queasy. I was either in a forest, or the forest was in the living room. I looked, then looked again. What my eyes told my brain made no sense. Like finding a penguin in the tub, zebra in a chair, lemur on a lamp, chipmunk in the fridge, cow jumping the moon, it was goofy. My mind and eyes were having a dispute.

"Something not right …"

"Forget it."

"Not right …"

"Ignore it, carry on."

"Something is wrong, have to wake up."

Then, I did. Standing on the upright was a tuxedoed tenor, ready for Carnegie Hall. Not shy, he seemed proud, bold and unmoved. On pearly legs, we had an uninvited guest. And he was staring me down. He was probably as shocked to see me, as I was him. By reputation, he was a recluse. He was also a pint-sized warrior, stealthy, fierce, and not much on music. He was not known for malingering, but he was malingering. Maybe he thought I mistook him for the mess around him. Maybe he was blending. Either way, he stayed. Sharp eyes glared from his white body, neon against the upright. A snowy owl would have hidden better. Standing atop our upright, with nerves of steel, was … *a white ermine.*

He eyed me hard. *Was it fear, wonder, curiosity – all three?* He was intense, had a motivated stare. Not to be outdone, I returned the stare. For one interminable moment, maybe a minute, we faced each other unblinking. He did not show any sign of ill health. Quite the reverse, he radiated royal indifference. If anything, he was put out with my arrival. The outdoors were cold, and he looked mighty comfortable, there on the piano. What was I doing here? He had a perch, 360-degree view, two stoves and peace. What more could an honest ermine want?

How long had he been there? I wondered. *How many times had I shuffled by, not seeing him? Had I missed him on my last circuit?* He was poised to jump if pressed. He had seen me first, decided to bide his time. Brilliantly, he assumed the posture of belonging. He waited for me to notice. *Well, he was noticed now.*

To be fair, a Maine ermine was worth observing. He wore white fur all winter – lovely. That he stood unmoving was remarkable. I had never seen one, except in books. Reputed to be clever, nimble, daring and resourceful – he obviously was. Made the species proud. He might not play piano, but he sure cut a profile. That said, it was time for action. He did not belong here.

Ermine molt from scruffy brown to white each fall. In spring, they molt back to brown, which takes more time. They match themselves to the seasons, white for snow, brown for mud, to avoid detection. They turn white from tail to head, brown from head to tail. Dead winter, they almost blend with the tusk keys of an upright piano, but not quite.

Rationality interceded. An ermine would be an inveterate pest, aggressive and problematic. He did not belong in our house, glorious as he was. The ermine's winter coat, once prized for capes and heraldic shields, gave way at twelve to a coat of pure brown weasel. In every season, they were predators. They could take down an animal three times their size. We had cats and rabbits. The ermine's presence was a problem.

I watched him with fascination, knowing he could not stay. He was a fine example of a gutsy, short-tailed weasel, hard to find when you are looking for them. He was a foot long and handsome at eye level, white coat pristine against our dark upright. His coat was tailored like an Italian suit, right down to the wispy, black tip. I knew he moved like a hummingbird.

Our truce persisted slightly longer, a rare interspecies equipoise. What he thought of me I do not know, cannot hazard a guess. Watching him was exciting, but had to end. I resolved to let him go, on my terms. I would practice physics. "A body at rest will remain at rest, unless …" Neither of us broke our gaze. Slowly, I slipped one hand around the telephone book. Imperceptibly – or maybe not – I prepared my sidearm throw. The objective was to deter a future visit. Even on cold nights, pianos are not meant for ermine. This could not become a regular thing. We might both admire the upright, but we lived in different places.

Suddenly, I whipped the phonebook in his direction. He knew his options. Any animal capable of eating something three times his size was not going to fall to a phonebook. The flapping projectile fluttered through space, and bounced off a bookcase. Long before it landed, he was gone. How he got out is a mystery, but he was down, around and out before my eyes could follow. What a day we had, we three – the upright, ermine and me. Time moved on, but I never ignored the upright again. Sometimes, I pictured the little guy there. Ebony and ivory, turned ebony and ermine.

42. Icicle War

You know the famous battles,
On Lipizzaner and Frisian,
The Carthaginian,
Peloponnesian.

Epic contests, bravely fought,
Combat, flashing steel,
Marathon and Agincourt,
No icicles, no zeal.

Oh yes, Hundred Year,
Shakespeare's praise,
History, hope and fear,
All that, the Olden Days.

We aimed somewhat higher,
In weather bright and bland,
Becoming horseless squire,
Frozen armaments in hand.

We took them off with care,
Held high, suspended there,
Imagined we were He
Of Edinburgh's Chair.

Knights, ice blades free,
Swords drawn dispassionately,
We swung and smashed,
Frozen sabers, exploding clashed.

"En garde!" blurted one,
Then wild, cascading cries,
Excitement punctuated
Every blade's demise.

Slivers flew like swallows
Cavorting on the breeze,

Gloved hands gripped tight
Just a temporary squeeze.

Slippery, fat and frozen,
Shrinking every blow,
These splendid fencing tools
Went ice, to stub, to snow.

Breathless now, laughing,
We gasped, once more
Surveyed eaves above
For implements of war.

In jest we skirmished,
Knuckles getting red,
From roof we plucked
Every frozen shred.

Then at last, we fell,
Giddy in our lore,
Maine's Roundtable,
Another icicle war.

43. Indoor Storms

Some winters, storms came inside. The ceilings sagged as snow mounded up, temperatures rose, and water came south – into the house. Suddenly, we were stepping around drips and over puddles. We were rearranging furniture, having family huddles, getting assignments. As circles grew, we put down pans, bottles and buckets.

Overhead, shoveling got top priority. Snow had to go. That was my job. I did not mind. I liked roof duty. Forbidden in other seasons, I was finally *invited* up there, late winter. Shoveling was the price of admission. And standing there, where Santa sometimes stood, I caught whispers on the wind, took in all the meadows and forest, Androscoggin's expanse. Then I leaned into roof duty, and shoveled.

Inside, everyone set to putting about water catchers, listened to footsteps on the shingles. They could hear my shuffling, and pounding of ice. Some years, a weather pattern hung off the coast for weeks, dropping snow every day. Rather than sliding, the snow piled up on our shallow, tar-shingled roof. That was a sign of things to come. And meant I was soon shoveling.

If snow did not slide by mid-March, it was not going to. It was coming through – not off – the roof. Warm days combined with woodstove heat, cold nights and re-freezing to create a glacier overhead. If temperatures fell fast enough, icepack became slush, then water. Even in light snow years, our roof was not designed for drainage. It was neither steep nor watertight. Why, I am not sure – but that was how it was. The North Atlantic snuck into our every room.

There was a routine. Water spots showed up first. If they turned yellow, dark and heavy, we could expect drips. Some years, they poured. We found ourselves fumbling and finding, placing and positioning, hauling and emptying buckets and baking bowls, sauce pans and juice cans, big and small Tupperware containers. We were shifting books wholesale, toting stacks of paper and vinyl records, wiping shelves and covering what could not be moved. We were mopping and toweling, sopping up spatter, in a phrase, managing an indoor storm.

Not all homes faced this predicament, although many did. If life unfolded under a metal roof, steep grade or tight flashing, the snow slid. If a roof was shallow, shingled or old, get out pans and pots. Roof shoveling was serious business, too. Done wrong, a shoveling Samaritan could break shingles, compounding the indoor storm. He might put a hole in the roof, or worse – come through. Visions of my boots dangling through sheetrock kept me focused. I worked shingles with care, tapping for studs. Getting snow down was the priority, with care.

When the whole ceiling started to bow, time really mattered. Given our shallow roof, action accelerated outside and in. With buckets and bowls, we deployed kitchenware, bread pans and pie tins, number eights and Campbell's cylinders, pitchers and vases, anything that would hold water. Outside, I got the ladder and shovel, propelled myself up – back to work. Before long, the indoor storms passed. By spring, they were forgotten – until next year.

These days, Mainers mostly have watertight roofs. Smart thing, too. If not steep, they are well shingled or metal capped. Somehow, ours never fell into those categories. We went with buckets and bowls, ladder and shovel. We manned the ramparts, until indoor storms passed and ceiling no longer sagged. Sounds silly, but back then, we watched the ceiling for signs, the way modern Americans monitor weather apps and global positioning. A shift in color, shade, texture, or bend, let alone a sag, meant an indoor storm was coming. So, we sprang into action.

44. *Doris Anne*

We often admire most in others what we do not have in ourselves, or have less in ourselves than we wish we had. Heroes are born of that sentiment, as are admired loved ones, closest friends, and sometimes mothers.

By definition, mothers bring us into the world, give us all they can, and center their working lives on an oath to survival, revival, encouragement and growth – ours. They never stop being who they once were, no matter the passage of time. We can never catch up with them, and wouldn't wish to. Fathers are special, too. As one, I can say we do our part, but this is about mothers, one in particular.

Doris Anne is in perpetual motion, always teaching children – hers and others – and recording life's beauty, chiefly in watercolors. She has met adversity with resilience, made ends meet on a school teacher's salary, forged her way with inner peace and outer resolve, and wearing a smile for the better part of 80 years.

In the process, she has piled up a mountain of returns, oceans of laughter, and more friends per acre than God allows blades of grass. Daily, she mixes dreams, reflections and earth tones, painting and teaching, teaching and painting. She can capture the quick surf mid-curl, a sunset in dabs and swirls, an old barn tipping precariously, young kids playing gregariously.

She transposes Katahdin's grandeur stroke by stroke, keeps streams gurgling forever, guzzling from trout ponds, just beyond. She records the blue heron's poise and dignity, motionless and drifting in flight, captures colors not seen by others, his resolution and will. From speckled feathers on a whimsical wash, end of fall, you hear the loon's haunting call. She has caught the ocean, which is a feat – in its moody blues and shifting hues.

She has painted hundreds of watercolors over 50 artistic years. From Pemaquid Point's long, metamorphic gray stones and igneous white dikes, preserved in cerulean blue, lamp black and Chinese whites, to the ancient cliffs of Grand Manan and Monhegan, rounded gabbro, shadows of cadmium red, burnt umber, gold ochre at sunset. They rise above crashing, splashing surf, surging in cobalt green and aquamarine.

From Western mountains to inland lakes, Moosehead to Androscoggin, she has recreated evergreens in vivid viridian, gentle mixes of cobalt blue and green, a touch of olive, nickel and manganese. Trees often tumble onto wide beaches of new gamboge yellow, met by waves of ultramarine, here and there a lonely glacial rock.

She is fond of young birch stands, tall birds and endangered animals, from dignified cranes and glowing egrets to sullen seagulls and burrowing owls, all of which feature in her children's books – of which there are now more than ten. She deposits plentiful peace in all these pictures, there to be found by those who pause to look around.

Nor has her work gone wholly unnoticed. Today, it lights homes and workplaces from Maine to Bermuda, from Canada to India, and has been on display in permanent collections and private galleries. Over five decades, she has run galleries in Wayne, Rockland, and Orr's Island, so she has had her time in the sun. But it's really about her connection to Maine's beauty, and the art she creates with love.

Over that same span of years, she taught elementary school, lower grades and remedial reading, while also teaching watercolors to adults on weekends and evenings. She has opened endless vistas to eager children, adding compassion and guidance, patience and second-mothering. Teaching hundreds of kids through more than four decades, she lifted countless hearts and brightened innumerable days.

As is the way with all good teachers, many of those she taught have never forgotten, later writing and visiting her. If you are a teacher, you know – your life is embedded in those minds and hearts. All begin small and doubting, but once taught love, grow large and strong. Anyone who has had a good teacher knows, that is their gift.

Somehow, she managed to raise four children, more or less on her own – with smiles and laughter, applying hope as eternal balm, best medicine for disaster. And when a need to retreat swept her, she staved off what rushed on, made sense of the senseless, by turning to her faith.

She is one of a kind, still rising each day to paint, and by painting still teaching – how to find ballast in life's wildly whipping winds. Across her works, you see those proud birds and vibrant flowers, cresting waves and evergreen towers, simple praise for the miracle of it all.

She is no veteran or hero in the ordinary sense, never carried a rifle or flew a plane, never took a mountain or island, except by leaving them where she found them. Her battles and buffets have been closer to home. And we, beneficiaries of her love, carry forward a bit of that perspective.

The artist's heart, infused with unseen purpose, understands that everyone must find their own hum and sources of harmony, but she has hers and shares them. That is the magic of her loving life: She takes in the world and gives it all away. Like mothers everywhere, she does what she can. That is the magic of Doris Anne.

Doris Anne (Holman), mother and artist, Circa 1997

One of Doris Anne's classic Maine seagulls, from her children's books

Doris Anne painting on the Maine coast, Circa 1970s

Doris Anne painting on Monhegan Island, observed by my siblings, young Charlie, Cynthia, Anita

Katahdin by Doris Anne

Birches by Doris Anne

Maine Coast by Doris Anne

45. Christmas Traditions

Christmas … There is magic in the word. Traditions, holy and secular, hallowed and simple defined the season. Everyone turned happy during Advent. Kids laughed, parents approved. The scent of evergreen flowed from freshly cut trees, homemade wreaths and garlands. Stoves rattled, people tried not to, and thoughts universally turned toward others.

No sooner were Thanksgiving dishes done, than Advent was upon us. We began imagining the Christmas tree, stringing lights, humming carols. By Christmas day, a little sleigh would be piled high with gifts, sitting on our dinner table. Red ribbons with names would be pulled, on cue. An old "grab bag" would await our digging and giving ritual, as it had for five generations.

Early December, young minds began plotting. Gifts had to be made and wrapped, cards written and read. Time accelerated. Mom was in high gear, so her four kids followed. She made cookies; we sprinkled them red and green for giving away – and eating. She baked apple, peach and blueberry pies for freezing; one was eaten by nightfall. The air grew rich with cinnamon, nutmeg, ginger, and chocolate. Cranberry candles showed up on the mantelpiece. Homemade applesauce bubbled on the stove. Bing Crosby sang "White Christmas" from spinning vinyl. People began to smile, without thinking about it.

Before long, lights were up. They adorned homes and trees, bushes and barns. Colors bobbed on evening breezes, scattered in fog, sprayed snow banks, lit dangling icicles and falling flakes. Strings of light jumped from house to house, and town to town. Every living room seemed aglow. Candles appeared in windows, and the world became one big tapestry.

White lights, especially, jumped out. You saw them in apple orchards and trimming farmhouses. They always struck me as pristine, like splintering moonlight, a bit of heaven brought to earth. Gambrel roofs turned elegant white, poignant and quieting, like monochrome wedding photos. On windless, silent nights, these little white lights warmed the darkness.

Elsewhere, rainbow lights spiraled and undulated under dark eaves, crisscrossing big lawns in radiant hues. Young eyes filled and thrilled to the festival, all these exotic colors, macaw red and finch gold, lorikeet blue, parakeet green, tang yellow, Garibaldi orange. We soaked up the feathers, blooms and bursts. *Christmas was coming!*

It was – as it had for centuries. That is how Christmas must have felt in 1933 – when my grandmother and grandfather were married. Exciting. Their hearts must have leapt. My grandmother had just finished Vassar, my grandfather Cornell. Two years later, he was hard at work – and a second lieutenant in the Army Reserves. Two more years, and my mother was born; another two and my aunt arrived. And then … tragedy. In 1941, as America went to war, my grandfather died – not in combat, but of cancer.

Suddenly, my grandmother was alone. She had two little girls, two aging parents, her two brothers in combat, and her nation at war. She rallied, as always, and so did our nation. She moved in with her parents, caring for them and her girls, learned to drive, took up teaching, eventually became a school principal.

My mother, then age four, was old enough to feel loss and disorientation. That Christmas, she asked for a Cocker Spaniel. She might as well have asked for the moon, or her father back, maybe her uncles home from war, or peace for the world. Santa did not see fit to bring her a dog – or peace for the world – that year.

The family struggled, but Christmas traditions were held high. The tree was warmly decorated. Stockings were hung along a mantel, twenty-two with visiting aunts and cousins. The kitchen buzzed and a feast followed. The family celebrated, laughed and played, sang and prayed.

In our youth, as in our mother's, Christmas music lifted the heart. Harmonious voices rose like wind instruments in a cathedral, dancing in the beams, ricocheting through the rafters, taking the chill out of cold stone. Like hearing Handel's "Messiah," voices awake in song elevated the soul. Even without the cathedral, music was buoyant. Kindness multiplied.

In our town, as across America, people seemed to suspend judgment at Christmas. For once, they put themselves in others' shoes. Missteps got waved off, vulnerabilities acknowledged, sensibilities protected, and foibles forgiven. The rough contours of human interaction became smooth. Why at Christmas only, I do not know. But the season touched us all.

Small towns, perhaps big cities, tightened at Christmas. Not perfectly, but predictably. People rose above what lay without, to celebrate what lay within. Once again, they cared for each other. They looked for ways to help, listened more closely, gave more reflexively. Miracles were hoped on, and seemed to happen. Old debts were unexpectedly forgiven, heavy burdens jointly borne, tolerances exceeded with grace, prayers murmured and hopes rekindled. Ironically, kids helped that process, recalling to adults the innocence of childhood. And whatever the lot of our neighbor, we knew John Bradford was right: "There but for the grace of God go I." We remembered this lesson most at Christmas.

As kids, we anticipated giving and getting gifts, looked for indulgence, and focused on the tree. One year, cutting the tree fell to us. We were literally commissioned to bring home that year's tree from the forest. *Talk about a thrill!* I was fourteen, my siblings younger. Sled in tow, our entourage set out. When we arrived at "the spot," we were in shock. Nothing around us fit the living room. The forest was all Sequoias, or seemed so. We passed through white pines, black and blue spruce, hemlock, mixed hardwoods. No luck. We just needed a short-needled tree, lots of branches, smaller than six feet. The forest had none.

We crunched in endless circles, until we had to stop. Anything would do. Eight eyes fervently hunted for that year's tree. Finally, we found one. Unanimity was important. We cut at snow line, then a few feet higher. We limbed the base, put it on the sled, took it home, and put it up. *Proud* is the only word.

Next came decorating. Every year, that tradition brought family together. Baubles got dug out, corncob dolls and hand-knit bells, baked ceramics, carved wood, glazed clay and breakable glass. We found flat, hand-painted Nutcrackers, and Styrofoam balls with ribbons and push pins. For garlands, popcorn and cranberries met construction paper. Old lights were hot, so we unplugged at bedtime. Some glass balls even had flecks of periwinkle, pearl and lavender. One shimmered with aquamarine, blown from glass made of ash.

Tree trimming was disorderly, but no one minded. Angels and elves were placed higher on the tree, along with little bulbs. Wooden ornaments and knits tended to go low, but away from lights. Tiny birds got hung above "cat level." Tinsel was supposed to be placed one strand at a time, but never was. We started with good intentions, but clumps were soon tossed and blown. Often the tree looked covered in Spanish moss. Next morning, all was neat – the work of Mom.

Gifts were handmade – by choice. Our mother – a teacher and artist – convinced us that things "made" counted as "art," and that people liked "art." Indulged in this way, we made lots of art and gave it away. We drew, painted, sawed, hammered, and sanded. We lacquered, sewed, wove and crocheted. We burned letters into wood, molded stones into ashtrays, and turned seashells to candlesticks. Then, we put our treasures under the tree.

Of course, we also made a mess. We had to scrape glue from the floor, put scraps in the woodstove, rewind yarn balls, and sweep up sawdust. The impulse to create was strong. Boards were hammered and sanded into step-stools and plaques, toast grabbers and boot-pullers. Cans were fancied-up to become pencil holders and flowerpots, while old socks were transformed into button-eyed puppets. Popsicle sticks turned into birdhouses, rocks got painted, sticks whittled, feathers and driftwood glued together. From little, we cobbled much.

One year, my brother Charlie stunned us all. Between weightlifting, distance running, school and work, he learned from our grandmother how to crochet. A one-time inspiration, he then produced thematic quilts for the entire family. Mine was of chessmen. I still use it. My sisters made endless potholders, crocheted scarves, mittens and tree ornaments. Cynthia was gifted with a paint brush and silkscreen, Anita on the chromatic harmonica. Her rendition of "Silver Bells" was ethereal.

One year, I discovered polyurethane. The urethane gloss on pine was like discovering honey on toast, and it looked about the same. Accordingly, I daubed wooden stools and flower boxes, picture frames and even a water ski. I shellacked rocks and mugs, tool handles and game pieces, neckerchief slides and belt buckles, walking sticks, leather pouches, a bicycle seat, door handles, and a horseshoe crab. The spirit – of polyurethane – moved me, to excess.

Sometimes, animated by Christmas, we embraced bigger risk. One year, we decided to equip Mom's car with a quadraphonic stereo, eight-track player, then state of the art. This was a huge secret. We pooled our money. Late on Christmas Eve, I proceeded to carve up Mom's car. By flashlight, I cut big holes throughout the interior – under the dash, in insulation and carpets, making gashes across the rear shelf. Suddenly, I realized this was irreversible. If it did not work, I had ruined Mom's car. *It had to work!* With freezing fingers, on crinkling seat covers, I finished the holes, completed wiring, splicing, tucking, taping, hiding, and attaching the speakers. Wires ran from back to front, dash to low-slung tape box.

I held my breath. Turning the key, then the knob, I got – complete silence. Under the dash I went again. Something was loose or unconnected, had to be. Had to find it. Finally, turning the knob, I got sound! Back inside, I reported success to my groggy siblings and slept the peace Santa must after Christmas.

Next morning, Mom said: "What in the world?" And we told her: "Turn on your 8-track tape player." She was in shock. From the speakers came her favorite, "*Johnny Cash!*" Then Roger Whitaker and Linda Ronstadt. We celebrated not being in Johnny's "ring of fire!"

Every Christmas Eve, of course, we attended church. Voices harmonized, bell ringers rang. Below the steeple, an outdoor manger came to life. We pondered the imponderable, the Great Miracle. We prayed for "peace on earth" and "goodwill among men." When the service ended, we walked with our candles, into the darkness. And back at home, we dreamed.

Next morning, we scrambled from bed to see what Santa had left, our hearts racing. Santa's footprints often proceeded from the fireplace; he never shook his boots. Cookies and milk, left for him the night before with a note, were consumed. Sometimes, Santa left a note, thanking us. In our big felt stockings, strung along the mantle, we found wind-up toys and marbles, silly putty, yo-yos and magnets, stencils, pencils and chocolate, twirling tops and for my sisters, dollhouse furniture. One year, my brother and I got jackknifes. Everyone got a candy cane. Protruding from each stocking top was a stuffed animal. Deep in each toe was a tangerine and two walnuts. Our stockings, made by Mom, sometimes seemed to be Christmas itself.

As presents were extracted from under the tree, eyes brightened. Everyone watched when someone opened. Wrapping paper was balled up and launched at unsuspecting targets. Kids laughed and tumbled about, while adults prepared the feast. My mother and Aunt Neetie (Anita) shared Thanksgiving and Christmas duties, giving us extra time with first cousins Eric and Duncan. Throughout the house floated an aroma of roast bird, giblet gravy, fresh bread and wood smoke.

When all were seated for dinner, grace was said. It was never pretentious, always clear and short. Adults sat at a big table, children at a smaller one. The two tables were side by side, serving bowls passed between them. Turkey was dark and light, embroidered with amber skin. Gravy was drizzled from a boat. String beans were piled up like split-rail fences, streams of hot butter trickling off mashed potato mounds. Then came pies, ice cream, plum pudding, coffee and belt-loosening.

Before sunset, gifts were pulled from the miniature sleigh, others selected from the grab bag, a tradition that involved one gift for each person, pulled youngest to oldest. Adults tumbled back into childhood, themselves laughing. As we grew, we poked good-naturedly at each other. Cynthia, with her kind heart for animals, denied her "stubborn streak," until we convinced her "the lady doth protest too much." Charlie produced belly laughs with puns and punchlines. Anita resolved to save the world, for which we ribbed her mercilessly, until she started doing so, one child at a time. Today, she and her genial husband Chris have five children, Duncan, Midhun, Cameron, Devki and Malvika. For me, the list of targets was long, big nose and ears, thinning hair, and my politics. All this made Christmas fun, sometimes producing so much laughter we struggled to breathe.

Now and then, we courted madness. One year, we dared each other to run barefoot around the house in snow up to our knees. We did it, but that tradition died fast. Another year, we donned outlandish hats, moose antlers, a blue wig. We thought we were hilarious, long after everyone else did. Another year, we took a family photo – with packing peanuts on every nose. We looked like frostbite victims or careless painters. The noses gave that year *je ne sais quoi*, and an air of absurdity.

To all this, we added gag gifts. A beautifully-wrapped box might hold a smaller one, and smaller, and smaller, until nothing – and then laughter. In a reverse, the smallest might hold a precious gift. The old flying snake wriggled from a can of mixed nuts every year, making the rounds. Visitors were fair game. Then Mom might suddenly adopt a sock, provide it with a mouth and make it talk, becoming an instant puppeteer. We would roar. Once she started, especially if Charlie joined in, there was no hope. No one could stop laughing.

On a more thoughtful note, we loved the tradition of Christmas cards – sending and receiving. We wrote by hand, read every card, and did neither fast. We wrote full sentences with looping letters, thinking about those to whom we were writing. Each card was a mini-visit. We addressed each envelope by hand, licking the flap and stamp, placing it in the mailbox, and then lifting the flag. That was one end of a tunnel – leading to the world. People had pride in their handwriting. We could pick out senders by their scrawl. Christmas cards were more like a rolling, annual conversation than a chore. Mass production, let alone email cards, did not exist. Card writing was an art.

Of course, all these Christmas traditions started *somewhere.* A quick backward glance puts the light on my grandmother, Mary Elizabeth Hassell, my mother's mother, the lifetime teacher and school principal – very same. She wore prescription glasses with style, was long on listening to grandchildren, overflowed with love and had a ready, hallmark smile. She was short on criticism, but had her views. Most importantly, she was the family rock. She fixed problems and untied knots, figurative and literal, with patience. Into her 80th year, she taught us grace, with no lectures. She never complained, despite a life of inordinate loss, including the love of her life, our grandfather, who left her at thirty-four.

She raised two young girls, cared for her parents, guided her sister's three daughters when cancer struck a second time. She refused to view herself as special, despite an early injury that forced her to rely on a brace and cane all her life. The condition did not matter to her, so should not matter to others. Life was a blessing, come what may. She personified resilience. Born in 1911, she managed through two world wars, a Great Depression, loss of family near and far, with perspective. She grew to become a much-revered principal – and wonderful grandmother.

One day, as I studied for the bar in her little home, she interrupted me. She asked if I could search for a small shoebox in her bedroom closet. I found the box. It was wrapped in faded ribbon. She asked me to open it, remove one of the envelopes. Inside the envelope was a letter, from my grandfather, Robert Francis Hassell.

Suddenly, I realized – she too had been young. She asked me to read the letter aloud. I did so. She asked me to read another. Finally, after a time, she said, "Thank you… That is enough." She asked me to put the box away, never asked again. I never forgot. Somehow, even in her later years, my grandfather's young love carried her forward.

Christmas, like her life, was all about family. She laughed along with us. Like us, she grew up with siblings, a sister and two brothers. Her childhood home, to which she returned after her husband died, was called Twenty One. It exists, still. It is located in Chevy Chase, Maryland. Local literature says it "was influenced by architecture of Frank Lloyd Wright, with stucco walls and long overhanging eaves." Funny, since it was built by my grandmother's father, my great-grandfather, Charles Cleveland Clark.

Mary Elizabeth's maiden name was Clark, of course. The Chevy Chase Historical Society observes: "During the Clark years, the main entrance [of Twenty-One] was West Irving Street, and the kitchen entrance was on Magnolia Parkway … there was a beautiful grove of pink dogwood trees at the Magnolia-West Irving corner of the property."

My grandmother was proud of those trees, and spoke about them fondly. Her father planted them, then grafted pink to white for variety. The old home, which came to life in 1911 with my grandmother, was surrounded by cutting gardens and rolling lawns. Today, those gardens have houses on them. But in the day, one senses they were grand. As was their Christmas.

On Christmas Day, cousins and aunts came and went, even at the height of World War II. Somehow, Santa got through, leaving each child a tangerine and two walnuts in their stocking. As my grandmother retold it, and mother and aunt corroborated, Christmas Day at Twenty-One was a wondrous affair, as all Christmases should be, centered on family, faith and nation.

Her father, with the initials CCC, was one of four brothers, all sons of Ezra Westcote and Sylvia Nodine Clark. He became a lawyer, eventually assistant head of the US Weather Bureau, predecessor of the National Oceanic and Atmospheric Administration (NOAA). While there, he was briefly sent abroad, to Italy.

His brother Eugene was an inventor. Eugene was another all-American sort, graduating from public high school, winning a chance to earn his Masters in Engineering from Cornell, in 1894. Putting that degree right to use, he patented the can opener, a new drill, steel wheels and axles, even a wood stove. In 1906, he founded a company, renaming it Clark Equipment Company in 1916.

That year was an inflection point for the Clarks, and for America. Scholars call 1916 "the end of American innocence." America was inexorably being drawn into the "war to end all wars," World War I. The life-shattering conflagration was consuming Europe. When it was all over, 37 million would be dead or wounded. In large numbers, Americans prayed on New Year's Eve not to be drawn in, but by April, 1917, America was at war.

As younger Clarks served in uniform, Eugene turned to inventing for the war effort. He produced transmissions, the first undercarriage for trolleys and subways, America's first fork lift, and utility vehicles for the US Army. His efforts supported peacetime activities also, but more capital was needed. Eugene turned to his brother, Charles (CCC), who invested his savings in Eugene's company. Back then, brothers did that.

The company went public in 1928, not the best year for an initial public offering. Nevertheless, by work and luck, Eugene weathered the Great Depression, which hit hard in 1929. Clark Equipment Company continued to grow, eventually winding up on the New York Stock Exchange.

In 1933, the same year my grandmother married, a *Cycle and Automobile Trade Journal* ran flashy cartoons of the dashing young Eugene Clark, dangling patents from a magnet. Caption: "The magnetic influence which has lifted the axle business to a higher plane." Text gave the Clark boys a nod: "It seems quite fitting that Washington, D.C. should be birthplace of a man who can trace his ancestry back to 1640, when John Clark, late of England, settled in New York," adding "Eugene Bradley Clark was son of a distinguished lawyer and Civil War Veteran." That would be Ezra Westcote Clark, who fought for the North. He is buried at Arlington National Cemetery, together with his son and Charles and Eugene's brother, Ezra Westcote Clark, Jr. Ezra Jr. fought in World War I.

Also in 1933, Eugene's company became "prominent in the development of electrical applications in the steel industry, and … development of automotive apparatus, especially of motor trucks." The motor trucks caught on, becoming a key to America's ground combat efforts in World War II. The second "war to end all wars" was just six years off.

Unfortunately, Eugene died in 1942, but his company survived. In the 1960s, Clark Equipment grew and was eventually bought by Ingersoll Rand in 1995. The family interest – like Twenty One – had long since been sold, but the Clark brothers had done their part, strived and been equal to their time. Until she died, I recall my grandmother holding a few shares of the old company.

If all this sounds like eclectic family history, it is. But that is what 20th Century America was about, risk, hope, patriotism, family and faith. This is how America grew, through millions of dreamers and hard workers, personal freedom and attention to civic duty. Family bonds were big, never more so than at Christmas. Together, Americans survived, holding fast to traditions.

As my mother tells it, before and during World War II, a simple check arrived in the mail at Christmas. It was always accompanied by two "Christmas pheasants." Check and pheasants were from Eugene, for Charles. The check was cashed for gifts, placed in the little sleigh and family grab bag. The pheasants became Christmas dinner.

And one last tradition. Christmas involved retelling stories. *Imagine that!* Maybe that is why I like telling stories. Somewhere along the line, my great-grandfather, CCC, and his wife ended up in Italy –briefly. This was a Christmas favorite. During their stay, former President Theodore Roosevelt visited Italy. A State dinner was held. Our great-grandparents were invited. The "Rough Rider" must have put on quite a show. One can only imagine the heraldry surrounding any dinner for Theodore Roosevelt.

That story has a charming end. By some misfortune, my great-grandparents found themselves on the wrong side of a diplomatic cordon. My great-grandmother approached the sentry, probably a U.S. Marine, observing that she and her husband belonged on the *other side* of the rope. Her appeal caught Theodore Roosevelt's attention. Ever the man of action, TR lifted the rope and escorted the two to dinner. In the process, our great-grandmother lost her corsage. Not missing a beat, TR gallantly retrieved it. The President was a hero for life, the "perfect gentleman." Her devotion never flagged, nor ours for the story. So such stories were also part of Christmas.

And one last. True to the family tradition of taking risks, in 1976, four gumptious kids took the biggest Christmas risk ever. I had just gotten my driver's license. From there, the plot quickly thickened. It would bring much joy or end in a spectacular failure.

Everything was set, but there was one rub. To pull it off, I needed the family car. Tentatively, I asked Mom on Christmas Eve for the car. This was more than unusual; it was borderline impossible. I explained that I needed it to "pick something up" – for Christmas. With grave reservations, she gave permission. We then embarked on our secret mission.

In the family car, equipped with the eight-track, we drove to the destination, plunked down every penny we had, and purchased – a baby Cocker Spaniel. To a one, we were giddy. And not sure how Mom would react. The family had never owned a dog. Mom had told us the Cocker Spaniel saga to teach a lesson: People do not always get what they want, and life can be unfair. Dreams do not always come true, even if hard work is a discriminator. We got all that. She taught well. Some barriers are immovable. We understood that.

But that night, we took aim at the unfairness. We aimed to even the score, to remove a barrier. We could not bring her father back, but we could deliver the other half of her childhood dream – a Cocker Spaniel. At the exuberant ages 10, 12, 14 and 16, we felt she had waited long enough. We consulted newspapers, wrote and made calls. We worked it out. Empowered by her own resilience, and that of our grandmother, we made it so.

Christmas morning, Mom became a child again. She was overwhelmed. Better than an eight-track, she had her living, breathing Cocker Spaniel. She finally *had* her pup! We were ecstatic too, just watching her. Sometimes, dreams do come true. Risks are worth taking, history is worth making. We had pulled it off. Mom kept her puppy, and named her Buffy.

For the next decade and a half, Mom and Buffy travelled everywhere together. They were inseparable. And when Mom played with Buffy, Christmas filled the air. They both wagged. Christmas … there is magic in the word.

Epilogue

Small towns are not perfect. Nor are the people who live in them, in any generation. Our town was not devoid of trauma, tension, tragedy, testiness or periodic debate. But those who called our town home comprehended a larger reality, whether they spoke of it or not. They seemed to feel privileged to share in it. It lifted them daily above inevitable disappointments and differences. They were strong, and by their personal resolve part of "one." In my youth, as in other times, America understood this idea – the binding force of ideals, personal sacrifice, conscious and difficult resilience, required to be "one."

In Nature, as in life, there are downdrafts, recurring storms. Life dashes and disappoints, tosses, stresses and tests. It also surprises and eases, elevates and empowers. The timeless challenge, from my perspective, is to see the goodness and use the freedom, to understand the blessings given, and thus to give and live fully while we are able.

Chris did that at the wheel of his plow. Richie did it in wartime Italy, and on his return to Wayne. Del did as a camp counselor, later saving lives in war-torn Germany. Ed did it setting up an epic summer camp, and later in Europe. George, Tom and Linc gave in the Pacific, then educated youth back at home. Ford gave to his family, and fatefully in Europe.

Vern served overseas, then as proprietor of the Wayne General Store. Harold, Vern's brother, worked in the crutch factory, then taught teens to roof, think and laugh. During and after World War II, brothers Peter, Richard and David – with John, Robert and Jimmy – served in uniform. So did brothers Charles, Bob and Bill. They all taught, in their own ways.

Mike was a mother and nurse, then she and Jeanie became an intergenerational force that guided teenagers toward the church. Tink went to war, then became the living embodiment of the US Postal Service, a cheerful voice that tied us to the world. Tink's wife Lila managed the town, as my friend Stefan later managed two towns, on return from the Peace Corps. Stefan and his wife, Lynette, raised their family where he grew up. My grandmother, mother and aunt, along with Priscilla, spent their lives as professional teachers, as did others in town. They gave and gave.

As kids, we learned to play, work and give from these leaders, whom we did not yet understand were leaders. Or I did not, anyway. They taught us the value in work, service and freedom, the goodness that lies in all three. This and more we learned from them, while drifting here and there, barefoot and tanned, under their protective wings, free by their will, oblivious to our luck.

My friend Will became a lawyer, accountant, and lifetime example of patience. My friend Carl, also known as Linc, flew C-17s, Blackhawks (Pavehawks) and other aircraft for America in combat, including over Afghanistan. My friend Perry flew F-4s, A-4s, and F-18s for our nation. Friend John, who worked at Androscoggin, became a Master Maine Guide. Friends Mark and Karl, outdoorsmen still, advanced the causes of geology and technology respectively. Binky empowered countless kids to act, while Liz ended up conducting human rights missions in Africa. My siblings Anita and Charlie teach professionally, Anita at the college level, when not raising her five kids, and Charlie at a public high school in Maine. Cynthia, like our mother, is an artist and businesswoman, dedicated to animals.

Small towns share one trait above others – they are *painfully authentic.* There is no room or any place to hide. Independent people become inextricably tied together, interdependent; they work at it. They live up to obligations assumed, and to the duties interdependence imposes. Most could go anywhere, if they wanted. They don't. Most could choose anonymity, if they wanted. They don't. Instead, they choose to give, live, work, and get old together, authentically.

Those who have once called a small town home know this feeling. They know what it means to have lifetime friends, that is, to live among people you will know all of your life, and all of theirs. They know accountability, shared responsibility for things small and large. They know a good deal about human nature, too. They are not afraid to hold opinions, to come to them on their own. They have no need to share them, unless you ask. They let others do their own thinking, expect it. They are not embarrassed by closeness to family, faith, country or honor, even if they talk little of such things. They prefer a slower place, but don't judge those who prefer a faster one. They know what it means to be connected to what is real, now and in the past. They care about the future. In Maine, the idea prevails, true or not, that this is how life should be.

In short, growing up in small town Maine made me one of the luckiest kids on earth. In our day, we had four seasons, plus the space, time and ambit to use them. People cared to steer us in the right direction, so we headed that way. They expected something of us, so we expected something of us. They encouraged our play, creativity, wonder and laughter. So we valued those sensibilities. People like my grandmother, mother and aunt – plus those who served in World War II and beyond – taught us to be other-regarding, to sacrifice and have resilience. Lucky does not begin to capture it. Blessed, that is better. To be sure, we grew up among eagles and evergreens. And just for me, borrowing from Robert Frost, "that has made all the difference."

About the Author

Robert "Bobby" Charles grew up in Wayne, Maine. After a rural childhood punctuated by woodland adventures, tutelage by aging veterans, and Maranacook High School, he graduated Dartmouth College (AB), Oxford University (MA, PPE), and Columbia Law School (JD). Professionally, he has served in the judicial, legislative and executive branches, privately litigated, and now runs a small company focused on national security. A ten-year naval intelligence officer (USNR), he volunteered for active duty on 9/11/01. In 2003, he was unanimously confirmed by the US Senate, and became an Assistant Secretary of State, under Colin Powell. In that capacity, he turned youthful Maine lessons toward setting up the Iraqi and Afghan police training programs, seeking security in Colombia, and managing other global security programs. Today, he and his wife and two children spend considerable time back where he grew up, in Maine. Their permanent residence is Maryland, but Charles writes on many topics, none with greater passion than love of Maine's woods and people. This volume weaves respect for Maine ways and people with tales of a formative, cheerful, sometimes rollicking and unpredictable Maine childhood.

CPSIA information can be obtained
at www.ICGtesting.com
Printed in the USA
BVHW07*0940221018
530871BV00009B/185/P

9 781943 424337